KRISHNA KUMARI

The Tragedy of India

KRISHNA KUMARI

The Tragedy of India

ENGLISH SUBBA RAO

Edited and Introduced by
RAHUL SAGAR

B L O O M S B U R Y
NEW DELHI • LONDON • OXFORD • NEW YORK • SYDNEY

BLOOMSBURY INDIA
Bloomsbury Publishing India Pvt. Ltd
Second Floor, LSC Building No. 4, DDA Complex, Pocket C–6&7,
Vasant Kunj, New Delhi 110070

BLOOMSBURY, BLOOMSBURY ACADEMIC INDIA and the Diana logo are
trademarks of Bloomsbury Publishing Plc

First published in India 2024
First published in Great Britain 2024

Cover design: Yan He, 2024
Cover image © "A Swooning Lady", The Metropolitan Museum of Art

This edition published with permission from Bloomsbury Publishing Plc,
50 Bedford Square, London, WC1B3DP, UK

A catalogue record for this book is available from the British Library.
A catalog record for this book is available from the Library of Congress.

ISBN: 978-93-61313-01-1
Series: Methuen Drama Play Collections

Typeset by RefineCatch Limited, Bungay, Suffolk
Printed and bound in India by Thomson Press India Ltd

To find out more about our authors and books
visit www.bloomsbury.com and sign up for our newsletters

For sale in the Indian subcontinent only

To English Subba Rao, the man who saw India

Contents

Preface

In 2020 I was working on a biography of Madhava Rao, the illustrious *dewan* (or prime minister) of Travancore, when a question began to gnaw away at me. Why had this statesman, celebrated for modernizing Travancore, been invited there in the first place? The principalities of nineteenth-century India were generally moribund, but Travancore had clearly chosen to be otherwise—why? Working through the early records, I concluded that Madhava Rao would not have been summoned to Travancore had the Maharaja, Uttaram Tirunal, not received a modern liberal education from *his* tutor, English Subba Rao. And so began my quest to uncover the story of this intriguingly named individual about whom British records were unusually silent.

As I rummaged through the archives, out tumbled revelation upon revelation. Subba Rao, I realized, was arguably the very first Indian to study and master English and certainly the very first to write a play in that language—*Krishna Kumari*. The discovery was electrifying—and puzzling. Why did Subba Rao write the play? Did the events it portrays really take place? Why had it been neglected all this time? Burning with curiosity, I immersed myself in the archives, collecting every scrap of information available about the playwright as well as the events and characters in his drama. As I assembled the fragments, Subba Rao's extraordinary life came into focus—as did his purpose in writing this play. *Krishna Kumari* it now became clear was nothing less than a pioneering study of our national character. Crafted by a man well-versed in the ways of the *darbar* (or royal court), the drama exposed the foolishness that had made the kingdoms and principalities of the subcontinent easy prey for the East India Company—which is precisely why the British sent the play and its author into oblivion. Convinced that this drama ought to be read by generations to come, I now place it before you. The introductory essay makes the case for its importance; I hope it does English Subba Rao the honor long due to him.

Rahul Sagar
Diwali
November 2023

Acknowledgments

In seeking to recover Subba Rao's *Krishna Kumari* I have incurred many debts. To begin at the beginning, this volume would simply not exist without the research funding provided by NYU Abu Dhabi and NYU Shanghai. I am immensely grateful to Hervé Crès, Joanna Waley-Cohen, Maria Montoya, Paula England, and Hannah Brückner for supporting my research. I am also much obliged to colleagues that helped manage the ensuing grants: Janet Kelly, Julie McGuire, Diana Pangan, Emily Del Monte, Sana Ahmed, and Nicoleta Nichifor at NYU Abu Dhabi, and Jinyi Ouyang and Xinyi Xiong at NYU Shanghai. I also want to express my deep gratitude to Martin Klimke and the members of the NYUAD Grant for Publication Program whose support made it possible for me to publish the maps and portraits in this volume and to Blaine Robbins and the Governance and Public Policy Research Cluster at NYU Abu Dhabi for a grant supporting travel to distant archives.

I began working on this volume during my time in Shanghai, the city that makes everyone a historian. For that invaluable opportunity, I am indebted to Joanna Waley-Cohen, Maria Montoya, Casey Owens, Alyshea Austern, Chris Ke, and Sally Ni at NYU Shanghai, to Hannah Brückner, Luisa Vallory, and Susan Wei at NYU Abu Dhabi, and to Zvi Ben-Dor Benite and Vivien Lee at NYU New York. Though the vagaries of the pandemic limited in-person interactions, I cannot forget the kind welcome from Almaz Zelleke, Ivan Rasmussen, and Xiaogong Wu.

I would not have been able to complete this manuscript without the research assistance provided by Nidhi Shukla, Khushi Singh Rathore, Jonah Elsey, Zilan Qian, Sowmya Baskaran, and M. Lakshmi Priya. When the pandemic brought travel to a halt, Jonah, Zilan, Sowmya, and Lakshmi saved the day by scanning many hundreds of records in the British Library, the New York Public Library, the Tamil Nadu State Archives, and the Kerala State Archives. Khushi typed up the play and the appendices, and helped tackle challenges ranging from identifying translators to deciphering archaic terms. Nidhi has been a tireless aide throughout the writing process, helping track down obscure texts and identify gaps in the narrative. She has proofread more drafts than I dare admit and patiently listened to me agonize over minute details. Truly, words cannot express my gratitude to Khushi and Nidhi. Of course, I am solely responsible for any errors in this volume and for the views expressed therein.

It is a great honor to have this volume published by Bloomsbury. I am indebted to Dom O'Hanlon for responding so warmly to my proposal and to Sam Nicholls for deftly guiding the manuscript through the production process. I am also deeply grateful to Sophie Beardsworth, Merv Honeywood, and Neil Dowden for producing the manuscript with such care, to Sebastian Ballard for the elegant maps, and to Yan He for the lyrical cover. I want to also express my gratitude to the four anonymous reviewers for their helpful comments on the original manuscript.

Several colleagues provided invaluable advice or encouragement along the way. I am, once again, indebted to Robin Jeffrey and Manu Pillai for being so generous with their boundless knowledge of Indian India, and to Rohan Mukherjee and Anit Mukherjee for slogging through multiple drafts. I am also very grateful to Pratap Bhanu Mehta, Devesh Kapur, Chandran Kukathas, Christine Dunn Henderson, Stephen Macedo, Corey Brettschneider, Melissa Schwartzberg, Shruti Rajagopalan, Milan Vaishnav, Kanti Bajpai, Constantino Xavier, Dinyar Patel, Parag Khanna, James Crabtree, and John Donaldson, for being sounding boards and givers of wise counsel. I also want to take this chance to express my thanks to cherished colleagues whose initiative and good humor have made NYU Abu Dhabi such a wonderful place to work: Christopher Paik, Leonid Peisakhin, Melina Platas, Eric Hamilton, Jeffrey Timmons, Abdul Noury, Ron Rogowski, Peter van der Windt, Andrew Harris, Adam Ramey, Muhammet Bas, Rachel Brule, Michael Harsch, Mario Chacon, Swethaa Ballakrishnen, David Cook-Martin, Toral Gajarawala, David Blakeslee, Samreen Malik, Sanjeev Goyal, Taneli Kukkonen, and Matthew Silverstein.

Finally, I want to thank friends and family. The anxieties of the pandemic era were eased by the companionship of Abhishek and Devika Rao, Arunabha Ghosh and Meghna Narayan, Kapil and Tamanna Kapoor, Arjun and Anjali Purkayastha, Shashi and Miranda Jayakumar, Douglas and Min Ang, Jonathan Fulton and Robyn Albers, N. Janardhan and Meena Janardhan, Vivek Sondhi and Nivedita Barthakur, Rohan and Shailey Hingorani, and Anit and Malobi Mukherjee. I want to express my deepest gratitude to my parents, Prema and Jyoti Sagar, and to my wife, Una, for helping shoulder the burdens of the pandemic era. As always, I am thankful, above everything else in this world, for my beloved daughters, Mia and Sophie, whose exuberance kept my spirits up in those days, and whose love continues to make every day a treasure.

Chronology

1775 Subba Rao born in Tanjore; Tanjore becomes a British subsidiary

1782 First Anglo-Maratha War ends; Marathas begin to dominate Northern India

1784 Raja Tuljaji grants land and money for an English school to be built in Tanjore

1790 Marathas become dominant in Rajputana; Sindhia–Holkar rivalry escalates

1793 Subba Rao graduates; appointed translator in the Tanjore *darbar*

1795 Travancore becomes a British subsidiary; Daulat Rao Sindhia attacks the Holkars

1798 Serfoji becomes Raja of Tanjore; Jaswant Rao Holkar combines with Amir Khan

1799 Subba Rao made preceptor; Krishna Kumari betrothed to Bhim Singh of Jodhpur

1803 Second Anglo-Maratha War begins; Bhim Singh of Jodhpur dies

1803 Jagat Singh becomes Maharaja of Jaipur; Man Singh made Maharaja of Jodhpur

1804 Man Singh seizes Ghanerao; Bhim Singh offers Krishna Kumari to Jagat Singh

1805 Second-Anglo Maratha War ends; British withdraw from Rajputana

1807 Jaipur and Jodhpur go to war; Amir Khan supports Jaipur then Jodhpur

1808 Amir Khan murders Sawai Singh; Jaswant Rao Holkar goes insane

1809 Subba Rao publishes *Balabodha Muktavali*; Amir Khan threatens Nagpur

1810 Jaipur and Jodhpur make peace; Krishna Kumari commits suicide in Udaipur

1812 Subba Rao appointed *Sarkil* of Tanjore

1815 Subba Rao resigns; Amir Khan dominates Jodhpur; Pindaris raid British India

1817 Third Anglo-Maratha War begins; Pindaris destroyed; Amir Khan joins the British

1818 Marathas and Rajputs submit to the British; Amir Khan made Nawab of Tonk

1820 Subba Rao appointed tutor to Swati Tirunal and Uttaram Tirunal in Travancore

1823 John Malcolm publishes *A Memoir on Central India*

1826 Subba Rao completes *Krishna Kumari*

1829 Swati Tirunal becomes Maharaja; James Tod publishes *Annals and Antiquities*

1830 Subba Rao appointed *Dewan* of Travancore

1840 *Krishna Kumari* published by the Government Press in Trivandrum

1841 William Cullen appointed Resident in Travancore

1842 Cullen forces Subba Rao to resign; Swati makes Subba Rao his preceptor

1846 Swati Tirunal dies

1848 Subba Rao passes away in Trivandrum

Illustrations

The Tragedy of India

Krishna Kumari is the first play written by an Indian in the English language. It depicts the true story of a princess in the kingdom of Udaipur who became the object of a fratricidal contest between the rulers of the neighboring kingdoms of Jaipur and Jodhpur, each vying for her hand in marriage. Faced with the prospect of Udaipur being engulfed in the ensuing hostilities, the princess was compelled to end the dispute by committing suicide. This tragic event, which occurred in 1810, made Krishna Kumari's name synonymous with selfless patriotism. Her sacrifice could not, however, undo the rash decisions previously made by her suitors. In their heedless attempts to prevail in the conflict, the rulers of Jaipur and Jodhpur had sought the support of infamous mercenaries known as the Pindaris. Having entered Rajputana, these "human locusts" proceeded to ravage rulers and ruled until, worn and weary, one and all submitted to the East India Company in 1818.[1]

Krishna Kumari was written in 1826 by Subba Rao (or "English Subba Rao," as he was colloquially known), one of the most important figures in nineteenth-century India. Incredibly, Subba Rao's life and accomplishments are hardly known in contemporary India. A distinguished polymath, he was among the very first "natives" to be schooled in English, following which he served as *sarkil* (or head minister) in Tanjore and as *dewan* (or prime minister) in Travancore where he laid the foundation for its later transformation into a model state. Subba Rao penned *Krishna Kumari* in the interval between these posts, when he served as tutor to Swati Tirunal and Uttaram Tirunal, the future Maharajas of Travancore. He wrote the play to educate his wards by vividly depicting the vices that had led to Rajputana's ruin.

It may be thought that because *Krishna Kumari* was written two centuries ago it could now only be of interest to antiquarians. Nothing could be further from the truth. The characters it pithily exposes—feeble dynasts, craven sycophants, scheming politicians, and parochial communities—continue to mar public life in India. There is, therefore, much to be learnt and much pleasure to be had from Subba Rao's skewering of these characters. The fact that the play is written in an easy, modern style only heightens its timelessness. Unfortunately, it is not easy to come by. Only three copies of the play, which was published in 1840, remain in circulation, only one of which is in India. There is a facsimile available online, but it is devoid of supporting material, leaving contemporary readers bewildered by the characters and context. Little wonder then that the play remains unknown, only being hazily recalled in encyclopedias as "the first Indo-Anglian drama."[2]

The purpose of this volume, then, is to rescue Subba Rao's *Krishna Kumari* from oblivion by showing why it deserves to be honored as a modern classic. To this end, this introduction begins by outlining the episode upon which the play is based. It details the grim sequence of events that prompted Krishna Kumari to sacrifice her life and the miseries that followed nonetheless. The essay then goes on to explain why a tragedy that occurred in Rajputana ended up becoming the subject of an English-language drama in distant Travancore. It does this by reconstructing Subba Rao's extraordinary life and career, shedding light on the events and personalities that shaped him and led him to produce this pioneering work. The essay concludes by explaining why Krishna Kumari's story, which was once read and cherished across India, especially in regional languages, has come to be all but forgotten, and why Subba Rao's English-language version of the story is especially deserving of being handed down to posterity.

Setting the Stage

Rajputana was shaped, Susanne Rudolph tells us, by a warrior-ethic, one that "stressed spirit, valor, and abandon."[3] At one time such a way of being served a great purpose. In the eleventh and twelfth centuries, it allowed the clans that would later come to be termed Rajputs to withstand repeated invasions from the northwest. Though compelled to retreat from the rich Gangetic plains to "less inviting country," namely the arid, hilly region that would later be known as Rajputana, the martial habits of these clans preserved them from oblivion.[4] Over the thirteenth and fourteenth centuries, the same habits then allowed the ablest of them to establish principalities, the most important of which grew to be Mewar (later Udaipur), Marwar (later Jodhpur), and Amber (later Jaipur).

This difficult birth granted the Rajputs, as K. R. Qanungo memorably put it, "the best of pedigrees—the sword."[5] It would have remained a commendable parentage had the Rajputs been able to transcend their clannish origins. But unfortunately, from the outset this community displayed an unerring tendency to be "split up" by "archaic wrangling" over points of honor.[6] And once they had drawn their swords, Rajputs struggled to sheathe them, because they made *vair* (vendetta) the "salt of life."[7] As a result, the "gratification of revenge" became something like "a moral obligation," pitting clan against clan, family against family, leading ultimately to an "interminable course of feuds."[8]

Such a culture, Rudolph notes, was never going to be "hospitable to successful statesmanship."[9] What preserved the Rajputs was sheer grit marshalled by meteoric personalities. Thus, the Delhi Sultanate, which dominated North India between the thirteenth and sixteenth centuries, was ever "plundering and slaying" in Rajputana, but it was not able to make a "serious impression" on the hardy inhabitants of this "difficult land."[10] And when the Delhi Sultanate began to decline, the Rajputs even formed a confederacy under Rana Sanga of Mewar who, at the cost of an eye, two limbs, and some ninety scars, obtained something like hegemony over his fellow chieftains.[11] But the enterprise was fragile. In 1526, Uzbeks led by Babur marched in from the northwest. The confederacy, led by Sanga, met them at Khanwa where Rajputana's "mounted splendor" was outmatched by the Uzbek's "furious artillery."[12] At this critical moment, instead of regrouping, the Rajputs splintered, with Sanga apparently poisoned by dissenting clans who "had no desire to renew conflict."[13]

Upon gaining control of Northern India, Babur's descendants, now better known as the Mughals, made it their mission to subjugate Rajputana, lest its inhabitants emerge from their desert strongholds at inopportune moments. The Rajputs helped the process along by once again failing to unite. When Babur's grandson, Akbar, invaded Rajputana in 1561, the Kachwahas of Amber, then a relatively minor clan, submitted "at once."[14] The Rathores of Marwar put up a fight, but alone could not resist the Mughals' by-now "colossal power."[15] In the end, both clans "purchased peace" by surrendering a daughter to Akbar's teeming harem, opening the door to profitable imperial service.[16] The Sisodias of Mewar, though unprepared for the contest, refused to surrender, for which reason they were brutalized. Akbar penetrated Mewar's fortresses and massacred tens of thousands of innocent civilians, prompting the ruling family to retreat to the hills. There they remained until Rana Pratap, the "savior of his race," ascended to the throne in 1572 and launched a grueling campaign to eject the Mughals.[17] To underscore that they alone had not bartered a daughter to obtain clemency and crumbs, the Sisodias henceforth refused to intermarry or even dine with the "effete" Kachwahas and Rathores.[18] But one man can only do so much. Rana Pratap died in 1597. Within a decade, Akbar's son, the emperor Jahangir, dispatched his forces to Mewar and, as the Kachwahas and Rathores docilely looked on, obtained its submission. The Sisodias were not, however, compelled to hand over a daughter, a "concession" that maintained their distinctive status amongst Rajputs.

By the end of the seventeenth century the Rajputs appeared to have learned their lesson when the fanaticism of Akbar's great-grandson, Aurangzeb, persuaded them to sink their "petty enmities" and unite "for a greater cause," namely, to preserve their ancestral religion and secure mutual protection against "capricious abuses."[19] The rising tide of rebellion, led by Jodhpur and Udaipur, left Mughal forces harried and worn. Later, even Jaipur, which had obtained preeminence in Rajputana by serving the Mughals, began to buck. In 1700 the three kingdoms even managed to form a "triple alliance," harkening back to Rana Sanga's stand against Babur.[20] So unified, the Rajputs met with success, expelling the Mughals from their lands during chaos that followed Aurangzeb's death in 1707. But when the Mughals regrouped and returned to the region in the following decade, the triple alliance gave way. Jaipur, greedy as ever, defected to resume imperial service, leaving Jodhpur and Udaipur, by now shadows of what they once were, to brood in cold silence.[21]

Over the next two decades, as the Mughal empire went into terminal decline, the balance of power shifted in favor of its vassals, which began to exercise independent control over territories they had previously governed on behalf of the suzerain. But barely had the Rajputs begun to assert themselves in Central India than the Marathas, the rising power in the Deccan, appeared on the scene. As they moved upwards, compelling the Mughals to surrender to them the right to exact tribute from ever-wider swathes of territory, the Marathas turned their eyes toward Rajputana. They recognized that the region's wealthy commercial centers, strategically located forts, and battle-hardened clans could bolster their growing empire. But the Rajputs, with their high opinion of themselves, and still relishing with their newly regained freedom, were not keen to be reduced to mere tributaries. Thus began a prolonged contest over the terms of submission. Unfortunately, to extract the best possible terms the Rajputs would need the skill they possessed least—the ability to act in concert.[22]

The Marathas did not find it difficult to insert themselves into the picture. In 1743 Sawai Jai Singh, the Maharaja of Jaipur, passed away whereupon his sons, Ishwari and

Madho, fell out over which of them was entitled to succeed. Ironically, this dispute originated in the terms of the aforementioned triple alliance forged against Aurangzeb, which had readmitted Jaipur and Jodhpur to "the honor of matrimonial connection" with Udaipur on the condition that the sons of Udaipur princesses would have precedence in the line of succession.[23] On this basis, Madho, born to an Udaipur princess, laid claim to the Jaipur throne, whereas Ishwari, being elder, insisted on the sanctity of primogeniture. Unable to prevail, both sides sought aid from the Marathas, who had by now seized control of neighboring Malwa. This was par for the course, as the Rajputs had previously permitted the Mughals to settle their disputes.[24] But the Mughals were a monarchy, whereas the Marathas were a confederacy. So where once there had been an appeal to an emperor, now there was an appeal to many *sardars* (chieftains), each of whom was hoping to build up a kingdom of his own.

Subsequent proceedings in Jaipur signaled what was to come. Madho offered Malhar Holkar, the leading Maratha *sardar* in Malwa, 2 lakh rupees to support him in battle. Ishwari countered by offering more to Holkar's fellow *sardar*, Ranoji Sindhia. Udaipur, which championed Madho as he was the son of an Udaipur princess, then upped the ante by offering 10 lakhs to the Peshwa, the head of the Maratha Empire, who ordered Sindhia to join Holkar. So combined, the *sardars* easily humbled Ishwari, from whom they then demanded 50 lakh rupees in indemnities. Unable to raise even half the sum, Ishwari made sure to commit suicide by swallowing arsenic, then inducing a bite from a cobra, and perhaps also ingesting gold dust. His rival did not feel much better. After placing Madho on the throne, Sindhia and Holkar proposed that he grant them "one-third or at least one-fourth" of Jaipur's territory.[25] Angered by the *sardars*' "insatiable greed," Madho responded by trying to murder them.[26] His plots failed but an orchestrated riot led to the massacre of some 1500 Maratha soldiers, an affront that the *sardars* only forgave after being promised 75 lakhs in cumulative tribute.[27]

So matters went for the next half century. The Marathas "became the general referees in all disputes" in Rajputana, which they usually "decided in favor of the highest bidder."[28] A succession dispute in Jodhpur, for instance, yielded more than 50 lakh rupees, while one in Udaipur netted them about 65 lakhs.[29] The Rajputs responded to such fleecing by invariably paying less than they had promised. This tactic eventually prompted the Marathas to seize valuable territories as sureties, which only exacerbated the harm done to the exchequer. For instance, when the previously mentioned Madho of Jaipur delivered up less than half of the 75 lakh rupees he had promised, he had to suffer a show of force, which ended with Holkar marching away with a 36-year lease on Rampura, a region yielding 3 lakhs in annual revenue.[30]

These exactions decimated Rajputana's finances. Jaipur, for instance, saw its annual revenue decline by a third over the latter part of the century, falling from about 1.2 crore to 86 lakhs.[31] Being "constantly in need of money" to support their sprawling militias, which were prone to revolting when their pay went into arrears, the Marathas could not afford to change their ways.[32] Hence, they sought, Jadunath Sarkar laments, "to draw blood out of stone," citing the pitiable condition of Udaipur, where the ruler was at one point reduced to borrowing money to cover his expenses.[33] Much the same happened in Jodhpur whose Rathores had earlier lorded over neighboring Gujarat but toward the end of the century "could not afford oil for lighting lamps in the evenings."[34]

More offensive than the Marathas' hungry ledger books was the narrowness of their vision. Because they never tried to draw the Rajputs into anything like a common enterprise, and instead sought only to build up moth-eaten territories to pass on to their families, the Maratha *sardars* gave Rajputana no reason to embrace them. Had they "utilized the Rajputs as the Mughals had done," A. C. Bannerjee observes, events might have "flowed through different channels."[35] To make matters worse, the Rajputs responded to the Marathas' carelessness in the least useful way. Rather than uniting to extract better terms, they sought deliverance from the outside, which only encouraged the Marathas to distrust them. They crossed a line in 1761 when they declined to aid the Marathas after Ahmed Shah Durrani of Afghanistan invaded India.[36] After Durrani worsted the Marathas at Panipat, the Rajputs added to the Marathas' misery by trying to expel them from Rajputana. Such maneuvers cost the Marathas dearly and made them ache for the chance to humble the Rajputs who were apparently ready to offer "obedience and service" to foreigners but not to their co-religionists from the Deccan.[37]

Toward the close of the century the Marathas were able to impose costs. By this time, under the de facto leadership of Mahadaji Sindhia, and his renowned French commander, Benoît de Boigne, the Marathas had revitalized their military, which now boasted drilled troops and modern artillery. After obtaining hegemony in Northern India, Sindhia marched on Rajputana in 1790.[38] Unable to persuade the British to come to their aid, the Rajputs replied with another one of their half-hearted confederations. But by now their combined numbers were not enough to compensate for their growing disadvantage in the military sphere.[39] With the Rajput nobility loathe to cede their customary role as the suppliers and leaders of troops, the Maharajas of Rajasthan had been able to do little in terms of modernizing their militaries in the interim, save for recruiting disjointed mercenary units.[40] Little wonder then that when the two sides met at Patan and Merta, the hail of bullets from Sindhia's "invincible army" made a bloody mess of Jaipur and Jodhpur's levies, who were then stripped of everything from their antiquated weapons to their cooking pots and ordered to pay tens of lakhs in indemnities. With this historic defeat it became clear that an era had ended: the Rajput on his horse had been shown, as G. S. Sardesai put it, the "utter futility of mere courage against discipline, and of the sword against bullets."[41] Going forward, Rajputana's peace and prosperity would have to depend on diplomacy or the prudent handling of external forces bearing down on the region.

The Curtain Rises

So far we have seen how imprudence repeatedly led to Rajputana's subjugation. Brave but conservative, the Rajputs did not prepare sufficiently for modern warfare; selfless but parochial, they did not combine to compensate for their declining power. These defects left them exposed to the war machines of the Mughals and the Marathas. What remains to be seen is why the Rajputs subsequently failed at diplomacy as well. And this requires that we take in two dramatic changes that occurred in Northern India in the opening decade of the nineteenth century: the fragmentation of the Maratha Empire and the emergence of an uneasy challenger to it, the East India Company.

Over the course of the eighteenth century, two slow-motion coups had transformed the Marathas from a monarchy into a confederacy. The first saw the Chhatrapatis, the descendants of Shivaji, the founder of the Maratha Empire, lose power to their more able ministers, the Peshwas. The second saw the Peshwas, whose talents waned after their own office became hereditary, cede power to their more able *sardars*, Sindhia and Holkar in particular. Because both these coups rewarded vitality, they were the cause of great good. Under sagacious Peshwas, the Marathas subverted the Mughals and gained a sprawling empire which ambitious *sardars* then preserved by putting down "insurgent Rajas" such as the Rajputs.[42]

But these coups also had a consequence that would ultimately prove fatal to the Maratha Empire. Because they dispersed power, these coups encouraged the *sardars* to act ever more independently of the central authority—the Peshwa's *darbar* (court) in Pune.[43] This characteristic became especially apparent in the closing decade of the

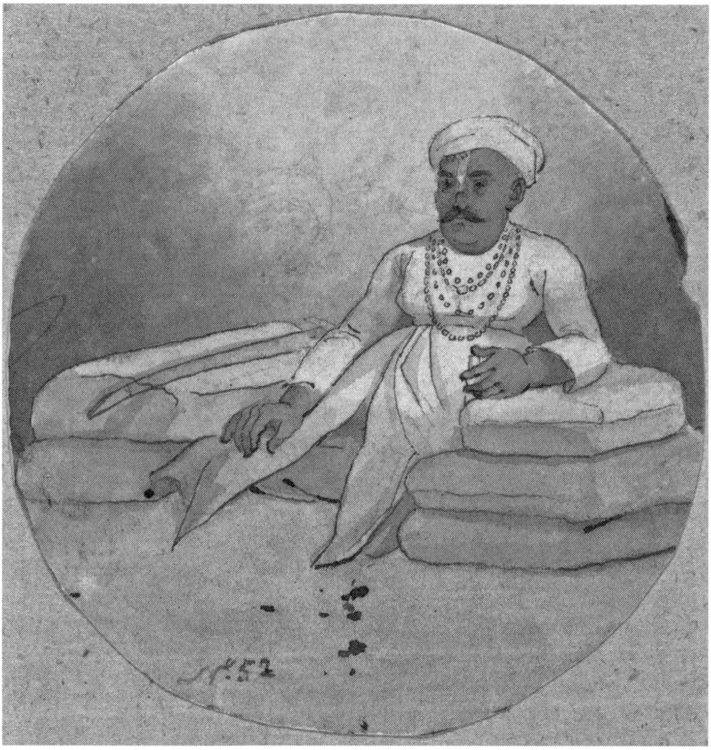

Mahadaji Sindhia.
© Robert Mabon, Paul Mellon Collection, Yale Center for British Art.

eighteenth century when Sindhia and Holkar, the leading *sardars*, came to blows. The two houses had long feuded over the division of spoils on which depended their militias and hence their stature. As both had their strongholds in the neighboring region of Malwa, control over lucrative tracts in Rajputana was a particular bone of contention, prompting Pune to establish a formula to divide the tributes obtained from there: of every rupee, six *annas* belonged to the Peshwa, and five each to Sindhia and Holkar.[44]

So long as the *sardars* were roughly on par in terms of men and material, this formula served its purpose. All this began to change when Mahadaji Sindhia appeared on the scene. By 1790, this hard-working man had humbled the Jats and the Rohillas, deterred the Afghans, the Sikhs, and the British, and routed the Mughals and the Rajputs, making him the nominal ruler of territories between the Sutlej and the Narmada. Painfully aware that Mahadaji's "long strides" had reduced them to a "second rate position," the Holkars belatedly sought to recover lost ground.[45] Led by Tukoji Holkar, they now hurriedly "westernized" their military by raising a properly drilled and regularly paid military force under the command of Chevalier Dudrenec, another of the many French adventurers that, like de Boigne, were circulating in Northern India at the time.[46] As the rivalry between the houses began to escalate, the Rajputs were caught in the middle. The breaking point came in 1792 when Mahadaji claimed, as the fruit of his aforementioned victory at Patan, the right to collect and distribute the tribute from Jaipur, a prerogative hitherto exercised by the Holkars.[47] Not wanting to pay the tribute of 17 lakhs twice over, Jaipur sided with Tukoji. This open challenge led to a series of battles between the *sardars* culminating in a showdown at Lakheri in 1793 where de Boigne's better trained and equipped forces routed Dudrenec's battalions.

Having overawed the Holkars, Mahadaji was in a position to dictate terms to Pune—a veritable turbaned Caesar. Since 1774, the Maratha Empire had effectively been governed by Nana Fadnavis, Regent to Madhava Rao II, the underage Peshwa. As Mahadaji's successes accumulated, Fadnavis had sought to preserve Pune's declining authority by tightening the purse strings and tacitly encouraging the Holkars. No longer willing to put up with this "imbecilic policy," Sindhia now demanded to be properly compensated for his troubles.[48] The sight of his gleaming battalions prompted a compromise: the Pune *darbar* pledged 5 crores toward his expenses and granted him "sole management" of Hindustan.[49] But just as Mahadaji was about to bring order to the weary residents of Indo-Gangetic plain, fate exposed his shortcoming—his failure to nurture a worthy successor. In February 1794 he was carried away by a sudden illness, leaving his vast dominion to a hastily adopted grandnephew, Daulat Rao, who "inherited the ambition, but not the judgment or talents of his uncle."[50]

Daulat Rao immediately set about trying to complete the political revolution that Mahadaji had begun. The death of Madhava Rao II, the young Peshwa, only a few months later, provided what seemed a suitable opening. Taking advantage of the military he had inherited from Mahadaji, Daulat Rao ensured that the office of Peshwa was filled in 1795 by Baji Rao II. The new Peshwa repaid Sindhia by backing his bid to reduce the Holkars to perpetual "vassalage."[51] Initially, Daulat Rao appeared certain to succeed, especially after Tukoji Holkar's demise in 1797 sparked a ferocious battle of succession that ended with Sindhia having killed or captured all the contenders to the Holkar *gaddi* (throne). But then in 1798 the hardiest of these contenders, Jaswant Rao Holkar, escaped from captivity and made his way to Malwa, where he set about trying to restore his house.

Lacking money and men, Jaswant recruited "adventurers of all kinds." Of vital importance was his decision to enter into an agreement with Amir Khan, a Pathan mercenary of some repute in Central India, wherein the two agreed to "unite in their fortunes and share equally in all future conquest and plunder."[52] Together they brought under Holkar's banner hordes of Pindaris—horsemen who formed predatory bands when there was no employment to be had as irregular cavalry units.[53] With the aid of these "brigand" Pathans and "wolfish" Pindaris, Jaswant undertook "roving campaigns" that plundered Sindhia's possessions in Malwa.[54] Once he had filled his pockets, Jaswant recruited the remnants of Dudrenec's modern battalions, and prepared to give battle. His plans were spoiled, however, when, on the eve of the confrontation at Indore in 1801, Daulat Rao bribed Dudrenec into switching sides. With Holkar's infantry and artillery in disarray, Sindhia's forces were able to have their way, compelling Jaswant to retreat toward Rajputana, where he and Amir set about replenishing their coffers by pillaging towns, raiding Hindu temples, and racking cultivators.[55] Then, in his typically brash way, Jaswant went on the offensive. In 1802 he made an unexpected, rapid march toward Pune with a view to becoming the "real custodian" of the Maratha Empire.[56] A showdown at outskirts of the capital ended with Baji Rao II fleeing toward Company territory, whereupon Jaswant sacked Pune and raised up a new Peshwa in the form of Amrit Rao.[57]

By this point in the story Rajputana had already suffered a great deal. Jaswant's relentless demands for contributions had inflicted unspeakable misery on the populace.[58] That no one was safe was made clear by the case of Nathdwara, the famed temple town in Mewar, where after "upbraiding Lord Krishna for his defeats while lying prostrate before his image," Jaswant seized treasures from the priests as *prasad* (blessed food) before plundering the inhabitants for good measure.[59] Daulat Rao's efforts to maintain his supremacy in the region only made matters worse. The lieutenants he sent in pursuit of Jaswant spent more time warring with each other and making themselves disagreeable by punishing communities that had given succor to Holkar.[60]

Just as it seemed the Rajputs' misery would never end, there was a glimmer of hope. At the very end of 1802 it became clear that the British intended to exploit the deepening civil war between the *sardars*. The Rajputs had been awaiting this moment. A quarter of a century earlier the Company had tried to unsettle the Marathas by influencing the contest for the office of Peshwa. This prompted the Marathas to unite against them, sparking the First Anglo-Maratha War (1776–82). Astute diplomacy by Nana Fadnavis led to an unprecedented confederacy of Native States that battered the British from all directions. Confronted with military defeats and then blockades that caused famine and financial distress, the British sued for peace, promising Pune in 1781 that going forward it was the "unalterable determination of the Company, of the King, and of the whole English Nation . . . of remaining satisfied with their possessions in this part of the World, without aiming at new conquests, but living in peace and amity."[61]

This promise of "everlasting friendship" was of course a ploy to buy time. The British were on the search for an empire in Asia that would "more than compensate for the loss of America."[62] As John Robinson, one of the leading figures in Parliament, wrote to Warren Hastings in 1781, "I am enthusiastic about India, and look upon it as the salvation, as the wealth, the grandeur, the glory of this country."[63] The Marathas broadly understood the challenge they confronted. The British, they discerned, were only temporarily vanquished and they intended to "divide and grab" the Native States by "enlisting the sympathy of one to put down the others."[64] The great question then was what the two sides could accomplish in the interval.

The British rose to the occasion. Under two successive Governor-Generals, Charles Cornwallis and John Shore, the Company devoted itself to the "great work" of establishing a "system of government on sound principles."[65] By inaugurating the rudiments of the rule of law and a modern bureaucracy, it was able to improve revenue generation and collection. This allowed it to obtain loans from Indian bankers at relatively lower rates of interest and also gave it the ability to pay its troops punctually.[66] In the uneasy Maratha camp, by contrast, revenue management was "too chaotic to yield an assured surplus," compelling the *sardars* to exercise an "impolitic parsimony" that exasperated their bankers and angered their troops.[67]

Having put its own house in order, the Company then set about dismantling the "coalition of opportunists" that had caused it such trouble in the First Anglo-Maratha War.[68] While Nana Fadnavis, the Peshwa's Regent, was occupied with managing the unmanageable *sardars*, the next Governor-General, Richard Wellesley, reduced Tanjore, Travancore, Hyderabad, and Mysore to the position of so-called subsidiaries, giving the Company control over the military and diplomatic policies of those Native States. He even ventured to "strike at the root" of the Maratha Empire by treating separately with the *sardars*, successfully peeling away the Gaekwars of Baroda in 1802.[69]

Having outperformed and encircled the Marathas, Wellesley waited to take renewed advantage of the worsening relations between the Peshwa and his *sardars*. Between 1798 and 1802 he keenly watched Sindhia and Holkar "weaken the power and impair the resources of each other."[70] Knowing that Baji Rao II dreaded being at the mercy of the victor of that contest, Wellesley repeatedly proposed secret treaties to "liberate" the Peshwa from his *sardars*.[71] Initially, the Peshwa entertained the offers only with a view to deterring Daulat Rao, his overweening patron. But when Jaswant routed Daulat Rao's forces and proceeded to raise up Amrit Rao as the new Peshwa, a panicked Baji Rao II decided to "purchase his security at the expense of his independence" by signing the Treaty of Bassein in December 1802, which invited the Company to restore him as Peshwa.[72] By April 1803 the Company had done the needful, with Jaswant and Amrit Rao fleeing Pune on the approach of Baji Rao II "backed by British bayonets."[73]

The scene was head-spinning: having taken their turns making and unmaking Peshwas, the *sardars* were now confronted with a Peshwa beholden to the Company. They reacted to the humiliation in the same way they had when the British had last meddled in Pune—by declaring war. But there was to be a fateful difference. Whereas previously the Maratha *sardars* had banded together against the British, this time around their brotherhood gave way. After calling on his fellow *sardars* to "combine" against the Company, Jaswant chose, at the very last time minute, to stay on the sidelines, hoping to see the British take Daulat Rao down a few notches.[74]

Jaswant's hope was more than realized. Ever since the First Anglo-Maratha War, Mahadaji had been diligently preparing for the coming showdown with the Company. Unlike his fellow *sardars*, who were notoriously tight-fisted, Mahadaji granted his commander, de Boigne, extensive *jaidads* (military fiefs) that the Frenchman managed well and used to build that rarest of things among the Marathas, "a contented and well-paid army," equipped and trained in the modern way, complete with cannon foundries, ambulance corps, and even pensions for the invalid.[75] However, all this planning, which Daulat Rao inherited, came to naught when the Second Anglo-Maratha War began in August 1803, due to the "notorious infidelity" of the European mercenaries on whom de Boigne's system depended.[76] De Boigne himself had already quit in 1796. Sensing that the Marathas under Daulat Rao were unlikely to prevail against the Company, and being "cold-blooded enough" to see that his only escape route ran through Company territory, as did the credit system that would allow him to siphon his enormous wealth back to Europe, the Frenchman elected to depart in good time.[77] Nearly all of de Boigne's subordinates made the same decision after the Company announced, on the eve of the Second Anglo-Maratha War, an amnesty for Europeans serving with the Marathas.[78] The ensuing desertions decimated Daulat Rao's officer corps.[79] In spite of this, his military performed remarkably well. At the pivotal Battle of Assaye in September 1803, several battalions fought down to the last man, and Arthur Wellesley paid heavily for underestimating the Marathas: 40 percent of the British contingent were killed or wounded, making it one of the bloodiest battles in Company history.[80] But tenacity could not make up for the loss in numbers and morale caused by Holkar's absence. Following a string of defeats to Arthur Wellesley in the Deccan, and to Gerard Lake in the North, Daulat Rao grudgingly signed the Treaty of Surji-Arjungaon in December 1803, surrendering control of North India to the Company and with it the right to collect tribute from Rajputana.

Up to this moment the Rajputs had not been able to take much advantage of the Company's contest with the Marathas. Though the Company had long viewed the Marathas' hold over Rajputana with a "jealous eye," the beating it had received in the First Anglo-Maratha War had taught it patience.[81] Thus, when in 1787 Jaipur and Jodhpur appealed to the Governor-General for protection from an avenging Mahadaji, Fort William "maturely" decided that it would be unwise to "involve the Company in trouble."[82] However, once the Second Anglo-Maratha War got underway, the Company's earlier policy of "non-intervention" in Rajputana was discarded on the usual grounds of "justice and necessity."[83] Aiming to reduce the Marathas' room for maneuver, Wellesley now set about wresting Rajputana from them. To wit, he presented Jaipur and Jodhpur with treaties requiring "reciprocal aid" against the Marathas.[84] Dreading a violent reaction from the Marathas, the Rajputs dithered for some months. But, as the Company's victories over Sindhia mounted, their confidence grew. Ultimately, in the same month that Sindhia signed the Treaty of Surji-Arjungaon,

Jaipur accepted the Company's offer of "firm and permanent friendship," and Jodhpur prepared to follow suit.[85]

What no one anticipated correctly was Holkar. Having thus far been "carefully left alone" by the British, Jaswant now decided to take advantage of what he presumed was a war-weary Fort William.[86] In April 1804 he placed before the Governor-General a set of "insolent proposals," including the right to collect tribute from Rajputana, which he followed up by ravaging Jaipur.[87] In this face of Holkar's "uncontrolled fury," Jodhpur quickly coughed up 20 lakhs in tribute and decided against ratifying its treaty with the Company.[88] This challenge to the Company turned out to be something of a miscalculation on Holkar's part. Though they were wary of Jaswant, the British were still keen to establish "tranquility" in Central India.[89] His unruliness only convinced them of the need to neutralize the "last messy remnant of Maratha independence."[90] But this endeavor turned out to be far costlier than they imagined. The British mocked Jaswant's promise that Company forces would not "have leisure to breathe for a moment" as little more than "insulting menace" from a ruler who could only "consider the ground on which he encamped his country."[91] But Jaswant was more than the "mere robber" they believed him to be; he was by this time a practiced guerilla.[92] After preemptively expelling (and in some cases, even beheading) his European officers, whom he declared *dhokebaaz* (or deceivers), Jaswant undertook "high-speed cavalry warfare" that harassed Company forces for months on end.[93] He periodically cut off their supplies and communication, and directed surprise assaults that caught them short, leading in one famous case to the destruction of an entire battle group.[94]

Jaswant's successes "created a sensation" in Northern India, especially after Lake lost thousands of men in botched sieges at Bharatpur in February 1805.[95] Daulat Rao, who had been licking his wounds, now saw "a ray of hope" when Jaswant urged that the *sardars* ought to give up "quarrelling among themselves."[96] Following secret contact between their officers, Sindhia and Holkar met in person whereupon, to the Company's great shock, they agreed to forge a "united front" for the "welfare of the Maratha Empire."[97] The terms included returning to the earlier custom of sharing equally the tributes collected from Rajputana. The principality of Kota was the first to feel the effects of their renewed brotherly feeling, being compelled to hand over 20 lakhs as tribute which was divided equally between the *sardars*.

Predictably enough, the alliance lasted only a few months. By August 1805 the Company was able to "detach" Sindhia from Holkar by promising to renegotiate the humiliating Treaty of Surji-Arjungaon.[98] Since he blamed his defeat at the Battle of Assaye on Jaswant's decision to sit out the contest, Daulat Rao was only too happy to repay his Maratha brother in kind. Abandoned, Jaswant went on the run, knowing that, having restored their advantage in numbers and resources, the British would now come after him with renewed vigor. Shadowed by Lake, Jaswant escaped via Jodhpur toward the Punjab. By December 1805, he was in Amritsar, where he offered to "embrace the Sikh religion" in return for Ranjit Singh's protection.[99] Should the Sikhs not support him, he warned them, he would go "to the extremity of turning Mohammadan" and seek refuge with their enemies, the Afghans.[100] More interested in striking a deal with

Ranjit Singh (*left*) with Jaswant Rao Holkar (*center*), and Amir Khan (*bottom right*).

the ambitious British than the distracted Afghans across the mountains, Ranjit Singh wasted little time in renouncing Jaswant, who was, he surmised, a "*pucca haramzada*" (a true rascal).[101]

At a loss, Jaswant now deputed his *vakils* (representatives) to Lake and prepared to submit to the Company. And then, at the very moment when the noose was around his neck, he obtained an amazing reprieve. It so happened that over the preceding months the Company's directors had concluded that Wellesley's so-called "forward policy" faced "extraordinary difficulties."[102] The prolonged contest with the Marathas had compelled the Governor-General to keep his military in the field for far longer than anticipated. With the Company's debt having doubled during Wellesley's tenure, and the pay for Lake's troops now five months in arrears, the directors began fretting over the "failure of public credit" should the increasingly desperate Jaswant find an ally and provoke a wider war at the very moment when Napoleon's highly publicized preparations to invade England made it impossible for Britain to send reinforcements to India.[103] In the event, the decision was made to recall Wellesley and revive the policy of "non-intervention."[104]

In October 1805 the execution of this policy had been entrusted to George Barlow, a senior civil servant, who became the Acting Governor-General. Seeking "the most rigid economy" in military spending, Barlow immediately set about negotiating treaties with the Marathas that would "conciliate them by concessions" and make it in "their interest to maintain amity."[105] Within a month, he concluded a revised treaty that returned to Daulat Rao several of his territories and gave him "a free hand" in Rajputana.[106] Barlow was even more generous to Jaswant, who wanted concessions "of a nature to make it appear to the world that his fortunes were not at so low an ebb as they really are."[107] Thus, two months later, in January 1806, Jaswant was given a "god-send" in the form of a treaty wherein the Company pledged to stay clear of his territory in Malwa and to sever its "connections" with Rajputana.[108] Then the news was broken to the Rajputs. Jaipur was now bluntly informed that the treaty it had concluded with the Company—only a month prior—stood annulled. The decision was made, Barlow promised the Maharaja, after "maturest deliberation."[109] And when Jodhpur hurriedly tried to revive the treaty earlier proposed by Wellesley, which it had not ratified under duress from Holkar, it was curtly informed that the arrangement was no longer "expedient."[110]

These rapid developments caught the Rajputs completely wrong-footed. As the Maharaja of Jaipur lamented in a letter to the Governor-General, "the future safety and tranquility of his possessions" would henceforth depend "upon the clemency and generosity of those enemies whom he had so highly irritated by his unfortunate connection with the British Government."[111] And clemency, everyone knew, was unlikely to be shown. Sindhia and Holkar were itching to settle scores with the unfaithful Rajputs, and to use Rajputana's remaining wealth as the means to pacify the unpaid creditors, hungry troops, and restless Pindaris that were conducting *dharnas* (demonstrations) outside their simmering *darbars*. And so began what was colloquially referred to as *gardi ka waqt* (time of troubles), the period when, as Jadunath Sarkar's melancholy observation has it, "Rajputana became a zoological garden with the barriers of the cages thrown down and the keepers removed."[112]

Map 1 British India in 1782 and 1805.

The Main Act

Thus far we have traced the factors that brought the Rajputs to the brink of disaster. In 1790 their long history of disunity culminated in their being routed by the larger and better prepared Maratha Empire. To this was added misfortune when in 1806 the Company's sudden withdrawal from Northern India left them diplomatically isolated and at the mercy of the Marathas. But even this background cannot fully account for the intensity of the horrors Rajputana would subsequently confront. To grasp the sequence of events that led to Krishna Kumari's sacrifice, we need to examine the characters involved because division and bad luck may have laid Rajputana low, but it was the imprudent choices of its Maharajas that turned adversity into tragedy.

The originator of the tragedy was Man Singh, the Maharaja of Jodhpur. When he ascended to the *gaddi* in 1803, Man Singh inherited an age-old headache. Jodhpur's size and stature owed much to clans who had "conquered lands with the strength of their own arms."[113] Since they believed they held their fiefs "by virtue of individual efforts," the heads of these clans considered themselves "chiefs in miniature," whose allegiance to the "central authority" was only voluntary.[114] The Maharajas of Jodhpur had long tried to disabuse the *thakurs* (chiefs) of this idea, but they had limited success because the "refractory nobles" were usually able to gain support from outsiders.[115] Initially, this succor came from the Mughal emperors, who gladly aided the *thakurs* whenever the Maharaja did not display sufficient featly.[116] Later, we have seen, it was the Maratha *sardars*, who supported either the Maharaja or his recalcitrant *thakurs* as the pay made it worthwhile.

Man Singh was intimately familiar with the consequences of Jodhpur's fragmented polity. His life had been profoundly shaped by one of the "dastardly" acts that his grandfather, Vijay Singh, had employed to cement his uncertain authority. It had involved inviting some of the rebellious "pillars" of the nobility to the funeral of his *guru* (preceptor) in 1760, whereupon the troublesome *thakurs* were seized and put to death.[117] This rash act inaugurated a blood feud that simmered for decades until Jodhpur was thrashed by the Marathas in 1790. The humiliating loss lowered Vijay Singh's standing and gave the heirs of the murdered *thakurs*, led by Sawai Singh of Pokhran, the opening they needed. In February 1792 they helped the Maharaja's grandson, Bhim Singh, seize power in a coup. Though Vijay Singh was eventually able to claw his way back onto the *gaddi*, it was only by promising the rebellious *thakurs* that he would be succeeded by Bhim Singh—and not by Man Singh, his other grandson and preferred heir.

A little more than a year later, Vijay Singh was no more. Never one to give up, Man Singh simply shrugged off his grandfather's promise and staked his claim to the throne, thereby inaugurating a "straight fight" with Bhim Singh.[118] For the next decade, Bhim Singh had the upper hand. He eliminated the *thakurs* that supported Man Singh, compelling his cousin to retreat to Jalore, a territory that Vijay Singh, the late Maharaja, had prepared for precisely such contingencies. Jalore contained a celebrated medieval-era fort whose "strong walls" held Marwar's "reserve treasury" and two "large tanks of sweet water."[119] These favorable features allowed Man Singh to withstand repeated

Man Singh, Maharaja of Jodhpur © British Library Board.

year-long sieges until October 1803 when, starving and demoralized, he announced his decision to capitulate. Then, miraculously, two days before Man Singh was to surrender, Bhim Singh dropped dead. Within days, Man Singh found himself transported from his exhausted fortress to the *gaddi* of Jodhpur.

On ascending to the throne, Man Singh still had to contend with the formidable group of refractory *thakurs* that had supported Bhim Singh. Foremost among these was Sawai Singh who held the office of *pradhan* (effectively, the leader of the nobility). What made the *thakur* of Pokhran a particularly grave threat was his sister, the Derawari *Rani* (queen), who had been married to Bhim Singh and now claimed to be expecting the late Maharaja's child. Ever one to temporize, Man Singh sought to placate Sawai Singh by giving a written undertaking that if the child proved to be a son, he would surrender the throne to him. As luck would have it, the *Rani* produced a boy, Dhonkal Singh, whereupon a dismayed Man Singh demanded proof that the infant was in fact Bhim Singh's offspring. Fearing that Man Singh had "evil intentions," Sawai Singh secreted his sister and her child out of Jodhpur and ferried them to Khetri, a fief owing fealty to Jaipur.[120] Angered at being outsmarted, Man Singh struck back hard. He launched offensives against Sawai Singh's adherents, and after defeating or killing several of them with the aid of mercenaries, he turned his attention toward Jaipur, seeking to punish it for supporting Dhonkal Singh. And thus came Krishna Kumari into view.

Krishna Kumari was the daughter of Bhim Singh, the Maharana of Udaipur. In 1799 the Maharana had her betrothed, at the age of five, to his namesake, Bhim Singh of Jodhpur. Given the singular status that Udaipur's princesses enjoyed in Rajputana as embodiments of purity, the engagement had greatly bolstered Bhim Singh's stature amid his contest with Man Singh. Little wonder then that when Man Singh came to power, he crossly declined the Maharana's offer to inherit the engagement and instead seized Ghanerao, a strategically important fief occupied by the Maharana's relations, who had refused to support Man Singh in his fight against his cousin. Man Singh's intention may have been to humiliate the Maharana, but his heavy-handedness backfired. Egged on by Sawai Singh's allies in Udaipur, the humiliated Maharana retaliated by drawing closer to Jaipur, to which end he offered Krishna Kumari's hand to Jagat Singh, the Maharaja of Jaipur.[121] As this move left him dangerously isolated, Man Singh demanded in November 1804 that the Maharana renew the offer for him to inherit the engagement with Krishna Kumari. But by this point the matter had become a triangular one. Having also recently ascended to the *gaddi*, the twenty-year-old Jagat Singh had gladly accepted the marriage proposal as it would "exalt" him and bolster his authority in the eyes of his subjects.[122] He was also persuaded by his counselors to see the Maharana's offer as a once-in-a-lifetime chance to underscore the primacy of the Kachwahas of Jaipur over the Rathores of Jodhpur.[123]

For some months the matter simmered. Letters and threats were exchanged between all the parties—to little avail. Then Sawai Singh's intrigues brought matters to a boil. In the summer of 1805, he arranged for his granddaughter to become one of Jagat Singh's many wives, a development that promised to bring Jaipur still deeper into Dhonkal Singh's camp. Naturally, Man Singh tried to stymie the wedding, citing the

Bhim Singh, Maharana of Udaipur © British Library Board.

indecorum of having a Rathore noblewoman betrothed to Jagat Singh, who was notorious for his abject devotion to a Muslim dancing girl in his *zenana* (women's quarters).[124] Sawai Singh had a retort ready: he humiliated Man Singh by asking how dare the Maharaja speak of the pride of the Rathores, having lost to Jaipur the prized bride that his predecessor had previously won for Jodhpur?[125]

The taunt, which underlined Man Singh's increasingly perilous situation—his neighbors and nobles working in concert against him—pushed the Maharaja to act. Being a tributary of Daulat Rao, Man Singh appealed to the Maratha chieftain to intercede and pressure Jaipur to decline the proffered engagement. But Jagat Singh was not easily intimidated. Convinced that his alliance with the Company, which had been formalized only a month prior, would give him the upper hand in the event of a contest with Daulat Rao, he pressed the Maharana of Udaipur to complete the formalities.[126] To ensure that the Maharana did not change his mind, in January 1806 Jagat Singh dispatched troops to "escort" a party carrying the *tika* (the vermillion used to symbolize blessing) to Jaipur.[127] Not wanting to be outmaneuvered, Man Singh countered by sending a sizable contingent that successfully prevented the *tika* from leaving Udaipur. With these *fait accomplis*, the dispute assumed a truly dangerous character. It now became a matter of honor, making it impossible for either side to back down.

As it had become imperative to prevail, both Maharajas reached out to the British for aid. Their timing could not have been worse. This was, we have seen, the exact moment when the British were about to surrender Rajputana to the Marathas. Thus, when *vakils* from Jaipur and Jodhpur arrived at the Residency (the office of the British resident or ambassador to the Mughal court) in Delhi, they were politely informed that the Company could not involve itself in disputes of a "private and family nature."[128] Left reeling, both sides then raced to win over the Marathas. With Holkar still dusting himself down in the Punjab, the Maharajas initially appealed to Sindhia. Predictably, Daulat Rao demanded they settle their "arrears" in tribute before he would resolve their "matrimonial tangle."[129] Having collected a few lakhs from both sides, Sindhia proposed that the Maharajas give each other a daughter in marriage and offered to solve the "connubial difficulty" by wedding Krishna Kumari himself.[130] The proposal had the makings of a masterstroke: by bringing the Sisodias and Sindhias into matrimonial alliance, it promised to bring peace to Udaipur while strengthening Daulat Rao against Holkar as well as the Company. Indeed, it could have changed the very course of history in Northern India. Unfortunately, the proposal was much too much for the Maharana to stomach. Embittered by decades of Maratha plunder, and unwilling to "pollute" his line by giving his daughter to a "scion of the plough," Bhim Singh demurred.[131] Once it became clear that the Rajputs were less than pleased with his offer, and that Holkar, bankrupted by war and seething at Daulat Rao for betraying him, was on his way to Rajputana, Sindhia smartly retreated.

Man Singh had much to hope from Holkar's arrival in Rajputana. Not only had he previously given Holkar's family refuge when the British were hot on his heels, he had also declined to ratify the treaty that his predecessor, Bhim Singh, had negotiated with the Company. Jaipur, by contrast, had done neither of these things. And so, sure enough, upon returning to the region Holkar gladly allowed his troops to fall upon Jaipur. Following weeks of rapine and pillage, the Jaipur *darbar* agreed to make amends by coughing up a tribute of some 15 lakhs.[132] By August 1806, with the threat of renewed violence hovering over it, the Jaipur *darbar* also agreed to a political compromise brokered by Holkar: Man Singh would marry Jagat Singh's sister, and Jagat Singh would marry Man Singh's daughter; neither would marry Krishna Kumari, and the Maharana "would not select her husband without their approval."[133]

This compromise, which allowed only Jodhpur to save face, was never going to last. Almost at once Jagat Singh set about rebalancing the equation. Over the next few months, he obtained Sindhia and Holkar's neutrality for 10 lakhs apiece. With the Maratha *sardars*' tacit consent he also recruited Amir Khan and four of Sindhia's captains, Ambaji Ingle, Jean Baptiste, Bapuji Sindhia, and Sirji Rao Ghatke, who brought with them large numbers of troops. Then in January 1807 Jagat Singh delivered what he thought would be the *coup de grace*: he formally recognized Dhonkal Singh as the rightful heir to Bhim Singh, an act that brought over to his side some of Jodhpur's most important *thakurs* led by Sawai Singh. Two months later, with this "gigantic coalition" in place, Jagat Singh went on the offensive.[134] After being worsted in early skirmishes, the bulk of the *thakurs* on Man Singh's side switched their allegiance to Dhonkal Singh.[135] In the event, it was not long before Jaipur's contingents were bearing down on Man Singh's encampment. Not knowing which of his remaining *thakurs* he could still trust, Man Singh abandoned his weapons, stores, and insignia and fled to Jodhpur where he holed up in the imposing Mehrangarh fort.[136]

This might have been the end of the matter but for Sawai Singh. He pressed Jagat Singh not to depart for Udaipur and marry Krishna Kumari before he had fulfilled his promise to eject Man Singh from Jodhpur and place Dhonkal Singh on the throne. Persuaded to complete his triumph, Jagat Singh entered Jodhpur in pursuit of Man Singh. Once again at the receiving end of a siege, Man Singh did what he did best: wait for the tide to turn. And turn it did. In a few short months the confederacy ranged against him started to break down. The Jodhpur *thakurs* were the first to become disgruntled, embarrassed by the "wanton depredations" that the mercenaries in Jagat Singh's employ were inflicting on their *watan* (homeland).[137] When the Jodhpur *thakurs* began to peel off, Jagat Singh tried to put a stop to the plunder and violence, leaving the mercenaries, Amir Khan in particular, with a "profound sense of grief."[138] Spying an opening, Man Singh promptly offered the Pathan a hefty bribe to switch sides. The offer was readily accepted, and Amir then went on the offensive on behalf of his new master. Consequently, by August 1807 the tables had turned. With the rapacious Pathan knocking on the gates of Jaipur, Jagat Singh had to give up the siege of Jodhpur and hurry home.[139]

Though he had once again outlasted his opponents, Man Singh was not yet ready to celebrate. His mind was fixed on a "living problem": in the course of his hasty retreat, Jagat Singh had left Sawai Singh and Dhonkal Singh ensconced in the strong fort of Nagaur.[140] A siege would be costly and prolonged, especially as the pair were jealously guarded by Bapuji Sindhia and Jean Baptiste who considered them surety for the

Jagat Singh, Maharaja of Jaipur © British Library Board.

money that Jagat Singh owed them. Unwilling to leave the reckoning to another day, Man Singh struck an expensive deal with Amir Khan: he promised the Pathan 35 lakhs (about half of Jodhpur's annual revenue) if he would eliminate Sawai Singh and Dhonkal Singh.

The former objective was accomplished sooner and more easily than either man anticipated. In March 1808, after feigning a rupture with Man Singh, Amir stomped off in the direction of Nagaur. After deliberately plundering some villages belonging to the Maharaja, he gave out his desire to once again side with Sawai Singh. As Man Singh had failed to make good on his dues, the Pathan loudly complained, he was willing to see Dhonkal Singh placed on the throne "for a due consideration."[141] While the suspicious *thakur* mulled over the offer, Amir set out about trying to remove Sindhia's generals from the scene. To wit, he instigated Bapuji's Afghan troops to mutiny on account of arrears in pay. Once the Afghans had subjected Bapuji to "considerable severities," Amir kindly intervened to offer him 3 lakhs to help with his debts, with an additional lakh for Baptiste who was owed so much by Jagat Singh. Their pockets sufficiently filled, Sindhia's generals quickly departed Nagaur, leaving Amir to focus on Sawai Singh.

Negotiations with Sawai Singh soon came to a head. Rightly doubtful of the Pathan, the *thakur* offered Amir 40 lakhs for his support—but only if he would "give him a guarantee on oath" as to his fidelity and goodwill.[142] It did not take Amir long to unite his officers in declaring that "to shed the blood of an enemy to the faith, by treachery, when necessary for the good of the general cause of the faith, and its army, or for the service of one's chief, was lawful."[143] With this preliminary out of the way, Amir met with Sawai Singh at the Tarkin *dargah* near Nagaur, the tomb of a venerated Sufi saint. There the men exchanged "presents, dresses and even turbans" and the Pathan swore "at the tomb of the saint, to be faithful to his new ally."[144] The following day Sawai Singh and his fellow *thakurs* arrived at Amir's camp in Mundwa, a short distance from Nagaur, to formalize and celebrate their renewed alliance. Once the guests had been seated in the handsome tent appointed for the purpose, Amir's officers excused themselves on the pretext of escorting their commander to the ceremony. Then, on Amir's signal, the tent was dropped, trapping the unsuspecting guests—forty *thakurs*, a couple of the Pathan's lesser relations, and various musicians and *nautch* (dance) girls—all of whom were then "inhumanly massacred by showers of grape and musketry from every direction."[145] Once the severed heads of Sawai Singh and his principal supporters had been paraded around the camp, they were boxed up and dispatched to Jodhpur.[146]

The gruesome end to the *thakur* of Pokhran did not entirely dispel Man Singh's worries. When news of Amir's treachery reached Nagaur, Sawai Singh's sons immediately spirited away the five-year old Dhonkal Singh to neighboring Bikaner. Hence, for the next six months, Man Singh's mind was focused on Bikaner whose ruler, Surat Singh, had long been a thorn in his side, having openly supported his cousin Bhim Singh and then Jagat Singh against him. Now, with Jaipur still smarting from the beating it had recently received, and with Sawai Singh's faction literally in pieces, it was the ideal time to settle scores. So off went Man Singh's mercenaries to Bikaner. Though Dhonkal Singh was once again able to give them slip, they soon had the capital under siege. With no hope of aid from Jaipur, Surat Singh quickly capitulated. In October 1808 he acknowledged Man Singh's sovereignty and offered up significant compensation.

These developments left Man Singh in what appeared to be a commanding position. All that remained was to bring Jagat Singh to forswear support for Dhonkal Singh and relinquish his plan of marrying Krishna Kumari. But this was no easy task given that Jodhpur's treasury was completely empty and its *thakurs* were worn out by the late war. Meanwhile, Amir Khan, who had by now invited himself into the Jodhpur *darbar*, was becoming ever more impatient about the many lakhs owed to him for services rendered. And so, in his usual way, Man Singh tried to make his problems solve each other. He now entered into a dangerous bargain. He conferred on Amir the title of Nawab (governor) and agreed to take one of Pathan's perennially mutinous brigades "into permanent service at an annual charge of thirteen lakhs of rupees."[147] In March 1809, this newly acquired brigade began making routine incursions into Jaipur territory, "plundering and devastating the countryside."[148] The pressure had the desired effect. Having already spent "at the lowest computation" 120 lakhs of rupees (or about twice Jaipur's annual income) on the fruitless contest with Jodhpur, Jagat Singh was not in a position to mount a sustained response to Amir's guerilla tactics.[149] When his appeals to the British for assistance went unanswered, his emissaries set about working out a compromise. After prolonged negotiations, in May 1810 Jaipur and Jodhpur entered a treaty of "mutual defense and friendship." Man Singh got what he most wanted: Jagat Singh promised to cease supporting the cause of Dhonkal Singh. The Maharajas were also able to preserve their honor by agreeing that they would both "refrain from aspiring" for the hand of Krishna Kumari, and instead partake in the double marriage previously proposed by Holkar wherein Man Singh would wed Jagat Singh's sister, and Jagat Singh would marry Man Singh's daughter.[150]

This outcome left one question to resolve: if neither Maharaja were permitted to marry Krishna Kumari, then who would she wed? The princess had now reached the more than eminently marriageable age of sixteen. Per the norm of the era, her father, the Maharana of Udaipur, would be disgraced if she remained unmarried much longer. But given that Udaipur princesses had traditionally been married to the Maharajas of either Jaipur or Jodhpur, allowing Krishna Kumari to marry into a minor Rajput clan, or (god forbid!) a Maratha clan, would violate precedent and cause political turmoil. In the event, it soon became clear that "the honour of all parties required the death of Krishna Kumari."[151]

And so moved Amir Khan to the center of the stage. Accompanied by some 20,000 troops, he forced his way into the capital in Udaipur in June 1810 where he placed the unvarnished facts before Ajit Singh, the Maharana's principal counselor. The quarrel that Bhim Singh had provoked by using Krishna Kumari as pawn "would never be settled, so long as his daughter lived," the Pathan announced. It therefore "behooved" the Maharana "out of regard for the interests of his Raj (or state), no less than for the honor of his family, to put her to death."[152] When this argument failed to move the Maharana, Amir did what he did best, which was to threaten the worst. If Bhim Singh did not remove Krishna Kumari from the scene, he warned, it would be his "duty" as Man Singh's proxy "to seize her by force and carry her away in a *palki* (palanquin) to Jodhpur, that the Raja may there complete his marriage with her."[153] This may have been an empty threat because the peace treaty recently concluded between Jodhpur and Jaipur forbade Man Singh from marrying Krishna Kumari. But there was no mistaking the implication: if Bhim Singh continued to dally, Amir would take matters into his own hands. In the event, the Maharana would witness "the effects of a more extended dishonor from the vengeance of the Pathan, and the storm of his palace by his licentious adherents."[154]

Seeing where matters were heading, Ajit Singh pressed a compromise. He advised Bhim Singh to choose the lesser of two evils: the death of his daughter rather than the sacking of his capital and the violation of the *zenana*. Simultaneously, to leave the Maharana with some shred of dignity, Ajit Singh asked the Pathan to pledge that Man Singh would return to Udaipur the fief of Ghanerao, whose forcible seizure had initiated the saga over Krishna Kumari's hand.[155] Once the parties had agreed, the Maharana and his counselors set about trying to dispatch his daughter with "as little odium as possible."[156] Initially, a quiet murder by knife was contemplated, but this proved quite impractical, as neither Krishna Kumari's cousin nor her brother, who had access to the *zenana*, could bring themselves to commit the dastardly deed. In the event, "a messenger" from Bhim Singh, which may have been either the Maharana's sister, Chandra Kumari Bai, or more likely his queen, Chawadi Bai, approached Krishna Kumari in her quarters and entreated her "to save her father, family, and tribe, from the struggles and miseries to which her high birth and evil destiny exposed them."[157] By all accounts, the princess acceded to the plea unhesitatingly, considering it her duty as a Rajputni. After bathing and dressing herself "in new and gay attire," she consumed a cup of poison.[158] Unfortunately, her misery was prolonged when the concoction made her retch and therefore failed.[159] After three such fruitless attempts, the princess was offered a drink containing an immense dose of opium.[160] The draught had the desired effect and the princess slipped away from this world with the heart-rending lament: "This is the marriage to which I was foredoomed."[161]

Krishna Kumari's death caused a storm in Udaipur. In the words of John Malcolm, the eminent Company officer and diplomat who interviewed the key actors, and reported the incident in *A Memoir of Central India*, no sooner did the news spread than "loud lamentations burst from every quarter, and expressions of pity at her fate were mingled with execrations on the weakness and cowardice of those who could purchase safety on such terms."[162] The howls were renewed when Krishna Kumari's mother, Chawadi Bai, expired a few days later, having fasted unto death.[163] But once the funeral pyres stopped smoking, Udaipur simply moved on. The Maharana and his counselors had rightly judged, a later chronicler dryly noted, that to their fellow Rajputs, who routinely practiced female infanticide, a girl's life was "of small account."[164] What really mattered to them was whether Krishna Kumari's sacrifice, described in the newspapers, as "the most important political event which has lately occurred in Hindustan," had been in vain or not.[165] Unfortunately, the answer was not what they hoped.

The Curtain Falls

We have now traced the sequence of events that led to Krishna Kumari's death. What remains to be seen is the grim aftermath. The Rajputs hoped, we have seen, that the princess would "by her death seal the peace" (or, as the British press put it, terminate the war "which this second Helen [of Troy] had excited").[166] They failed to consider, however, what Amir Khan wanted. The Pathan, they soon learnt, wanted not to roam Rajputana but to rule it. As it happens, the Rajputs were not the only ones to misjudge circumstances. On his part, Amir failed to consider what the British wanted. The Company, he would learn, was prepared to save the Rajputs in order to save itself from his vaulting ambition.

When Amir first learnt of the contest over Krishna Kumari, he was gleeful about having "pigeons to pluck."[167] To wit, he advised Jaswant Rao Holkar in 1807 that they ought to alternately take the side of Jaipur and Jodhpur and thereby "turn the conflict to our own purposes, spinning it out at pleasure, till the resources of both were exhausted, and both were in our power."[168] It all went according to plan—for Amir. This was because shortly after Amir set about fleecing the Rajputs, Jaswant went from half to completely mad. He holed himself up in his fort in Bhanpura where, fortified by brandy and the many lakhs he had received from Jagat Singh to betray Man Singh, he set about preparing for a "vaster war" against the Company.[169] Taking his cue from what De Boigne had done for Sindhia, he drilled his troops incessantly and established cannon foundries where he personally helped cast "over two hundred brass guns" in a matter of months.[170] At first, these feverish proceedings were considered typical. But then evidence of a more serious mental infirmity became apparent as Jaswant's vigor gave way to violent paroxysms. By early 1808 the Holkar *darbar* concluded his "insanity had reached an extremity" whereupon Jaswant was "bound fast with ropes like a wild beast" and kept that way as he gradually "lapsed into idiotcy."[171]

This astonishing development gifted Amir Khan a long-awaited chance to outgrow his humble origins. Born in Sambhal in 1768 to a Pathan family from Buner in Afghanistan, the early decades of his life had seen Amir do no better than become a "petty mercenary leader" who was "not unfrequently in want of even a meal."[172] And it was not his stomach alone that had to be filled. He grappled constantly with the problem that "his followers were always more numerous than he had the means of paying."[173] And it was not as if Amir could simply overawe his fellow Pathans. Considering him "low and coarse," they mocked him as more of a serpent than a lion.[174] It was only his alliance with Jaswant in 1798 that had changed the picture. His assistance to Jaswant, who was then at his lowest ebb, had led the Maratha to grant him the title of Nawab and the *jagir* (fief) of Sironj, which came with an annual income of 3 lakhs.[175] This gift associated Amir with the celebrated "house of Holkar" and thereby solidified his "precarious rank."[176] But Amir still seems to have doubted his prospects, for when the Second Anglo-Maratha War broke out in 1803 he secretly tried to defect to the British.[177] Negotiations with the Company fell through, however, and so the Pathan was forced to stay on in Jaswant's service. It was only the unexpectedly fruitful end to Second Anglo-Maratha War—the result of the Court of Director's orders to Barlow to make peace with

Amir Khan, Nawab of Tonk © Victoria and Albert Museum, London.

the Marathas—that gave Amir a new lease of life. Barlow's generosity to Jaswant allowed the latter to grudgingly reward Amir with the fertile *parganas* (revenue subdivisions) of Tonk and Pirawa in 1806, increasing the Pathan's annual income by another two lakhs.[178]

Despite these gains, Amir could not rest easy. By 1806 he had an army comprising over 20,000 men to support, which cost, at minimum, half a lakh a month.[179] As the revenue grants from Holkar were nowhere near enough to cover his bills, the Nawab was regularly mobbed and assaulted by his "famished praetorians."[180] Nor could he hope for further largesse from Holkar. Like so many of the Pathan's previous employers, Jaswant was growing ever more wary of Amir's "intriguing nature." Toward the close of the Second Anglo-Maratha War Jaswant had even tried to poison his "inconvenient and overpowerful ally."[181] Though Amir "forgave" Jaswant after discovering the plot, the incident left the Pathan in no doubt that Holkar would prefer to keep him and his undisciplined corps "at a distance."[182]

These difficulties were a key reason why Amir involved himself so keenly in Rajputana's squabbles. But the enterprise was not as profitable as he hoped. The contest over Krishna Kumari certainly helped Amir "fatten his followers," but the wretched condition of the Rajput kingdoms meant there was only so much meat on the bones.[183] From Jodhpur, for instance, he was only able to extract for himself *parganas* worth about 4.5 lakhs per anum.[184] And like generations of Marathas before him, Amir rarely received what the Rajputs promised. Thus, when the full extent of Jaswant's derangement became clear, Amir spied an opportunity to improve his circumstances by exploiting his connection with Holkar in a radically new way. Barely months after Jaswant had been placed in restraints, Amir occupied lands belonging to the neighboring Maratha kingdom of Nagpur and issued a demand for a little more than 11 lakhs, claiming that he had been permitted by Holkar to seek reparations for losses Nagpur had caused him during the Second Anglo-Maratha War. Badly outnumbered, Nagpur appealed to the Company, which scrambled to respond. To wit, in October 1809, Lord Minto the Governor-General wrote to Amir asking him to explain himself. Taken aback by the intervention, Amir replied forcefully. Having forsworn involvement in Maratha territory, the British had no right to involve themselves in this "domestic dispute" he complained. Did they, he asked, wish to "rekindle the flames of war?"[185]

Startled by the menacing language the Governor-General wrote to Jaswant asking if he had in fact permitted Amir to press Nagpur.[186] The reply, ostensibly from Jaswant, but in fact from his Maratha counselors, now led by his mistress Tulsi Bai, disowned Amir's actions. "My health being infirm," Jaswant lamented, the Nawab "has done, and continues to do, whatever he chooses."[187] Upon being informed by Minto of this disavowal of his actions, Amir responded with pretended fury. "Finding that princes are capable of uttering such falsehoods," the Nawab announced, he intended to "separate" from Holkar.[188] He would much prefer, he announced, to "pass the remainder of my life in the service of the British Government," which was the "fountain of equity and justice."[189] All he wanted was "eight annas in the rupee" (or half the revenue of any district it assigned him).[190]

Being least interested in disturbing the treaties the Company had only recently signed with the Marathas, Minto ignored Amir's renewed offer to switch sides, and advised the Pathan to give up the "absurd notion" that the Company would grant him a *jagir*.[191] But Minto was also not willing to let Amir attack Nagpur. By this time, multiple Company officers were coming to the conclusion that the ultimate ambition of this "active and enterprising" chief was to seize Nagpur and thereby obtain "a country by conquest."[192] Thus, after confirming that Holkar's *darbar* would not object to the Nawab being cut down to size, in February 1810 the Governor General had his forces "chastise" Amir by marching toward his *jagir* of Sironj.[193] With his rear exposed, Amir had to beat a hasty and humiliating retreat.

Having learnt that the Company would not allow him to range beyond Malwa and Rajputana, Amir henceforth devoted himself to extracting all he could from these long-suffering territories. He started with Malwa where in April 1810 he effected a revolution by wooing away the cream of Holkar's military with promises of handsome pay—and then disbanding the remainder.[194] This realignment of forces permitted him to browbeat Tulsi Bai into authorizing him to collect tributes from Rajputana on "behalf" of Malhar Rao, the infant heir to Jaswant.[195] Still, his control over the Holkar *darbar* was tenuous because Sindhia, realizing that Amir intended to "reduce him to a state of secondary power," had begun supporting Tulsi Bai.[196] Thus, to beat down Sindhia, whose finances were already in shambles, the Pathan now sought to deny him any further income from Rajputana. With this began a new round of violence in Rajputana, which was inaugurated by Amir forcing his way into Udaipur in June 1810.

When Amir Khan entered Udaipur, he had hoped to kill three birds with one stone—Krishna Kumari. The princess's death would earn him Man Singh's gratitude, which he would exploit by asking the Maharaja to ignore the recently signed treaty of mutual defense that pledged Jodhpur to come to Jaipur's aid in the event of attack.[197] Simultaneously, by obtaining for Bhim Singh the fief of Ghanerao in exchange for Krishna Kumari's death he would prove his worth to Udaipur and thereby obtain a footing there as well. And then, having humiliated and isolated Jagat Singh, he would be able to dictate terms to Jaipur, the wealthiest of the Rajput kingdoms.

Little went as planned, however. In the wake of Krishna Kumari's death, Amir demanded 11 lakhs from Udaipur, nominally to support a brigade that would help the Maharana "enforce the collection of his revenues."[198] But by this time, Udaipur was so impoverished that even the Pathan's very real threat to demolish the Maharana's family temple of Eklinga could not produce the desired monies.[199] Frustrated, Amir moved on to Jaipur, leaving behind his rapacious son-in-law, Jamshed Khan, to squeeze out of Udaipur whatever he could. Though Jagat Singh was left "trembling for the safety of his capital and person" on Amir's approach, he was saved at the last minute by Sindhia who dispatched troops to prevent the Pathan from overpowering the valuable principality.[200] The unexpected development forced Amir to retreat, having acquired only a promise of 17 lakhs for his troubles. This was no small amount (nearly a third of Jaipur's rapidly shrinking annual revenue), but it was a far cry from his original plan of "seizing" control of Jaipur.[201]

Daulat Rao Sindhia © Victoria and Albert Museum, London.

These setbacks compounded Amir's financial difficulties. His military, now swollen with Holkar's cavalry and artillery, whom he had won over with extravagant promises, became so disorderly that he was routinely placed "under restraint" by his "hungry followers."[202] For many months the *akhbars* (newspapers) buzzed with reports of his imaginative escapes from their clutches, such as the time he evaded one set of jailors by hiding in a lieutenant's *zenana*. As the humiliations mounted, Amir became ever more reckless. Jodhpur was the first to feel the effects of his desperation. Between 1812 and 1815, Amir continually extorted land and jewels until Man Singh was bankrupted. When Man Singh's *guru* (preceptor) and *dewan* (prime minister) urged the Maharaja to seek Sindhia's help, Amir had his Pathan troops murder them in the palace. This show of force left Man Singh so fearful for his safety that he began feigning insanity and gave up power to a regency led by Chattar Singh (his degenerate son) and Salim Singh (heir of the beheaded *thakur* Sawai Singh).[203] Consequently, by early 1816 the *akhbars* were reporting that "with the exception of a few miles" around the capital, the "ancient race" of Rathores had submitted to the government of Amir Khan, his *thanas* (toll booths) dotting the landscape.[204] Udaipur had it even worse. Running battles between Jamshed Khan (representing Amir) and Bapuji Sindhia (representing Daulat Rao), each of whom claimed to be the *subadar* (governor) of Udaipur, left the ancient kingdom in ruins.[205] By 1816, of Udaipur's 50,000 houses only about 3,000 were still occupied and the Maharana's income had shrunk to a pitiful 40,000 rupees.[206]

Jaipur meanwhile teetered on the precipice. Having emptied the treasury of Jodhpur, Amir returned to Jaipur in 1816.[207] The pillaging spared nothing: utensils, clothes, grain, goats, fowl, and even ropes and shoes were taken.[208] Famine was the inevitable result.[209] Jagat Singh responded to the crisis by holing himself up inside his capital whereupon Amir parked the 200 cannons he had inherited from Jaswant outside the city walls and let off cannonades that reached the palace walls.[210] Unable to unite his *darbar*, Jagat Singh utilized a desperate feint. He made "importunate supplications" to the British, who prepared a squad to relieve him.[211] At the same time a gallant Jaipur *thakur* raided one of Amir's strongholds and took members of his extended family hostage.[212] These twin developments unsettled the Nawab, compelling him to accept Jaipur's promise of money and retreat to the countryside and plot anew.[213]

These dramatic events finally made the British sit up. Previously, they had dismissed Amir Khan's "temerity" with a wave of the hand. When he had challenged Nagpur in 1809, they had confidently declared that he could be "brought to his senses without much trouble."[214] But now, with the Nawab evidently "bidding fair to establish a Mussalman dynasty on the ruins of the Rajpoot states," the British perspective changed.[215] The cumulative value of the crown lands of Jodhpur, Jaipur, and Udaipur, they estimated with a gulp, amounted to well over a crore.[216] Were the "extraordinary rise" of the "famous Ameer Khan" to continue, the British press now anxiously reported, "he may, like Hyder Ali, become a serious thorn in our side before long."[217] Amir's growing proximity to his "bigoted co-religionists" in Rohilkhand, such as Sayyid Ahmed Barelvi, an officer in his army who was spearheading Wahhabism in Northern India, only deepened these fears.[218]

The threat posed by Amir was seriously exacerbated by his increasingly close relationship with the Pindaris (indeed many a Company officer considered him "a Pindari with ambition").[219] A kind of irregular cavalry, the Pindaris had emerged in the Deccan where the Sultanates employed them to hound their opponents. The Marathas borrowed this method of guerilla warfare when they moved up into Central India, cultivating their own "bands of freebooters" to harass the Mughals and then the British.[220] Until the Second Anglo-Maratha War, the Pindaris in Central India had generally served either Sindhia or Holkar. But the continual decline of these Maratha *sardars* had resulted in the Pindaris come under the leadership of a handful of mercurial "chiefs" who were now beginning to ravage Rajputana and Malwa of their own accord. The consequences for the *ryot* (tenant cultivators) were terrible: a Pindari visitation unfailingly meant rape, loot, murder, and arson.[221] Worries about Amir's relationship with the Pindaris had emerged as early as 1809, when they accompanied him on his expedition against Nagpur, and increased after 1811, when he began using them to harass Sindhia.[222] By 1815, the Pindaris had grown to number between 50,000 and 70,000, a fearsome figure given their "enterprising nature."[223] Now the fear arose that Amir would follow in Jaswant's footsteps and turn the Pindaris into "ready auxiliaries."[224] "With some degree of discipline" instilled in them, Charles Metcalfe, the Company's Resident (or representative) in Delhi, warned all who would listen, the Pindaris could become "a most formidable instrument in the hand of an able and ambitious chief."[225]

For a number of years, London rejected these warnings. The Board of Control declared time and again that were "unwilling to incur the risk of a general war for the uncertain purpose of extirpating altogether predatory bands."[226] These refusals caused much heartburn in Calcutta. The Board failed to see, the Governor-General privately fumed, that the Company's possessions in India "are not precisely like an estate in Yorkshire."[227] London's calculus began to shift, however, once Rajputana had been bled dry and the Pindaris began foraying into British India. Between 1811 and 1816, the Pindaris brought "fire and sword" to districts in Bengal and Madras.[228] Initially, the British tried defensive measures, using outposts and patrols to detect and chase off Pindari *tolls* (contingents). But this proved of little avail as the need to cover vast tracts left Company forces "stretched precariously thin."[229] Nor could the British hope to launch punitive attacks since the Pindaris' "sudden expeditions" ended with them recrossing the Narmada and taking refuge in abandoned forts in Central India.[230] Company officers briefly tried "outsourcing pacification" by arming and garrisoning village folk, but ordinary cultivators were no match for the battle-hardened Pindaris, making "mass flight" the more common response.[231]

Following a devastating raid by some 10,000 Pindaris in 1815 that netted them 25 lakhs and left 92 villages burning and more than 4,000 wounded or tortured, and then another in 1816 by more than double the number, who caused nearly a crore worth of loss and "threw the whole southern part of the peninsula into a state of alarm," the Marquis of Hastings, who had taken over as Governor-General, decided the time had come to secure the "permanent tranquility" of India.[232] His deputies lent their pens to the cause. The ability of the Pindaris to turn up in far corners of the peninsula and commit "wanton atrocities" had awakened the "hopes of the turbulent and disaffected," they warned London.[233] This was the time to strike, they underlined, because the Marathas, who had "fostered" the Pindaris as "an instrument for our annoyance" and "secretly rejoiced" their successive incursions into British India, were in complete disarray—Holkar's annual income, for instance, had shrunk from some 36 lakhs in 1808 to a mere 4 lakhs by 1817.[234]

After wringing an approval out of London, in October 1817 Hastings marched on Central India at the head of two massive armies, comprising 113,000 soldiers and 300 guns. His objective was to create "an iron net" that would "envelope the usual haunts of the Pindaris" and overawe any of the principalities "disposed to countenance them."[235] In the end, there was hardly any fighting. The only two powers that mattered in Central India were Daulat Rao Sindhia and Amir Khan. When the British arrived in Malwa, Sindhia, "did not even raise his little finger."[236] Seeing as the Pindaris had been raiding his territories in connivance with Amir, he was prepared to see them extirpated. As to Amir, the Company knew from past exchanges exactly what he wanted.[237] The Nawab was invited to give up his "Pindari habits" in return for the "guarantee of past gains."[238] Specifically, he would be allowed to keep the *jagirs* previously awarded to him by Jaswant and given 5 lakhs for his artillery and 3 lakhs to bribe his troops into disbanding.

Sensing that he was approaching the "evening of life," Amir was more than ready to accept the Company's offer.[239] This inclination of his did not sit well with his officers who, unwilling to give up their predatory ways, "abused him for truckling with the English."[240] And so the Nawab had to employ his "indefatigable cunning" once again. He had his *vakil* sign an agreement with the Company in November 1817 but gave that out to his subordinates that he was simply stringing the British along. Meanwhile, he encouraged Holkar's *darbar* to resist the British, and when Tulsi Bai tried to follow Sindhia and "come to terms with the English," his confederates deposed and beheaded her, freeing up the hotheads in the *darbar* that wanted war.[241] As Amir fully expected, the Company trounced Holkar's forces within a matter of days. The beating deflated his own officer corps, allowing him to enter "heartily" into the British cause.[242] To further grease the wheels, the Nawab gave his subordinates "delusive hopes" that they too would receive generous grants from the British.[243] Then, leaving them with overdrawn checks to the amount of 9 lakh rupees, he took refuge in the Company's camp.

In the end, it was left to the British to clean up the mess, which they did by absorbing the more "serviceable" of Amir's troops as a "temporary expedient" and "convincing" the remainder to take up other vocations.[244] The bulk of the Pindaris, meanwhile, melted away or were "hunted" to extinction.[245] A handful, who had worked closely with Amir, smartly followed his lead and offered the Company "early and unconditional" submission, for which reason they too were treated with "consideration and liberality," being allowed to take refuge in the Muslim principalities of Bhopal and Awadh, where they obtained small estates.[246] The entire exercise was so successful it became a template: over the next two decades, nine-tenths of princely and private militias in India would be disbanded through a similar mixture of recruitment, bribes, and compulsion.[247]

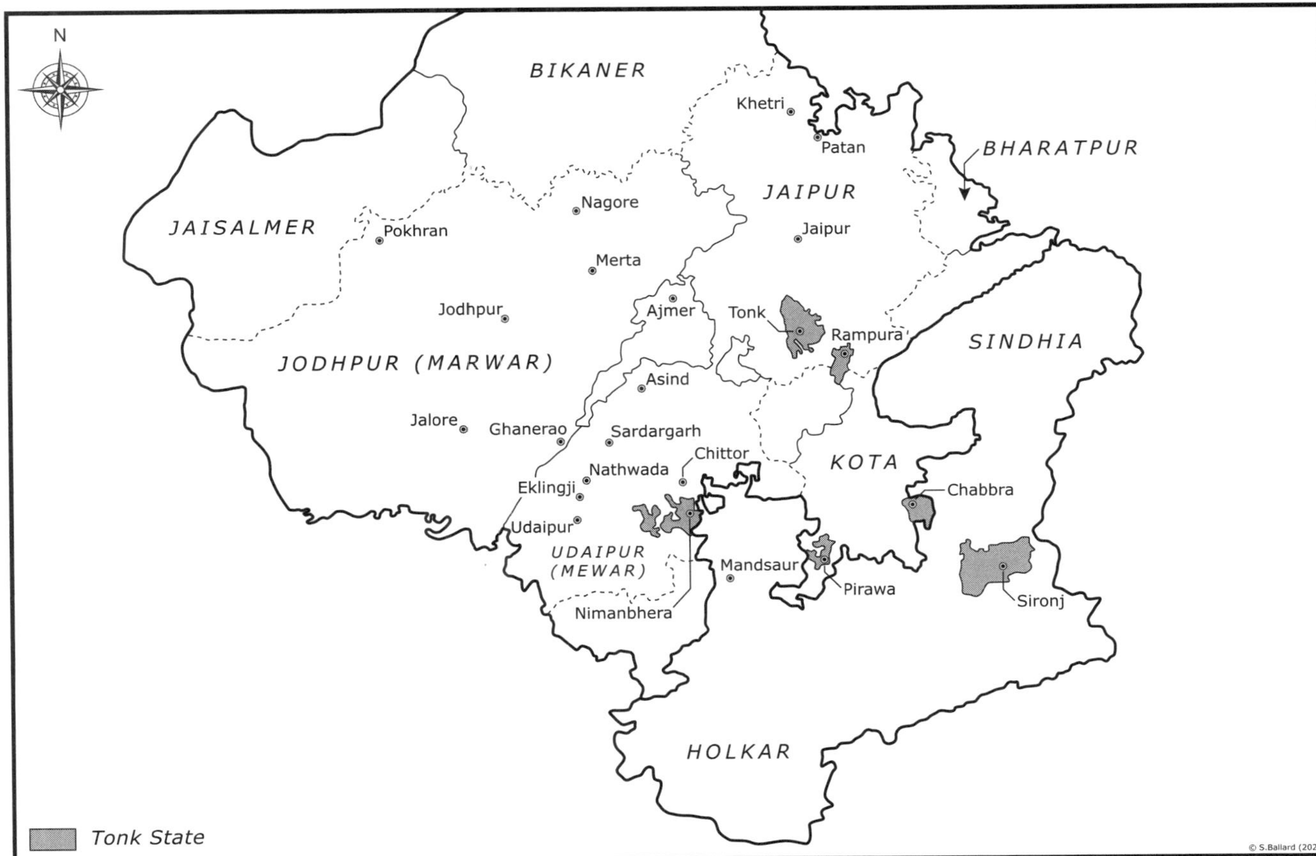

Map 2 Rajputana in 1818.

While these events were unfolding in Central India and the Deccan, the Company was busy negotiating treaties with the by-now "petty states" of Rajputana. As soon as Sindhia and Holkar had been rendered prostrate, and then compelled by treaties to surrender their right to collect tribute from the Rajputs, Metcalfe proceeded to finalize arrangements. By the middle of 1818, every Rajput principality was brought under the Company's protection, which gladly inherited the tribute the Rajputs used to pay the Marathas. Rajputana would no longer be, the British press now exulted, "a nursery for freebooters," an outcome that allowed Hastings to proudly declare that the Company had "reared the bulwark of security round the humble hovels of the helpless."[248]

It went less well for the Maharajas. Jagat Singh, having overstrained mind and body, expired within months of submitting to the British. Man Singh, the perennial survivor, miraculously cured himself of his insanity and then gripped by a "demonical spirit of revenge" set about fighting the *thakurs* whose alliance with Amir had "driven him to seclusion"—until the British ultimately forced him to retire.[249] Meanwhile, Bhim Singh, born into a family that claimed to be "the direct representative of Rama," lived to be remembered as the Maharana under whom Udaipur "definitely, formally, and effectually" lost its independence.[250]

The saga did not only shake sovereigns; it made some too. Amir Khan became the Nawab of Tonk, a "straggling principality" comprising lands snatched from the Rajputs and the Holkars. The Nawab may be "rude and uncouth," the British press murmured, but "if the main object of his exertions has been the attainment of an independent principality, then his ambition is now crowned with success."[251] Armed with annual income of 15 lakhs, Amir was able to take up the "arts of peace," becoming "one of the chief centers of financial support and asylum" to the Wahhabi movement.[252] The "Mussalman interest so created," the Company's officers exulted, "had the effect of introducing a counterpoise to the predominant influence of the Hindoos" in Central India.[253] Of course no one did better than the Company whose "sway was prodigiously extended" by the events set in motion by the contest over Krishna Kumari.[254] As H. H. Wilson would confess once the dust settled, the "continued contests of the native princes operated favorably for the extension of British ascendancy" over Central and Western India because "they disposed the weaker to welcome the approach of foreign protection, and they disabled the stronger from offering effective opposition."[255]

The Playwright

We have now examined the causes and characters behind Krishna Kumari's death and the painful consequences that followed it. But why, we may wonder, did Subba Rao, a Maratha Brahmin from Tanjore, serving as English tutor to the princes of Travancore, decide to write a play about this tragic event in distant Rajputana? To grasp Subba Rao's intention, we need to examine his life and the times in which he lived, and the pedagogical challenge that led him to craft *Krishna Kumari*.

Subba Rao was born in 1775 in Tanjore, exactly a century after the principality had been founded by the Maratha general Venkoji Bhonsle. It was also the moment when Tanjore became the Company's "subsidiary," an event that transformed the lives of the Marathi-speaking Brahmin clans that had followed in Venkoji's train. Like their compatriots in Madras, they began acquiring the rudiments of English by serving as *dubashes* (or intermediaries) for Company officers and British merchants.[256] This would likely have been Subba Rao's career path too had Tanjore not received succor from an unusual source: English-speaking Germans.

Once Tanjore came under the Company's "protection," missionaries streamed into the principality. The most enterprising of these was Christian Fredrich Schwarz, a Prussian who had started his missionary work in Danish-controlled Tranquebar (or Tharangambadi) before entering the Company's employ in Madras. In 1779, Schwarz settled in Tanjore, where he doubled as the interpreter for John Sullivan, the Company's Resident.[257] Sullivan quickly became frustrated by the constant need for aging Schwarz's services, and hence began urging the missionary, who had previously established schools for British orphans, to establish an English school in Tanjore so that "a freer intercourse would be opened between natives and Europeans."[258] By 1784 Sullivan had his wish. With the support of the Tuljaji Bhonsle (the learned Raja of Tanjore) and the Company, Schwarz was able to launch an English-medium school for "natives"—the very first of its kind in the subcontinent. Foremost amongst the eager pupils was Subba Rao, whom Schwarz considered "a most apt and docile student."[259] Under the supervision of his multilingual German teachers, Subba Rao's aptitude for languages became apparent. He studied Sanskrit, Marathi, Tamil, Hindustani, and Persian, and even picked up a little French and Latin. But it was his "superior knowledge" of English that stood out, leading his classmates to nickname him "English" Subba Rao, the moniker by which he would henceforth be known "in Native circles."[260]

Upon graduating in 1793, Subba Rao followed in his family's footsteps, taking up a "subordinate" position as a translator in the Tanjore *Raj*.[261] He was soon propelled up the ladder. In 1798 the Company settled a succession dispute in favor of Serfoji Bhonsle, the former Raja's adopted son, who had been educated at Vepery Mission in Madras. In return, Serfoji grudgingly ceded control over his territories, which reduced his writ to "a small circle" around Tanjore Fort.[262] Unhappy at being emasculated, Serfoji set about investing in scientific and cultural ventures, hoping to make Tanjore "a center of enlightenment" that would contribute to a wider Maratha revival.[263] And so opened the door to Subba Rao: with the Raja keen to have "all persons filling high situations" well acquainted with the English language, Subba Rao was inducted into *darbar* (or royal court) as a *shesho* (preceptor).[264]

Before Subba Rao could entirely settle into this new role, which involved "incessantly" reading English books to the Raja, he was swept up in broader events.[265] In 1803 the Second Anglo-Maratha War broke out. Following Sindhia's defeat at Assaye, the Governor-General dispatched Josiah Webbe, the Marathi-speaking Chief Secretary of Madras, to negotiate terms. Seeking a *munshi* (or secretary) to manage the voluminous Marathi and English correspondence that the new position would

English Subba Rao © P. Shungoonny Menon.

entail, Webbe requisitioned Subba Rao, whose linguistic abilities were by now well known in Company circles. Within a matter of months, the twenty-eight-year-old was in the thick of things. Under the gaze of some of the greatest figures of the Company era, including John Malcolm, Subba Rao drafted and translated documents, kept the minutes of conferences, and was even deputed to conduct interviews with Sindhia and his ministers.[266] The ringside seat to the destruction of his clansmen was not for him, however. In October 1804, correctly sensing that the Company had underestimated Holkar, whose irregular cavalry had already begun despoiling the countryside to provoke a famine, he sought leave. Angered by his *munshi* wanting to "quit his station at a time of difficulty," Webbe summarily sacked Subba Rao, bringing his career in the Company to a sudden and ignominious end.[267]

After returning to Tanjore, Subba Rao became intimately involved in Serfoji's endeavors to revitalize Maratha culture. In 1806 he was tasked with having "works of merit" translated from English into Marathi. He began by translating William Guthrie's 1771 *Geographical Grammar*, a best-selling work that synthesized the political and historical knowledge generated in Europe over the eighteenth century. This translation was prepared alongside, and contributed to, *Devendra Kuravanji* (The Fortune-Teller Play of the King of Gods), a Marathi-language "geographical opera" that introduced Tanjoreans to concepts and facts about the globe and the solar system.[268] Shortly after this came *Balabodha Muktavali* (String of Pearls), Subba Rao's rendering of Aesop's *Fables* into Marathi, which was published in 1809.[269] The first English-to-Marathi translation to be published in the subcontinent, *Balabodha Muktavali* became a standard textbook in Tanjore's schools and the means by which its young "engaged with Europe."[270] These literary assignments brought Subba Rao into Serfoji's inner circle and led to administrative duties as well. Eventually, in 1812, he was appointed *sarkil* (or head minister). It was not an enviable position. By this point, Serfoji was openly chafing at the restrictions that the Company had placed upon him, and the British were responding in their usual way, by placing spies in the *darbar* and encouraging the Raja's vassals to rebel. Unwilling to go along with Serfoji's overzealous courtiers and family, who wanted to confront the Company, an approach he considered suicidal in view of the Raja's "very scanty powers," Subba Rao stepped down in 1815 and returned to his books.[271]

The next turning point came in 1819 when Rajaraja Varma, the *Koil Thampuran* (or Royal Consort) of Travancore began searching for an English tutor for his sons, Swati Tirunal and Uttaram Tirunal. Established in the first half of the eighteenth century by Marthanda Varma, Travancore's prospects had dimmed considerably after it sought the Company's aid to fend off Hyder Ali and Tipu Sultan of Mysore. As elsewhere in the Deccan, the alliance ended with Travancore reduced to the role of a "subsidiary," a development that made it important for its princes acquire fluency in English. The *Koil Thampuran* thus pushed to hire the storied "English" Subba Rao of Tanjore.[272] Anxious about what Rajaraja Varma, their *bête noire*, was up to, the Company kept a close watch on the proceedings. The delicacy of Subba Rao's role was underlined by the Company's Resident in Travancore who politely warned him upon his arrival there in January 1820:

> I am hopeful that you will by your care and attention to the morals as well as the learnings of the young princes, make them both good and respectable men, patterns of excellence to the people whom God has called them to govern at some future day. Everything depends on early impressions in the mind of youth, how the character of a man is formed, and the importance of this truth will, I am persuaded, stimulate you to the most careful solicitude and reflection as to the best means of training the minds of these youths in all that is respectable and praiseworthy.[273]

As Swati was already seven years old by this point, Subba Rao knew he had to move quickly. The princes were promptly placed under tutors for Tamil, Telugu, Kannada, Hindustani, and Marathi, the last of which was taught by Subba Rao. Naturally, "English studies" were the centerpiece of the curriculum. Here there was much to be done. Prior to Subba Rao's arrival in Travancore, the princes could only speak a few coached sentences in English. Over the next four years, Subba Rao's "onerous labors" ensured that the princes made "considerable progress" in English as well as mathematics, logic, and the sciences. He did not neglect aesthetics either. In keeping with the distinctive humanism fostered by the Rajas of Tanjore, he "modernized" Swati's training in music, introducing him to the "refined form" of Carnatic music current in Tanjore, and to the *swarabat* (a rare stringed instrument) of which Subba Rao was an "acknowledged master."[274] He also called to Travancore musicians and dancers that had flourished under Serfoji's patronage in Tanjore. Their performances floored Swati and Uttaram, aiding the "efflorescence" of their "musical genius."[275]

By 1825 the devoted teacher and his talented pupils were in deep harmony. In a letter to his brother, Thiagaraja, Subba Rao declared, with evident pride, that the progress his pupils had made in their learning was "very rapid."[276] But time was precious. With only three years remaining before Swati ascended to the throne, his "labours in storing their minds with the knowledge worthy of their exalted situation," he wrote, were "unremitted."[277] The great question before him was *what* Swati and Uttaram ought to focus in the little time that remained. British officials invited to view the princes in their classroom in Trivandrum Fort had strong feelings on the matter. One such review in 1825 acknowledged that under the supervision of the "all-round scholar" from Tanjore, the princes had "greatly improved in mind" and were "lads of very high promise."[278] The now thirteen-year-old Maharaja-in-waiting, who had "sedate and dignified manners" and was "very fond of study," could sketch out Euclid's propositions and exhibited remarkable "linguistic acumen," being "equally clever" at several languages.[279] Even so, the report card was mixed because the princes' spoken English was apparently "inelegant and ungrammatical." Part of the problem was that with "so many studies on hand," they could "never read enough English to correct their idiom."[280]

The criticism was not entirely groundless, but it failed to grasp Subba Rao's objective. Fluency in writing and speaking in English were important because they would allow Swati and Uttaram to express themselves clearly and communicate directly with Company officers. But, from Subba Rao's perspective, the purpose of their "English studies" was intellectual rather than social; what he cared about was "improving the mind" rather making pleasant conversation.[281] As a result, he made the princes focus on a few books that would stimulate their intellect. The significance of this decision is something the princes would acknowledge throughout their lives. As Swati would later declare, "I love English, not only on account of its beauty, but for the sake of its utility, because my knowledge of English books . . . has proved to be a kind of strong barrier against many prejudices and false notions."[282]

There was a particular set of "false notions" that Subba Rao was especially keen to explode. This concern was reflected in the books that he made Swati and Uttaram read with special care. These books, which ranged from Aesop's *Fables* to John Malcom's *A Memoir of Central India*, may appear quaint and disparate, but the selection was careful and deliberate. In Subba Rao's view, no subject was more important for a prince to master than *niti shastra* (or ethics). This was because success in any great venture required moral knowledge—an individual had to "understand that human traits like being humble or cruel, content or greedy, sagacious or foolish, shy or bold, cunning or naive, all of these virtues and vices are helpful at some times and problematic at other times."[283] Such knowledge, Subba Rao underlined, could be the difference between life and death:

> To give an example, when a person who is following *niti shastra* sees a tiger on his way, he will say that, "it is in tiger's nature to attack and eat man, God has endowed us with intellect and common sense, but has not given us the strength to kill a tiger with our bare hands," hence he will retreat from tiger's path and hide. By contrast, a person who has no knowledge of *niti shastra*, or even if he has, but has not imbibed it, will rely on God and will think that "this life is the result of past deeds (*karma*) and if my death is written at the hands of this tiger, I won't be able to escape." And hence he will think that there is no need to hide from tiger. Alas! There will be no doubt that such a fool will be walking straight into the jaws of the tiger.[284]

Now, where might one learn how to avoid being consumed by a "tiger"? The requisite moral knowledge could only be gained, Subba Rao argued, by "taking counsel from experience." Traditionally, such counsel had been conveyed to students through fables such as *Hitopadesa* (Book of Good Counsel), *Panchatantra* (Five Treatises), *Simhasana Dvatrimsika* (Thirty-Two Tales of the Throne of Vikramaditya), and *Vetalpancavinsati* (Five-and-Twenty Tales of Vikram and the Vetal).[285] Subba Rao admired this technique, which distilled human experience into "easy-to-understand short stories relatable to daily life."[286] As he had previously observed in the preface to his *Balabodha Muktavali*:

> It is well known that by practicing a sport, a person maintains good health. If a person sits idly at home, he will only feel lazy, and it will bring him sickness. If exercise is available in a playful, joyful manner, then he will want to do it and it will bring him good health. To give an example, on their hunting trips, even kings sweat it out in chasing their hunt. There is no need for a king to go hunt in the forest. But a king goes on hunting trips because it brings him joy. Similarly, the

> teaching of *Niti* shouldn't be done in a cold, drab way. It should be made as exciting and enjoyable as possible by teaching it through the medium of stories. If the *Niti* is taught in this joyful way, it will act as medicine for those learning it.[287]

As much as Subba Rao valued this classical tradition, he fretted that "the discipline of *niti shastra* had fallen way behind with the changing times."[288] Hence, it became necessary to draw on fables from other traditions and languages. Subba Rao justified this course of action on the grounds that "the dictums of *niti shastra* are universal."[289] It was for this reason that he and Serfoji had selected Aesop's *Fables* as the first English work to be published in Marathi, and why he subsequently made Swati and Uttaram read *Arabian Nights* and *The Tales of the Genii*. But even this broadminded search for materials could only help so much. The pickings were slim because contemporaneous European literature on the subject of "moral improvement" was of a "crushingly moral character," frequently taking the form of sermons or bowdlerized accounts.[290] Mary Stockdale's *Children's Journal* and L. M. Stretch's *The Beauties of History*, both of

John Malcolm, author of *A Memoir of Central India*.
Courtesy of the National Army Museum, London.

which Subba Rao assigned, would not teach Swati and Uttaram the ways of the world. François Fénelon's *The Adventures of Telemachus* was more useful in this regard, but it demanded substantial knowledge of ancient Greek lore.

Thus, to supplement the traditional approach to moral education, Subba Rao turned to the study of history. As was the norm in Europe, ancient history provided much material in the way of moral education. Here Subba Rao drew upon the wide array of books he had read with Serfoji, such as Oliver Goldsmith's *The History of Greece*, Edward Gibbon's *The History of the Fall and Decline of the Roman Empire*, and David Hume's *The History of England.*[291] Swati found this material much to his taste. For instance, in a private letter he described the pleasure he had taken in reading *The History of Cyrus* in Charles Rollin's bestselling multi-volume *Ancient History*, saying that he found "properly delineated in it many exalted virtues of that Great King, such as courage, liberality, philanthropy, and magnanimity of mind, and it appears to me that he is an archetype of all good kings, who are renowned for their glorious deeds, and consequently, the perusal of his life is of very great use to me."[292]

But there was to be more. Subba Rao did not want to only familiarize the princes with archetypes of virtue but also with archetypes of vice. And here his distinctive contribution was to direct his wards' attention toward contemporary Indian history, which British writers were starting to bring into view. In doing so, he was building on what he had learnt during this time in Tanjore. Back there, Subba Rao and Serfoji had familiarized themselves with well-known histories of medieval India, such as Alexander Dow's *The History of Hindustan* (a popular English translation of Firishta's Persian-language *Tarikh-i-Farishti*). But what they found much more interesting and useful were contemporaneous accounts such as William Thompson's *Memoirs of the Late War in Asia*, Edward Moor's *A Narrative of the Mahratta Army*, and John Malcolm's *Sketch of Political History of India.* The work that affected them most deeply was Robert Orme's *A History of the Military Transactions of the British Nation in Indostan*, which they discussed extensively. This "valuable work" by the Company's first official historian, which the Raja had acquired in 1806, "opened" the duo's eyes to the "the field of history," revealing to them the "political proceedings" that had "contributed to terminate every event entirely in favor of the blessed British Nation."[293]

Malcolm's *Central India*, which was published in 1823, was the natural counterpart to Orme's earlier *History*. Whereas Orme explained how the Company had established itself in the Deccan by expelling the French, Malcolm illuminated how it had consolidated its hold on the Deccan by subjugating the Marathas. Now, what could be more useful to Swati and Uttaram than understanding the transactions that had sealed the fate of their fellow princes? Where better, in other words, to learn about the "tiger" prowling the land—the hungry animal that Subba Rao had seen up close when serving as Webbe's *munshi*? Thus became Malcom's *Central India* the centerpiece of Swati and Uttaram's "English studies."

But invaluable as it was, this two-volume work posed a pedagogical challenge. A dense narrative history, brimming with "minute details" about distant peoples and places, was unlikely to have an enduring impact on the Travancore princes or their circle. Indeed, Malcolm himself admitted that the volumes were "fatiguing" and that he "despaired of attracting general readers."[294] What was needed then was a pithy tale summarizing the moral of the mammoth work. As it happened, Subba Rao had a model to inspire him. This was *Devendra Kuravanji*, the "dance-drama" that he had helped Serfoji with back in Tanjore, which imparted knowledge of "world geography," such as details about continents and countries, and oceans and rivers, through "melodious songs" and "conversational exchanges." By employing the popular *kuravanji* (or dance-drama) tradition, this simple but striking production had taken geography from its "dreaded place" in the classroom to the "sweet realm" of music and poetry.[295] Of course Subba Rao's audience in Travancore was far more sophisticated than his students in Tanjore. Therefore, he needed to prepare a work that could rise to the occasion. And so was born *Krishna Kumari* (or *Kishun Koovur: A Tragedy in Five Acts* as it was originally titled), a compact "dramatic piece" written for "private amusement" that encapsulated the vices that had led the Rajputs to be despoiled by the Marathas and the Pindaris and then subjugated by the Company.[296] Building on the teenage princes' interest in theatre, and English drama in particular, the play focused their attention on the "subject" that had made an especially "deep impression" on the "author's mind," namely the "train of events, which had led to the tragical fate of Princess Krishna Kumari."[297]

Subba Rao's knowledge of the "train of events" in Rajputana was not perfect. As channels of communication were limited during this time, he had to rely almost entirely on Malcolm's depiction of the characters and the proceedings. Alternate accounts, such as James Tod's *Annals and Antiquities of Rajasthan* and Amir Khan's *Memoirs of the Puthan Soldier of Fortune*, which depict Bhim Singh, the Maharana of Udaipur, in a darker shade, had not appeared in print by this time; nor had eyewitness accounts that depict Sawai Singh and his fellow *thakurs* as having put up a mighty fight when ambushed by Amir Khan.[298] These limitations affect the historicity of Subba Rao's drama, but only very slightly. The broad outline Malcolm provided in *Central India* was undoubtedly true, and it was therefore perfectly adequate for Subba Rao's purpose, which was to write "a Tragedy" that could teach Swati and Uttaram that, since God was evidently content to "let virtue be the victim of vice," they "must not cherish foolish hopes of any help from above."[299]

The Audience

Having comprehended Subba Rao's purpose in penning *Krishna Kumari*, what remains to be seen is why, despite being the first English play written by an Indian, it barely registered in the public mind. The answer, we shall see, is that it was ill-timed. Published at the very moment when the Company was deeply at odds with Travancore, it was roundly ignored by the British Indian press. Consequently, it was other versions of the tale, especially those written in regional languages, that kept Krishna Kumari's memory alive until the middle of the twentieth century.

When it first began circulating in Travancore, Subba Rao's *Krishna Kumari* met with a favorable reception. David Newall, the Resident, received his copy on New

Year's Day in 1827. His reaction was encouraging. The play was, he declared, "well executed, and got up with spirit" and hence "very creditable to your dramatic talents."[300] Newall, who had taken part in hostilities against the Pindaris, was untroubled by the subject matter. He concurred, he wrote to Subba Rao, that "the incident stated in Sir John Malcolm's *Central India*, regarding the princess of Udaipur, afford interesting subject for a dramatic work."[301] Meanwhile, "several English gentlemen" known to Subba Rao also expressed "favorable opinions."[302]

These friendly readers may not have fully grasped Subba Rao's objective. They can be forgiven for assuming that his play was intended to inculcate in Swati and Uttaram an appreciation for the Company having relieved Rajputana from "intolerable evils," namely the exactions of the Marathas and the rapine of the Pindaris.[303] But Subba Rao's intention was quite different. He hoped that by showing how Rajputana's misery was the consequence of particular decisions made by particular characters, *Krishna Kumari* would encourage Travancore's princes to eschew the fatalism so characteristic of Native States. Henceforth, when confronted with "setbacks and failure," such as the arrival of a "tiger" in their neighborhood, they would "not blame their fate" or "blame God," instead, they would "restart their efforts with new vigor."[304] Only by reflecting on Indian history, in other words, would Swati and Uttaram develop the fortitude required to remake Travancore.

Subba Rao knew perfectly well that Madras would view such thoughts—which he had publicly expressed only in Tanjore and only in Marathi—as subversive. Hence, unlike in *Balabodha Muktavali*, the preface to *Krishna Kumari* steered clear of any discussion of *niti shastra*. In fact, it disavowed intentions of any kind, literary or otherwise, with Subba Rao declaring more than once that his "puny attempt" at "English dramatic composition" had been undertaken as "recreation in his leisure hours" merely in order "to comply with the wishes of some of his friends."[305] This disclaimer did not fool Subba Rao's critics, however. Company officers had long fretted over his being selected by, and closely associated with, the *Koil Thampuran*, who was openly hostile to the British. Up to this point, these critics had been silenced by Thomas Munro, the Governor of Madras, who ordered Newall to conciliate Travancore. But then, a mere two months after Subba Rao had sent Newall a copy of *Krishna Kumari*, the Resident's health suddenly gave way. A few months after that it was Munro's turn to drop dead. Now unshackled, Company officers, led by the new Resident, William Morrison, began pressuring Swati to dismiss Subba Rao. The young Maharaja flatly refused, setting in motion an epic contest that eventually drew in the Governor in Madras, who sided with Swati, and the Governor-General in Calcutta, who sided with Morrison. In the end, shrewd maneuvering by Subba Rao meant that he not only stayed on in Travancore but was made *dewan*—and Morrison was the one shunted out.

The victory was pyrrhic, however. From this moment on, Company officials went out of their way to stymie the Maharaja and his *dewan*, who were busying themselves with modernizing Travancore. The establishment of the Government Press in 1836, the first press in Travancore outside the control of Christian missionaries, was an important milestone in these plans. On Swati's orders, *Krishna Kumari* became the Press's second publication, copies of which were then dispatched to the Royal Asiatic Society via the *dewan's* "English friends," principal among whom was John Caldecott, the Royal Astronomer of Travancore. Lauded there as a "well-written tragedy," *Krishna Kumari* was one the reasons why the Royal Asiatic Society went on to elect Swati an Honorary Fellow, deeming him as among "the most enlightened sovereigns in Asia and in Europe."[306] In Madras, however, these accomplishments were met with frosty silence. Not only was there no native press to fall back upon, the number of Indians who could read English was vanishingly small, nearly all of whom were in the Company's employ. Consequently, *Krishna Kumari* was only ever publicly reviewed in London, where it was received as a curiosity, being described as "the first instance of a dramatic work that has appeared in English from the pen of a Hindoo."[307] From the self-congratulatory perspective of the British press, the fact that Subba Rao had been educated by Christian missionaries was more interesting than anything he had to say.

It is very likely that had Swati lived on, his patronage would have allowed *Krishna Kumari* to find new audiences, as the number of English-speaking Indians was about to explode. But it was not to be. In September 1841 Travancore received a new Resident: William Cullen. A gruff military officer, Cullen could not have been more unlike the Maharaja and his *dewan*. The dislike was mutual and instantaneous, with Cullen quickly agreeing with his predecessors that Subba Rao had instilled in the Maharaja "the most erroneous impressions" about the British.[308] Thus began another epic contest, but this time the odds were stacked against Travancore, as both Madras and Calcutta wanted to see the Maharaja and *dewan* "kept in order."[309] By 1842 Subba Rao had been forced into retirement and warned to stay out of sight. Eventually, worn down by the deaths of his father and sister, and by Cullen's constant threats to depose him and deport his cherished advisor, Swati's health collapsed. In December 1846 the thirty-three-year-old succumbed to an infection that overwhelmed his gaunt frame and depressed mind. Subba Rao never recovered from the sudden loss of his beloved protégé and patron, and himself passed away in January 1848.

Following Subba Rao's demise, his *Krishna Kumari* was purposefully consigned to oblivion. The last public reference to it came in his official obituary. Among the examples of the "superior talents" that had led the *shesho* to be "universally respected," it declared, was his "dramatic work" *Krishna Kumari*.[310] The only notable instance of patronage hereafter was Travancore's decision to display Subba Rao's *Krishna Kumari* at the Madras Exhibition of 1855 (where the Travancore Government Press's list of exhibits was diplomatically headed by Cullen's dry "Memorandum on Museums").[311] Following this, Subba Rao's production more or less disappeared from view. The copy reviewed by the Royal Asiatic Society eventually made its way to the British Museum and from thence to the British Library. In India, meanwhile, a copy could be found in the Government Central Museum in Madras, but the volume was not added to the Imperial Library in Calcutta or to the India Office Library in London. Things were more dire still in Travancore. Given Cullen's legendary prickliness even the name of his former nemesis was not uttered in public again. And, as luck would have it, Cullen would become the longest-serving Resident in Travancore, staying in harness until he was forced to retire in 1860, by which time Subba Rao was a distant memory.

Consequently, luck alone kept his *Krishna Kumari* in circulation. One specially bound copy reached Mountstuart Elphinstone, the celebrated Governor of Bombay, from whose library it made its way, somehow, to the University of Washington in Seattle. Another copy, which Subba Rao had gifted to Dr. G. J. Shaw, a British army surgeon stationed in Travancore, traveled down to Allardyce Nicoll, the British theatre historian, who microfilmed it for his encyclopedic *English and American Drama of the Nineteenth Century*, an act that ensured its longer-term survival, albeit in the shadows.

Subba Rao was not, however, the only one to be affected by the account of Krishna Kumari in Malcolm's *A Memoir of Central India*. Malcolm's incredible "oriental tale" found many takers in nineteenth-century Britain where it came to be seen as emblematic of the "high but mistaken notions of honour entertained by the Rajpoots" and as illustrative of the "degenerate days" that had overtaken a previously valorous people.[312] Thus, in 1828, the poetess Catherine Eliza Richardson, having returned to Scotland after nearly three decades in India, published "Kishen Kower," a short story eulogizing the "martyred" princess.[313] Then in 1832 Elizabeth Smith briefly recounted the tale under the title "The Three Moons" in her *East India Sketch-Book*.[314] Two years later came "Kishen Kowur" by J. L. Mowatt in the much-admired *Bengal Annual*, which further embellished the story of the "lovely victim," and "Kishen Kower" from the noted poet Letitia Elizabeth Landon, which appeared in *Fisher's Drawing Room Scrap Book*.[315]

Malcolm's successors in British India did not let their contemporaries forget the "pathetic and melancholy account" either.[316] In 1844, that hard-charging soldier, Henry Lawrence, weighed in, alongside his wife Honoria Marshal, lamenting in the pages of the *Calcutta Review*, the most widely read Anglo-Indian periodical of the time, the "sad chronicle" of "murdered innocence."[317] Two years later, Henry Prinsep, the prominent civil servant and historian, published *Ballads of the East*, wherein he promised the readers of his poem "Kishen Koomaree" that the princess's "honoured name will be remembered long, while aught remains in Rajasthan of history and song."[318] In 1848 came James Mill's expanded *The History of British India*, which carefully detailed a "quarrel" so unusual as to "be paralleled only in the poetical tradition of distant ages."[319] George Cameron's "Kishen Kower" followed a decade later, with the military hero's imaginative recitation sending the story of the "Maid of Odeypoore" to new dramatic heights.[320] In 1875, the tale received particular attention in George Malleson's *A Historical Sketch of the Native States of India*. Given his unique vantage point as guardian to the Maharaja of Mysore, Malleson's volume was reviewed widely. His recollection of the "extraordinary" Krishna Kumari, the "struggle for whose hand ruined Rajputana," caught a new generation of British reviewers unaware, leaving them aghast at what they termed the "strangest and saddest incident" of the century.[321] The publicity around Malleson's volume meant that when Queen Victoria assumed the title of Empress of India in 1877, the story of Krishna Kumari was recounted in overviews of the history of British India as the only "purely native event" from recent decades that could inspire "heroic emotion."[322] The episode was, one prominent retrospective declared, "a page from the Mahabharata quickened into life."[323] And even at the end of the century, the tale was still circulating in British India's club rooms, with no better example than "Krishna Kumari" in *Rhymes of Rajputana* by George Herbert

Trevor, the Agent to the Governor-General for Rajputana, who mournfully announced that the "tale wherever it is known/must move methinks a heart of stone."[324]

The version of the tale that had the greatest effect on Indians was the one in James Tod's *Annals and Antiquities of Rajasthan*. The volumes were perfectly timed, arriving in 1829 as the Company was on the verge of ramping up support for English education. By the early 1850s, Tod's *Annals*, now viewed as the "chief authority" on "all that pertains to the Rajasthan of former days," was being devoured by the graduates of newly established schools and colleges in India, who naturally came away full of admiration for "Rajput chivalry."[325] When these pioneers subsequently tried to challenge India's subjugation, they were understandably drawn to the bravery shown by those "Rajput heroes" of days past who could "never be brought to submission."[326] By drawing parallels between the story of Krishna Kumari and the mythical figures of Iphigenia and Virginia (famously put to death by their fathers in the cause of Greece and Rome respectively), Tod's poignant account encouraged passionate young Indians to see her as a particularly striking example of "female courage and patriotic devotion."[327]

Among the earliest to be affected by Tod's presentation was Bengal's premier poet and dramatist Michael Madhusudan Dutt. In 1860, upon the urging of his patrons to craft "a drama on an entirely Hindu subject," Dutt began "poring over the tremendous pages of Tod" hoping to "cull out" something from the "history of the Rajputs."[328] In a few feverish weeks he produced *Krishna Kumari*, the first tragedy in the Bengali language. Dutt was "quite in love" with his *Krishna Kumari* and had his "heart set upon" seeing it performed on the stage as "it would create a deeper sensation than any play yet produced." "I, a most hard-hearted rascal," Dutt wrote in a letter to a contemporary of his, "have cried over many scenes while correcting the proofs."[329] His patrons were less certain, however. They worried the play "would not succeed on the stage" because it lacked "comic" elements and required too many "good female actors."[330] Convinced that he was "born an age too soon," an offended Dutt withdrew from playwriting.[331] But his *Krishna Kumari*, which was published in 1861 with the support of the philanthropist Jatindra Mohan Tagore, subsequently took on a life of its own.[332] In 1867 it was performed at the Shobabazar Theatre in the presence of "many respectable citizens" including Tagore, who also sponsored a performance at his family's Jorasanko Theatre.[333] Then the play found a much larger stage. In February 1873 it was hosted at one of the most important cultural venues of the era, the Hindu Mela, a festival devoted to raising Hindu consciousness, whose proceedings were widely reported. This was followed by performances in Calcutta at the National Theatre in April and July 1873 and then at the Grand National Theatre in January 1874. Dutt's premature death in June 1873 arrested further uptake but the performances still led to reviews in native-owned publications like *Hindoo Patriot* and *Amrita Bazaar Patrika* that were starting to circulate the country, bringing Krishna Kumari's story to the attention of an emergent pan-Indian audience.[334]

As others read Tod, the tale of Krishna Kumari spread still further. Soon she was on the mind of litterateurs like Soshee Chandra Dutt, who penned the "Flower of Rajasthan," and scholars and poets like Ganesh Shastri Lele, Narayan Vasudev Juvekar, Dikshita Satarkar, Govind Shastri Parikh, and Narmada Lalshankar Dave, who memorialized her in Marathi and Gujarati.[335] Reviews of the handsome and well-priced edition of Tod's *Annals*, published in 1873 by Higginbotham & Co. of Madras, brought the "dreadful drama" to still wider attention.[336] Before long, her story, which "eclipses any romance", the reviews gushed, was appearing in literary competitions in Bombay and Hyderabad, in school textbooks on Indian history, on college reading lists in Bombay and Madras, and on the lips of *ayahs* (nannies) putting their wards to bed out in the districts.[337] Little wonder, then, that before the century was over, Krishna Kumari was being described as one of the "Heroines of Ind" and a "Hindoo female celebrity," with her own entry in the *Cyclopedia of India*.[338]

Not everyone was pleased by Krishna Kumari's new life, however. Discomfited by the emergence of Indian nationalism and the growth of Hindu consciousness, British imperialists and Christian missionaries portrayed the episode rather differently. According to them, it exposed, in Alfred Lyall's words, the "barbaric chivalry" and "primitive" political order that existed before the British graced India.[339] Such scorn had little effect on Indians, the more patriotic of whom now began producing easily digestible versions of the tale in regional languages. One notable example was Rajanikanta Gupta's 1883 *Arya Kirti* (Noble Victories) which, drawing on Tod's *Annals*, recounted various examples of Hindu valor. Tracing the "dismal circumstances" leading up to the "sacrifice of the innocent" Krishna Kumari, Gupta promised that the "ever glorious deed" of the "daughter of Rajasthan" would be "forever remembered on earth."[340] *Arya Kirti* proved immensely popular. There were multiple editions in Bengali, and it was translated into other languages, the most notable being C. Vasudevaiah's 1896 Kannada edition, which became a standard college textbook in Madras and Mysore.[341] Thus it was that in the closing decade of the nineteenth century Narendranath Datta, better known as Swami Vivekananda, could hold up a copy of Tod's *Annals* and declare that "two-thirds of the national ideas now in Bengal have been gathered from this book."[342]

Such fame notwithstanding, the tale of Krishna Kumari began to fade away after the turn of the century. In Britain, the story was still "well known" among "India hands," Flora Steel wrote in 1909, but increasingly "only for the strangeness of such an incident being possible in the nineteenth century."[343] Part of the problem was that though the "romantic spell" of Rajasthan was "still powerful," Tod's *Annals* was by now "practically unknown" in England.[344] The fearsome size of his magisterial volumes meant that publishers were not willing to take on the risk of publishing new editions. The few copies remaining in circulation were so "prohibitive" in cost that "not one in a hundred" libraries in England could afford to purchase a copy.[345] Hoping to keep memories alive, Anglo-Indians recounted every so often the "characteristically Oriental" story from Tod's "glowing pen" about the "accursed deed" responsible for the "melancholy of the House of Udaipur."[346] There was a wider but all-too-brief revival in 1924, when "The Flower of Rajasthan," an abridged version of her story by Francis Judd, was featured in the *Calcutta Review*, and *Krishna Kumari*, a play by

Edward Thompson, well known for translating Rabindranath Tagore's works into English, was published in London. The appearance of these works, the latter of which was widely reviewed, owed something to renewed British interest in Rajasthan following reports on the valor shown by Rajput troops in the First World War, and the republication in 1914 and 1920 of Tod's *Annals*. But by now the forward march of history was too rapid to sustain the British public's interest in an increasingly distant period in an increasingly troublesome possession. At a time when "the mere mention of India is enough to empty the smallest lecture room in the university," reviewers complained, Thompson's drama involved "too many allusions" to "Indian tribal history" to be of interest to the general reader.[347]

In India too the past was being buried. For a while, Krishna Kumari's story continued to find expression in regional languages. Notable examples included Bhogaraju Narayana Murthy's 1908 *Krishnakumari* (in Telugu) and Sitaram Shastri's 1913 *Krishna Kumari Nataka* (both in Telugu), P. Seshadri's 1915 *Krishnakumari* (in English), V. L Narasimha Rao's 1919 *Krishnakumari* (in Telugu), D. R. Bendre's 1922 *Krishnakumari* and B. R. Rau's 1931 *Krishnakumari* (both in Kannada) and Ullattil Sankarankutty Menon's 1937 *Krishnakumari* (in Malayalam).[348] There was also a pioneering edition in Hindi, published in 1922 in Ganga Pustak Mala's popular "Hindi Books for Ladies" series, which featured short biographies of legendary heroines such as Sita and Draupadi.[349] The tale was well known enough to also become the subject of two early silent films, *Daughter of Shripur* in 1924 and *Flower of Rajasthan* in 1930, with advertisements for the latter boldly urging colonial-era Indians to "wake up" and "take thy lessons from the chivalry and sacrifice" from their "sister" of yore.[350] All this activity notwithstanding, the wider milieu was undoubtedly becoming less hospitable. The rousing nationalism that emerged in the first decade of the twentieth century had been firmly repressed by the British in the run up to the Great War. As a result, by the time the war ended, new ideals—pacifism, cosmopolitanism, and communism—were ascendant. To these utopian ideologies, Tod's martial Rajputs were wholly unappealing examples. The resulting change in taste was discerned perhaps earliest in Bengal where by 1925 reviewers could see that Dutt's *Krishna Kumari* was becoming "more obscure by the day."[351]

The downward trajectory only continued over the following decades as theatre increasingly focused on "progressive" themes, especially combating "social evils."[352] To wit, the postcolonial era has witnessed only a few works on Krishna Kumari, most notably Govind Das's 1948 *Krishna Kumari* (in Hindi) and S. Balakrishnan's 1964 *Krishna Kumari: Princess of India* (in Tamil).[353] With the support of publicly-funded Sahitya Akademis, earlier editions of the tale were reprinted, most notably C. Vasudeviah's *Arya Kirti* in 1954, Bendre's *Krishnakumari* in 1957 and 1990, and Menon's *Krishnakumari* in 1993.[354] Unfortunately, all these editions proved short-lived with linguistic barriers splintering audiences and leading to small print runs. Today, only Dutt's *Krishna Kumari* remains in print, and like the other regional language editions it has never been translated into English.[355] As a consequence, declining numbers are aware of Krishna Kumari—her story has been relegated to the margin in her own land.

A Revival

Once acquainted with Krishna Kumari's tale no one is likely to deny that it deserves to be passed down to posterity. But why, we might wonder, should Subba Rao's dramatic work be the version that we ought to revive? What makes it worthy of being considered a classic? One reason, we shall see, is that it challenges longstanding views on the arrival of English learning in India and the use to which it was put. The other is that it focuses attention on the *collective* lesson to be learnt from Krishna Kumari's tragic end, making it the progenitor of a *national* theatre.

The introduction and spread of English literature in India has long been viewed as a moment when high culture was used to serve low ends. According to critics steeped in postcolonial theory, the principal means by which the British secured the quiescence of the colonized was by impressing upon them the "rationality" of English literature. By promising to impart such "true knowledge" to "uncivilized natives," the East India Company was able to present its rule to them as both necessary and beneficent.[356] English learning thus served, Gauri Viswanathan has famously argued, as an "ally" of the colonial enterprise, helping the British "in maintaining control of the natives under the guise of a liberal education."[357]

Over time this grim conclusion has come under question. One problem is that it does not track the facts. The reality is that Indians began acquiring the capacity to read and write in English well before the Company established its hold over India and much before it introduced public instruction in that language. A long-established tradition of multilingualism in South Asia, Vinay Dharwadker has shown, helped Indians of the late eighteenth and early nineteenth centuries acquire English through their social and economic links with British traders and soldiers.[358] Another weakness of postcolonial theory relates to the perspective it adopts. By focusing on "the operations of power" employed by colonizers, Suddhaseel Sen writes, it neglects the "mechanisms of resistance" employed by the colonized, leading to the latter's "invisibilisation." When we examine not what the British wanted to accomplish by teaching English literature but what Indians actually did with what they learnt, it quickly becomes clear that the latter were far from "passive" imbibers of colonial discourse.[359] As Dharwadker notes, figures like Cavelli Venkata Boriah and Rammohan Roy, who acquired English "outside the circumference of colonial domination," used it to "talk back," that is, to articulate Indian traditions and defend them against British critiques.[360]

Subba Rao's *Krishna Kumari* supports these counterclaims. Having been written by a native and for natives, only to then be stifled by the British, its very existence underlines that Indian writing in English was certainly not "homogenously a literature of complicity, collaboration, or mimicry."[361] But *Krishna Kumari* does more than prove that Indians successfully employed English learning to reflect on their circumstances. It also challenges longstanding claims about *where* and *when* such purposeful writing emerged. For more than a century, scholars have held that Indo-Anglian writing originated in British-dominated urban pockets, and in Bengal in particular. For instance, Srinavasa Iyengar's influential *The Indian Contribution to English Literature* proclaims that when it comes to English learning other parts of India were "content to follow in the footsteps of enterprising, energetic, and ever-experimenting Bengal."[362] *Krishna Kumari* shows up this bold claim. It embodies the fact that modern learning began not in Calcutta but in Tanjore and Travancore, where a series of learned Rajas supported the establishment of pioneering English-language schools.[363] The *babu*, the Anglicized native who spent his days "currying favour" with colonial authorities and exhibiting "enthusiastic loyalty" to England, may have been the most visible product of English learning in Calcutta, but the same books produced a different outcome in the Native States.[364] There modern education helped rulers and their counsellors preserve sovereignty and devise reforms needed to take advantage of an emergent modernity. As successive Residents in Travancore warned Calcutta, what made Subba Rao a threat to the Company's interests was his being "not unacquainted with our policy."[365]

Subba Rao's *Krishna Kumari* particularly complicates our understanding of how English learning shaped Indian theatre. The initial spur for modern theatre in India is usually traced to the late eighteenth and early nineteenth centuries when the British established theatres in Calcutta and Bombay that exposed the upper echelons of these cities to productions current in London. Fascinated by the spectacle, these elites sponsored productions of their own, such as *Uttara Rama Charita* (1831) and *Vidya Sundar* (1835), which married extant classical stories with modern stagecraft.[366] The next stimulus came with the opening of Company-backed schools and colleges in Calcutta and Bombay. In these institutions, which emerged in the second quarter of the nineteenth century, students were encouraged to read and perform plays "in a proper European style," which is to say, in English.[367] Hereupon arrived Shakespeare, with *Julius Caesar*, *Othello*, and the *Merchant of Venice* becoming the earliest English plays to be acted out by Indians.[368] But the tutelage apparently sparked a reaction. Searching for a "self-identity that could take them beyond the humiliation of being ruled," dramatists in Bengal and Bombay began to translate Sanskrit dramas into English, with Kalidas's works leading the way.[369] Then came the critical phase. As they began to tire of English plays that were either imported or translated, critics began demanding a "national" theatre that addressed pressing common concerns in the vernacular.[370] This is when, we are told, playwrights began appearing on the scene, with Krishna Mohan Banerjee's *The Persecuted* (1831), Michael Madhusudan Dutt's *Rizia* (1849), Jyotirao Phule's *Tritiya Ratna* (1853), and Ramnarayan Tarkaratna's *Kulin-Kulasarvasva* (1856) in the first crop.

Subba Rao's *Krishna Kumari* gives reason to doubt the narrative outlined above. To begin with, it challenges the claim that modern theatre in India was simply the product of a forceful stimulus from the colonizer followed by an imitative reaction from the colonized. Long before the denizens of Calcutta and Bombay were being dazzled by British theatre, much less studying it in Company-backed schools and colleges, the Rajas of Tanjore and Travancore, and their *shesho*, Subba Rao, were pouring over Elizabethan and Georgian dramas collated in Richard Cumberland's *British Drama* and Elizabeth Inchbald's *The British Theatre*. This background explains why scholars are mistaken in declaring Banerjee's *The Persecuted* (1831) as the "true commencement of Indian drama in English."[371] This is not a question of dates: there can be no doubt that *Krishna Kumari* was written well before *The Persecuted*. More important is the gulf in quality. *The Persecuted* exhibits, Ananda Lal notes, a "certain amateurishness." The hurried output of an overwrought eighteen-year-old, it features a number of "imperfections," including "dated" English and lengthy "bookish" monologues. Though clearly inspired by the Shakespearean five-act format, it runs out of steam as it goes along, coming to an "abrupt conclusion."[372] It is, Banerjee himself acknowledges in his preface to the play, more of a harangue than a drama. *Krishna Kumari*, by comparison, is written in strikingly modern English and follows the Shakespearean five-act format with fidelity. This polish is not an accident. Subba Rao's play draws back the curtain on the vibrant court cultures of Southern India where British drama was not stimulated or imposed by British schoolmasters but independently cultivated as a source of pleasant learning (indeed Tanjore and Travancore had been actively fostering and experimenting with dance-dramas in the vernacular since the seventeenth century).[373] As a result, *Krishna Kumari* suggests that the commencement of modern Indian drama in English may owe a little less to British tutelage in British India, and a little more to native ingenuity in the Native States than scholars have hitherto realized.

The fact that *Krishna Kumari* draws on Shakespeare brings us to a still deeper point. Because Shakespeare was a compulsory element of the curriculum in Company-backed schools and colleges, where his works were taught as the exemplar of "civilized" literature, and because questions about his works commonly featured in examinations that regulated entry into the British Indian civil service, the Bard has come to be described in postcolonial theory as the primary channel by which "the Indian was encouraged to become a surrogate Englishman."[374] So deeply was he impressed on the minds of the colonized, it is said, that as the nineteenth century proceeded it was Shakespeare rather than Victoria that became "the true and vital link between India and England."[375] This history has led to the gloomy conclusion that Shakespeare's popularity in India may have stemmed not so much from his merits as from the "anxious pedantry" of the native who memorized the Bard in a quest to obtain "validation as civilized and refined."[376] If there is a redeeming feature in this account, it is that Shakespeare eventually came to be clad in "loin cloth" as Jasodhara Bagchi has memorably put it.[377] That is, his plays were "localized and hybridized," as Indian dramatists began to freely adapt his plays and borrow his techniques.[378] They came to see the Bard, Poonam Trivedi writes, "as part of a global repertoire that offers templates to build upon," making his presence in India a result of exchange rather than imposition.[379]

Subba Rao's *Krishna Kumari* invites us to question both this criticism and this defense of the Bard. The criticism is unwarranted for reasons touched upon previously. The briefest examination of Serfoji's private library or Swati and Uttaram's syllabus will reveal that the rulers of these principalities were studying Shakespeare long before students in British India felt compelled to cram him. The belief that Shakespeare only arrived in India on the back of bayonets is therefore false. When we ask whence lies the Bard's appeal to these readers, who sought him outside the confines of British India, the answer lies not in pitiful mimicry but in the domain of aesthetics. Shakespeare was fascinating to the courts of Tanjore and Travancore not because he belonged to the conquering race, but because of his vivid portrayal of human nature, and the tragic in particular. Here we need to understand that Hindu aesthetics, as codified in Bharata's age-old *Natya Shastra* (Treatise on the Performing Arts), did not countenance tragedy. Why this was the case has been the subject of much discussion. G. K. Bhat's *Tragedy and Sanskrit Drama* lists a number of explanations, ranging from the nature of royal patrons and court audiences, who presumably sought pleasurable comedies and enchanting romances, to common philosophical and religious beliefs, which encouraged theatrical performances that would help the viewer "transcend turmoil and attain composure."[380] Whatever the precise cause, so carefully was the *Natya Shastra* obeyed in the centuries that followed that the "happy end" became a defining feature of Hindu drama. There were "tragic middles," moments of acute grief and suffering, but "tragic outcomes" were eschewed, with divine or supernatural intervention ensuring that the plot did not terminate with "death, conflict, and downfall."[381] The binding code, V. Raghavan sums up, was that:

> The spectacle of virtue defeated and evil triumphant, which frustrates the soul and makes it callous, should never be held up. Nor should the last curtain fall on corpses and the audience depart from the hall as from a cemetery. It is the example of a heroic character overcoming evil, of character triumphing over degradation, that Sanskrit drama sets as the most befitting theme for this art.[382]

The moral and political logic behind this aesthetic is unimpeachable. But the absence of tragedy in Sanskrit drama was, as Bhat writes, itself a tragedy, because it disabled Hindu drama from portraying, and preparing audiences for, the miseries of our existence.[383] Perhaps the greatest of these miseries is that we live in a world of "suffering virtue," where detestable tyrants can turn out victorious.[384] Far from being punished, Amir Khan—violator of oaths, plunderer of temples, ravager of the defenseless, murderer of women—was rewarded by the "civilized" British with a principality of his very own. Shakespeare's oeuvre showed the *shesho* a way to portray the events leading up to this galling outcome and to thereby vividly impress on his students that such miseries were never distant.

The broader point to note here is that Subba Rao's *Krishna Kumari* shows that Indians did not wait until the late-colonial or postcolonial era to self-assuredly use Shakespeare as a template. This should not be surprising because to the refined intellect, the aesthetic is above the political: excellence is to be admired wherever it may be found and appropriated whenever necessary. This was as true for Subba Rao at the start of the century as it was for Michael Madhusudan Dutt and Bankim Chandra Chatterjee toward its middle and its end. All three *litterateurs* considered Shakespeare to be a "literary model par excellence" who belonged not to Britain but to humanity, and whom there was no shame in imitating in order to "throw off the fetters" forged by their compatriots' "servile admiration" of the *Natya Shastra*.[385]

So far we have seen how *Krishna Kumari* challenges longstanding notions about the use to which English learning was put in India, particularly in the theatre. This should hopefully be enough to establish the play's *historical* significance. But what about the play itself? Does it only deserve to be recalled because of when and where it was written—or does it have some *intrinsic* merits that make it a classic? Arguably, it does:

Krishna Kumari deserves particular attention because in at least two respects it marks the beginning of a national theatre.

The first point to reflect upon is the choice of language. It is striking that plays would later claim to be "national theatre," particularly dramas that recalled the glories of the Rajputs and the Marathas, were invariably cast in regional languages. The use of regional languages made these plays authentic expressions of the search for a common identity, but it also made them unintelligible beyond regional boundaries. These playwrights spoke *for* the nation that was coming into being but were unable to speak *to* the nation that came into being. This sad irony is brought home by the fate of Dutt's *Krishna Kumari*. Dutt hoped that his play, which was written in Bengali, would become "the foundation stone of our National Theatre."[386] But the play was never translated into English and this goes some way toward explaining why it is hardly read outside Bengal.[387] By writing his *Krishna Kumari* in English rather than in Marathi, Subba Rao cast his net much more widely, foreshadowing English's emergence as India's *lingua franca*. Though the Company's enmity, and a great deal of bad luck, prevented his drama from being more widely known around the country, the wisdom of his linguistic strategy is borne out by how Krishna Kumari's story eventually became famous—recall that Dutt and his contemporaries learnt of her from Tod whose *Annals* obtained a pan-Indian readership precisely because it was written in English.

The other reason why Subba Rao's *Krishna Kumari* should be considered the starting point of a national theatre relates not to *mutual intelligibility* but to *collective norms*. Ever since Malcolm and Tod made the world aware of what transpired in Udaipur in July 1810, poets and dramatists have focused on the agonizing choices confronting Bhim Singh and Krishna Kumari. The objective in these works has been to understand "what are the obligations between the individual and society" and whether it is "better to let a daughter nobly die or see her live in shame."[388] These "disturbing" questions about *individual* morality are intended to "shake the reader and spectator" by exploring the human condition.[389] So exclusive has the focus been on this element that most works, including Dutt's *Krishna Kumari*, embellish the story with fictitious characters and events, all with a view to heightening the drama around the moment when Bhim Singh chooses to sacrifice Krishna Kumari and his daughter chooses to follow her father's command.

This is not what Subba Rao does. In his version of the tale, Bhim Singh and Krishna Kumari only appear in the closing scenes. The bulk of the play is devoted to dramatizing the machinations leading up to the princess's death. Why? By focusing less on the princess's grim choice and more on the characters that forced the grim choice upon her, Subba Rao teaches his readers a profound lesson in *political* morality. He directs attention not toward the nobility in this Indian tragedy but toward the tragedy of the Indian nobility. At the head of this order we find Maharajas, *sardars*, and *thakurs* consumed by jealousy and intrigues. Below them we see favorites, sycophants, and family members whose utter selfishness makes "falsehood and absurdity" the "current coin in all *darbars*."[390] And then at the very bottom of the heap we find upright servants such as Man Singh's *Bakshi*, Jagat Singh's *Munshi*, and Holkar's *Dewan* that are left to laugh bitterly at the heedless desires that hold court before them. The rottenness of the resulting edifice is laid bare by the *Khansama*'s summary of the Udaipur *darbar*:

> It consists of inconsiderate and barbarous generals, a rash soldiery, rapacious civilians, tyrannical ministers, superstitious Brahmins, crafty priests, deceitful astrologers, intriguing courtiers, prodigal nobles, ignorant relations, designing sycophants, abject slaves of both sexes, and lastly of blockheads and knaves of all descriptions.[391]

What is striking about Subba Rao's drama then is that it encourages introspection. The misery it focuses upon is not the vagaries of fortune or the "blindness of the divine decree" that destroys the innocent princess, but the impotence of the "Hindu Raja" who has been reduced to "a poor helpless creature."[392] And herein lies the play's deep and continuing relevance: unlike the "national theatre" that emerged in the late nineteenth century, which devoted itself to decrying colonialism and reviving Hindu pride, *Krishna Kumari* exposes the painful truth of what Hindu principalities looked like after the Mughals had declined but before the British obtained sway.[393] It was not foes outside the walls, but immorality within, it teaches, that did the most damage to these principalities.[394] It is thus precisely because this drama studies precolonial India that it is so useful to postcolonial India. The British have come and gone but feeble dynasts, craven sycophants, scheming politicians, and parochial communities remain. And so we are still what we were then—easy prey. This is the tragedy of India. Until we change, we will have need for Subba Rao's *Krishna Kumari*.

Notes

1 Jadunath Sarkar, *Daulat Rao Sindhia and North Indian Affairs, 1810–1818*, Bombay: Modern India Press, 1951, vi.
2 *The Book Collector*, Vol. 57, No. 4, Winter, 2008, 601; Sisir Kumar Das, *A History of Indian Literature: Western Impact: Indian Response, 1800–1910*, New Delhi: Sahitya Akademi, 1991, 474; Amritjit Singh, Rajiva Verma, and Irene M. Joshi, *Indian Literature in English, 1827–1979: A Guide to Information Sources*, Detroit: Gale, 1981, 67.
3 Susanne Hoeber Rudolph, "The Princely States of Rajputana: Ethic, Authority, and Structure," *The Indian Journal of Political Science*, Vol. 24, No. 1, 1963, 15.
4 *The Rajputana Gazetteer, Vol. 1*, Calcutta: Superintendent of Govt. Printing, 1879, 37–8.
5 K. R. Qanungo, *Historical Essays*, Agra: Shiva Lal Agarwala & Co. 1968, 63.
6 *The Rajputana Gazetteer*, 39–40; Alfred C. Lyall, *Asiatic Studies: Religious and Social*, London, John Murray, 1884, 189.
7 K. R. Qanungo, "The Rajput and his Vendetta," *Modern Review*, Vol. 101, 1957, 199–200.
8 Ibid., 199–200.
9 Rudolph, "The Princely States of Rajputana," 16.
10 *The Rajputana Gazetteer*, 40.
11 A. F. Pinhey, *History of Mewar*, Calcutta: Government of India Printing, 1909, 19–20.
12 *The Rajputana Gazetteer*, 42–3.
13 Gopi Nath Sharma, *Mewar and the Mughal Emperors*, Agra: Educational Publishers, 1951, 44; Satish Chandra, *Essays on Medieval Indian History*, New Delhi: Oxford University Press, 2003, 367.
14 Pinhey, *History of Mewar*, 24–5.
15 J. C. Brookes, *History of Mewar*, Calcutta: Baptist Mission Press, 1859, 14.
16 William Patrick Andrew, *India and Her Neighbours*, London: W. H. Allen, 1878, 14.
17 Brookes, *History of Mewar*, 14.
18 Pinhey, *History of Mewar*, 26–7.
19 Qanungo, "The Rajput and his Vendetta," 199. For a contrary view see Robert Hallissey, *The Rajput Rebellion Against Aurangzeb: A Study of the Mughal Empire in Seventeenth-Century India*, Columbia: University of Missouri Press, 1977, 47–58.
20 Pinhey, *History of Mewar*, 32–3.
21 Ibid., 32–3.
22 For an overview of the period see Raghubir Sinh, *Malwa in Transition: The First Phase, 1698–1767*, Bombay: D.B Taraporevala, Sons & Co., 1936, 229–30; Rev. John Robson, "Scenes from Rajput History, No. VII: The Triple Alliance," *United Presbyterian Magazine*, July 1, 1873, 300–1; V. S. Bhargava, *Rise of the Kachhawas in Dundhar: From the Earliest Times to the Death of Sawai Jai Singh*, Ajmer: Shabd Sanchar, 1979, 157–9.
23 Brookes, *History of Mewar*, 15.
24 Chandra, *Essays on Medieval Indian History*, 401.
25 Jadunath Sarkar, *Fall of the Mughal Empire, Vol. 1*, Delhi: Orient Longman, 1964, 180–8.
26 Sarkar, *Fall of the Mughal Empire, Vol. 1*, 188.
27 James Tod, *Several Short Accounts of Different States of Rajputana Their History Statistics and General Information Relating to Them* (British Library, Mss. Eur. Mack Private, No. 81, 1815–16, 5); Kalpana Sahu, *Maratha–Rajput Relations During the Eighteenth Century*, PhD dissertation, University of Delhi, 2002, 144–6.
28 Brookes, *History of Mewar*, 17; Pinhey, *History of Mewar*, 35.
29 Parihar, *Marwar and the Marathas*, 88–9; K. S. Gupta, *Mewar and the Maratha Relations*, Delhi: S. Chand & Co. 1971, 98–100; Pinhey, *History of Mewar*, 37.
30 Sahu, *Maratha–Rajput Relations During the Eighteenth Century*, 145–6, 152.

31 Anil Chandra Bannerjee, *Rajput Studies*, Calcutta: A. Mukherjee and Bros., 1944, 210.
32 Bannerjee, *Lectures on Rajput History*, 142.
33 Ibid., 156.
34 Sahu, *Maratha–Rajput Relations During the Eighteenth Century*, 2002, 161.
35 Bannerjee, *Rajput Studies*, 217–19.
36 Parihar, *Marwar and the Marathas*, 92–4.
37 Gupta, *Mewar and the Maratha Relations*, 75–7.
38 "Notes Relative to the Affairs of Native and Foreign European States" (British Library, IOR/H/606, 157).
39 Bannerjee, *Lectures on Rajput History*, 148; "Notes Relative to the Affairs of Native and Foreign European States," 169.
40 Jadunath Sarkar, *Fall of the Mughal Empire, Vol. I*, 197; Ananda Bhattacharyya and Jadunath Sarkar, eds., *A History of the Dasnami Naga Sannyasis*, New Delhi: Routledge, 2018, 238.
41 G. S. Sardesai, *New History of the Marathas, Vol. III*, Bombay: Phoenix Publications, 1968, 220.
42 A. R. Kulkarni, *The Marathas and the Maratha Country*, Pune: Diamond Publications, 2008, 179; "Notes Relative to the Affairs of Native and Foreign European States," 156.
43 "Changes in the Maratha State from the Time of Sivaji" (British Library, IOR/H/MISC/242, 197–98).
44 Sudhindra Nath Qanungo, *Jaswant Rao Holkar: The Golden Rogue*, Lucknow: Abhinava-Bharati, 1965, 50.
45 Sardesai, *New History of the Marathas, Vol. III*, 205.
46 Kaushik Roy, *War, Culture and Society in Early Modern South Asia, 1740–1849*, New York: Routledge, 2011, 116.
47 S. C. Misra, *Sindhia–Holkar Rivalry in Rajasthan*, Delhi: Sundeep Prakashan, 1981, 116–24.
48 Qanungo, *Jaswant Rao Holkar*, 48; A. Macdonald, *Memoir of the Life of the Late Nana Furnuwees*, Bombay: American Mission Press, 1851, 84–6; R. G. Pandey, *Mahadji Shinde and the Poona Durbar*, Delhi: Oriental Publishers, 1980, 122–8.
49 C. A. Kincaid, and D. B. Parasnis, *A History of the Maratha People, Vol. III*, London: Oxford University Press, 1925, 165–9; Poonam Goel, "Maratha Policy Towards the States of Northern India during the 18th Century," PhD dissertation, Aligarh Muslim University, 1981, 443.
50 An Officer in the Service of the Honorable East India Company, *Origin of the Pindaries*, London: John Murray, 1818, 79–80; Qanungo, *Jaswant Rao Holkar*, 51; Pandey, *Mahadji Shinde and the Poona Durbar*, 153–4.
51 Qanungo, *Jaswant Rao Holkar*, 50.
52 S. N. Qanungo, "Decline and Fall of the Maratha Power (1799–1818)," in R. C. Majumdar, ed., *The History and Culture of the Indian People, Vol. 8: The Maratha Supremacy*, Bombay: Bharati Vidya Bhavan, 1958, 489–92; Henry Beveridge, *A Comprehensive History of India: Civil, Military, and Social, Vol. 2*, London: Blackie & Son, 1870, 743.
53 D. H. A. Kolff, "The End of an Ancien Regime: Colonial War in India 1798–1818," in J. A. de Moor and H. L. Wesseling, eds., *Imperialism and War: Essays on Colonial Wars in Asia and Africa*, Leiden: Brill, 1998, 28–9.
54 Misra, *Sindhia-Holkar Rivalry in Rajasthan*, 138.
55 D. R. Mankekar, *Mewar Saga: The Sisodias' Role in Indian History*, Delhi: Vikas Publishing House, 1976, 126; Qanungo, *Jaswant Rao Holkar*, 54.
56 P. C. Gupta, *Baji Rao II and the East India Company, 1796–1818*, Oxford: Oxford University Press, 1923, 28–9.

57 G. S. Sardesai, *The Main Currents of Maratha History*, Bombay: Keshav Bhikaji Dhavle, 1933, 196.
58 James Baillie Fraser, ed., *Military Memoir of Lieut.-Col. James Skinner*, London: Smith, Elder & Co., 1851, 195–6.
59 Misra, *Sindhia–Holkar Rivalry in Rajasthan*, 144; Qanungo, *Jaswant Rao Holkar*, 282–3.
60 Misra, *Sindhia–Holkar Rivalry in Rajasthan*, 145–6; *The Imperial Gazetteer of India, Vol. XV*, Oxford: Clarendon Press, 1908, 412.
61 "Peace Proposed to the Marattas" in *Maratha Affairs 1786–1804* (British Library, IOR/H/241, 159). Also see Mukund Wamanrao Burway, *Mahadji Sindia*, Indore: Mukund Wamanrao Burway, 1921, 182.
62 "Extracts from a Pamphlet by John Macpherson entitled First and Second Letters to a Noble Earl" in *Maratha Affairs 1786–1804*, 149.
63 John Robinson to Warren Hastings, February 9, 1781 in *Maratha Affairs 1786–1804*, 154.
64 Kulkarni, *The Marathas and the Maratha Country*, 158; Rajat Kanta Ray, "Indian Society and the Establishment of the British Supremacy, 1765–1818," in P. J. Marshall, ed., *The Eighteenth Century*, Oxford: Oxford University Press, 1998, 519; Sardesai, *The Main Currents of Maratha History*, 184–5.
65 John Robinson to Warren Hastings, February 9, 1781 in *Maratha Affairs 1786–1804*, 155; N. K. Sinha, "Progress of the British Power (1795-1798)," in Majumdar, ed., *The Maratha Supremacy*, 477–9.
66 Ray, "Indian Society and the Establishment of the British Supremacy, 1765–1818," 516–17, 521.
67 Ray, "Indian Society and the Establishment of the British Supremacy, 1765–1818," 516–17, 521; "Notes Relative to the Affairs of Native and Foreign European States," 160–1.
68 Y. N. Deodhar, *Nana Phadnis and the External Affairs of the Maratha Empire*, Bombay: Popular Book Depot, 1962, 82.
69 Goel, "Maratha Policy Towards the States of Northern India," 362–3.
70 "Considerations on the Policy of the Treaty of Bassein" (British Library, IOR/H/241, 635–6).
71 Gupta, *Baji Rao II and the East India Company,* 62–6.
72 Beveridge, *A Comprehensive History of India*, 747.
73 Misra, *Sindhia–Holkar Rivalry in Rajasthan*, 149.
74 *Papers Concerning Political, Military, Administrative and Legal Matters, 1803–1805* (British Library, IOR/H/481, 1194–5).
75 Shelford Bidwell, *Swords for Hire: European Mercenaries in Eighteenth-Century India*, London: John Murray, 1971, 159; Sidney James Owen, "Benoit de Boigne," *The English Historical Review*, Vol. 3, No. 9, 1888, 63–82; Jean Marie Lafont, *Indika: Essays in Indo-French Relations, 1630–1976*, Delhi: Manohar, 2000, 182–6; Desmond Young, *Fountain of the Elephants*, London: Collins, 1959, 115–37.
76 Dirk H. A Kolff, "The End of an Ancien Regime," 35–8.
77 Bidwell, *Swords for Hire*, 77.
78 *Brief Remarks on the Mahratta War and the Progress of the French Establishment in Hindostan Under Generals De Boigne and Perron*, London: Cadell & Davies, 1804, 14–18; *Second Maratha War, 17th August to 5th September 1803* (British Library, IOR/H/485 274–276).
79 Kaushik Roy, "Military Synthesis in South Asia: Armies, Warfare, and Indian Society, c. 1740–1849," *The Journal of Military History*, Vol. 65, No. 3, 2005, 673; Bidwell, *Swords for Hire*, 184–86; William Thorn, *Memoir of War in India Conducted by General*

Lord Lake, London: T. Egerton, 1818, 108–9; "Lord Lake to General C. Perron" in *Second Maratha War, 17th August to 5th September 1803*, 257–9 274–5, 285–8, 359–65.

80 Roy, "Military Synthesis in South Asia," 672–3; Huw J. Davies, *Wellington's War: The Making of a Military Genius*, New Haven: Yale University Press, 2012, 61–4.

81 "Notes Relative to the Affairs of Native and Foreign European States," 160.

82 Ibid., 161.

83 "Memorandum on the Subject of Extension of British Territory in India, 1797–1806" (British Library, IOR/H/481, 1160–61).

84 Anil Chandra Banerjee, *British Alliance with Marwar*, Calcutta: A. Mukherjee & Bros., 1944, 310–12.

85 H. C. Batra, *The Relations of Jaipur State with East India Company (1803–1858)*, Delhi: S. Chand & Co., 1958, 18–22.

86 P. E. Roberts, *India Under Wellesley*, London: G. Bell and Sons Ltd., 1929, 239.

87 Roberts, *India Under Wellesley*, 240.

88 *Papers Concerning Political, Military, Administrative and Legal Matters, 1803–1805*, 1240–1; U. N. Chakravorty, *Anglo-Maratha Relations and Malcolm, 1798–1830*, Delhi: Associated Publishing, 1937, 65; "War in India," *The Sun*, September 24, 1804, 3.

89 Roberts, *India Under Wellesley*, 239–40; *Substance of Papers Respecting the War with Holkar, 2nd March 1804* (British Library, IOR/H/491, 333).

90 Davies, *Wellington's War*, 70–1; *Papers Concerning Political, Military, Administrative and Legal Matters, 1803–1805*, 1195.

91 *Papers Concerning Political, Military, Administrative and Legal Matters, 1803–1805*, 1197; G. H Barlow to G. Lake, November 15, 1804 (British Library, IOR/H/485, 602).

92 Chakravorty, *Anglo-Maratha Relations and Malcolm,* 66.

93 Roy, "Military Synthesis in South Asia," 674.

94 Davies, *Wellington's War*, 72.

95 Chakravorty, *Anglo-Maratha Relations and Malcolm,* 68.

96 Ibid., 68–9.

97 Ibid., 68–70.

98 *Cessions by Sindhia and Restorations, Sir George Barlow's Policy Compared with that of Gerard Lake and Lord Wellesley* (British Library, IOR/H/242, 258–60).

99 Chakravorty, *Anglo-Maratha Relations and Malcolm*, 79.

100 Ibid., 79.

101 Qanungo, *Jaswant Rao Holkar*, 283; John William Kaye, *The Life and Correspondence of Charles, Lord Metcalfe, Vol.1*, London: Richard Bentley, 1854, 190.

102 George Barlow to William Bentinck, December 17, 1805 (Bentinck Papers, Pw Jb 68, 271). I am grateful to Rebecca Hickman for carefully scanning the Bentinck Papers for me.

103 Ibid.

104 Ibid.

105 George Barlow to William Bentinck, December 17, 1805 (Bentinck Papers, Pw Jb 68, 266-270); Chakravorty, *Anglo-Maratha Relations and Malcolm*, 83.

106 Chakravorty, *Anglo-Maratha Relations and Malcolm*, 85.

107 *Substance of Papers Respecting the War with Holkar, 2nd March 1804*, 337.

108 Chakravorty, *Anglo-Maratha Relations and Malcolm*, 81–83; Percival Spear, *The Oxford History of Modern India, 1740–1975*, Oxford: Oxford University Press, 1965, 113–16.

109 *Dissolution of the Defensive Alliance between the East India Company and Jagat Singh Raja of Jyenagur (Jaipur)*, Examiner's Office, December 1806, (British Library, IOR/F/4/195/4431, 27).

110 Banerjee, *British Alliance with Marwar*, 314; Bengal Proceedings (Secret), Political, December 24, 1806 (British Library, IOR/P/BEN/SEC/198, No. 69); Bengal Proceedings (Secret), June 26, 1806 (British Library, IOR/P/BEN/SEC/191, No. 33).
111 Chakravorty, *Anglo-Maratha Relations and Malcolm*, 84; Bengal Proceedings (Secret), May 22, 1806 (British Library, IOR/P/BEN/SEC/188, No. 38).
112 Jadunath Sarkar, *Fall of the Mughal Empire, Vol. I*, 131.
113 R. P. Vyas, *Role of Nobility in Marwar (1800–1873 A.D.)*, New Delhi: Jain Brothers, 1969, 5.
114 Robert Stern, *The Cat and the Lion: Jaipur State in the British Raj*, Leiden: Brill, 1988, 3–4, 8–10; Vyas, *Role of Nobility in Marwar*, 8; V. S. Bhargava, *Marwar and the Mughal Emperors*, Delhi: Munshiram Manoharlal, 1966, 175–6.
115 Bhargava, *Marwar and the Mughal Emperors*, 78.
116 G. D. Sharma, *Rajput Polity: A Study of Politics and Administration of the State of Marwar, 1638–1749*, New Delhi: Manohar, 1977, 30–1.
117 Vyas, *Role of Nobility in Marwar*, 18–19.
118 G. N. Parihar, *Marwar and the Marathas, 1724–1843 A. D.*, Jodhpur: Hindi Sahitya Mandir, 1968, 135.
119 Padmaja Sharma, *Maharaja Man Singh of Jodhpur and His Times (1803–1843 A.D.)*, Agra: Shiva Lal Agarwala, 1972, 29–32.
120 Ibid., 43–9.
121 Basavan Lal, *Memoirs of the Puthan Soldier of Fortune: The Nuwab Ameer-Ood-Doulah Mohummud Ameer Khan, Chief of Seronj, Tonk, Rampoora, Neemahera, and Other Places in Hindoostan*, trans. Henry T. Prinsep, Calcutta: G. H. Huttman, 1832, 296.
122 N. B. Roy, "Princess Krisnakumari and the Conflict Amongst the Princes of Rajasthan," *Modern Review*, Vol. 71, April, 1942, 369.
123 Ibid., 369.
124 John Malcolm, *A Memoir of Central India, Vol. I*, London: Kingsbury, Parbury & Allen, 1824, 331.
125 Gaurishankar Hirachand Ojha, *Udaipur Rajya Ka Itihas, Vol. 2*, Ajmer: Vaidik Yantralay, 1931, 695–6.
126 *Dissolution of the Defensive Alliance between the East India Company and Jagat Singh Raja of Jyenaghur (Jaipur)*, 17–18.
127 Parihar, *Marwar and the Marathas,* 144.
128 A. C. Banerjee, *British Alliance with Jaipur*, Calcutta: A. Mukherjee and Bros., 1944, 229–30; *Dissolution of the Defensive Alliance between the East India Company and Jagat Singh Raja of Jyenagur (Jaipur)*, 84–6.
129 R. K. Saxena, *Maratha Relations with the Major States of Rajputana, 1761–1818 A.D.*, New Delhi: S. Chand, 1973, 199–203.
130 John William Kaye, *The Life and Correspondence of Henry St. George Tucker*, London: Richard Bentley, 1854, 196.
131 James Tod, *Annals and Antiquities of Rajasthan, Vol I & Vol. II*, Calcutta: The Society for the Resuscitation of Indian Literature, 1902, 198–9, ff.
132 Parihar, *Marwar and the Marathas,* 148.
133 Nirmala M. Upadhyaya, "Raids of Pindari Chief Amir Khan in Jodhpur State," *Rajasthan Institute of Historical Research*, Vol. 6, No. 1, 1971, 29–30; Tej Kumar Mathur, *Feudal Polity in Mewar, 1750–1850*, Jaipur: Publication Scheme, 1987, 74–83.
134 Roy, "Princess Krisnakumari," 371; Madras Proceedings (Secret), March 26, 1807 (British Library, IOR/P/BEN/SEC/201, No. 1).
135 Madras Proceedings (Secret), May 23, 1807 (Tamil Nadu State Archives, Secret Files, Vol. 30, 1851–60).

136 *Morning Herald*, December 14, 1807, 3; Madras Proceedings (Secret), May 23, 1807 (Tamil Nadu State Archives, Secret Files, Vol. 30, 1861–7).
137 Saxena, *Maratha Relations with the Major States of Rajputana,* 211–14.
138 Ibid., 215–17.
139 Banerjee, *British Alliance with Jaipur*, 245–7; Nirmala Upadhyay, *The Administration of Jodhpur State, 1800–1947 A.D.*, Jodhpur: International Publishers, 1973, 18–19.
140 Parihar, *Marwar and the Marathas,* 155–6; *Political Letters Received from Bengal, Vol. 3*, March 29, 1808 (British Library, IOR/L/PS/6/19, 519-20).
141 Vyas, *Role of Nobility in Marwar*, 39–40.
142 Lal, *Memoirs of the Puthan Soldier of Fortune*, 352.
143 Ibid., 352–3.
144 Malcolm, *A Memoir of Central India, Vol. I*, 329–42.
145 Malcolm, *A Memoir of Central India, Vol. I*, 329–42; "Meer Khan," *Government Gazette*, March 8, 1810, 2; "Memoirs of Ameer Khan," *The Asiatic Journal and Monthly Register*, Vol. XVIII, September-December, 1835, 263; D. C., "Some Account of Abdool Messee, a converted Mahometan, Now Employed in Hindoostan," *Panoplist & Missionary Magazine*, Vol. 11, No. 2, February, 1816, 84–6.
146 *Political Letters Received from Bengal*, Vol 4, September 27, 1808 (British Library, IOR/L/PS/6/20, 163–4).
147 Sharma, *Maharaja Man Singh of Jodhpur and His Times*, 97.
148 Ibid., 87.
149 Malcolm, *A Memoir of Central India, Vol. I*, 332.
150 Sharma, *Maharaja Man Singh of Jodhpur and His Times*, 88.
151 Malcolm, *A Memoir of Central India, Vol. I*, 329–42; Ojha, *Udaipur Rajya Ka Itihas, Vol. 2*, 695–9.
152 Lal, *Memoirs of the Puthan Soldier of Fortune*, 399.
153 Ibid., 399.
154 Tod, *Annals and Antiquities of Rajasthan,* 198–203.
155 Vyas, *Role of Nobility in Marwar*, 43–4; B. D. Sharma, "Amir Khan and Krisna Kumari Episode," *Journal of Rajasthan Institute of Historical Research*, Vol. 6, No. 1, 1970, 38–9.
156 Lal, *Memoirs of the Puthan Soldier of Fortune*, 359–60.
157 Malcolm, *A Memoir of Central India, Vol. I*, 329–42. Shyamaldas, the doyen of Rajasthani historians, recommends the account in Tod's *Annals* (see his *Vir-Vinod: Mevad Ka Itihas*, Vol. 2, Part 3, New Delhi: Motilal Banarsidass, 1986, 1736–9).
158 Lal, *Memoirs of the Puthan Soldier of Fortune*, 359–60.
159 Ojha, *Udaipur Rajya Ka Itihas, Vol. 2*, 695–9.
160 Tod, *Annals and Antiquities of Rajasthan,* 202.
161 Malcolm, *A Memoir of Central India, Vol. I*, 329–42.
162 Malcolm, *A Memoir of Central India, Vol. I*, 341–2; Shyamal Das, *Vir-Vinod: Mevad Ka Itihas*, 1739.
163 Shyamal Das, *Vir-Vinod: Mevad Ka Itihas*, 1739.
164 See the footnote by Henry T. Prinsep in Lal, *Memoirs of the Puthan Soldier of Fortune*, 400. On infanticide see, A. J. O'Brien, "Female Infanticide in the Punjab," *Folklore*, Vol. 19, No. 3, 1908, 261–75; Mahima Manchanda, *Kudi-Maar: The Vexed Question of Infanticide in Punjab, A Colonial and Post-Colonial Perspective*, MPhil thesis, University of Birmingham, 2014.
165 *Asiatic Annual Register 1810–1811*, London: J. Debrett, 1812, 49–50.
166 Tod, *Annals and Antiquities of Rajasthan,* 202; "Death of the Princess of Oudipore," *The Times*, April 21, 1811, 4.
167 Lal, *Memoirs of the Puthan Soldier of Fortune*, 276.

168 Ibid., 309–10.
169 Edward Thompson, *The Making of the Indian Princes*, Oxford: Oxford University Press, 1943, 152.
170 Thompson, *The Making of the Indian Princes*, 152.
171 Malcolm, *A Memoir of Central India, Vol. I*, 249–51.
172 "Tonk State," *Imperial Gazetteer of India*, Calcutta: Superintendent of Government Printing, 1908, 297–9; James Mill and Horace Hyman Wilson, *History of British India from 1805 to 1835, Vol. 1*, London: James Madden, 1848, 77.
173 Fraser, *Military Memoir of Lieut.-Col. James Skinner*, 67.
174 Fraser, *Military Memoir of Lieut.-Col. James Skinner*, 69–70; John Malcolm, *Report on the Province of Malwa, and Adjoining Districts, Submitted to the Supreme Court of British India*, Calcutta: Government Gazette Press, 1822, 213.
175 *Madras Courier*, May 28, 1811, 2.
176 Fraser, *Military Memoir of Lieut.-Col. James Skinner*, 68–9.
177 *Papers Concerning Political, Military, Administrative and Legal Matters, 1803–1805*, 1231–2.
178 "Tonk State," *Imperial Gazetteer of India*, 298; Lal, *Memoirs of the Puthan Soldier of Fortune*, 287.
179 George B. Malleson, *An Historical Sketch of the Native States of India*, London: Longman, Green, and Co., 1875, 78–80; S. M. Abdul Moid Khan, *The Rulers of Erstwhile Princely State of Tonk*, Tonk: Rajasthan Maulana Abul Kalam Azad Arabic Persian Research Institute, 2012, 37.
180 Valentine Blacker, *Memoir of the Operations of the British Army in India during the Mahratta War of 1817, 1818, & 1819*, London: Black, Kingsbury, Parbury, & Allen, 1821, 28.
181 K. R. Qanungo, *Historical Essays*, 108; Lal, *Memoirs of the Puthan Soldier of Fortune*, 292–3.
182 Fraser, *Military Memoir of Lieut.-Col. James Skinner*, 68; Malcolm, *Report on the Province of Malwa, and Adjoining Districts,* 134–5.
183 G. B. Malleson, *An Historical Sketch of the Native States of India in Subsidiary Alliance with the British Government with a Notice of the Mediatized and Minor States*, London: Longman, Green, & Co., 1875, 80.
184 Sarkar, *Daulat Rao Sindhia and North Indian Affairs, 1810–18*, 49.
185 Richard Jenkins to N. B. Edmonstone, November 13, 1809 in *Correspondence Regarding Ameer Khan and the Raja of Berar* (British Library, IOR/H/597, 303–8).
186 Lord Minto to Meer Khan, December 16, 1809, Lord Minto to Jaswant Rao Holkar, December 18, 1809 in *Correspondence Regarding Ameer Khan and the Raja of Berar* (British Library, IOR/H/596, 171–6).
187 Sarkar, *Daulat Rao Sindhia and North Indian Affairs, 1810–18*, 50–1.
188 Meer Khan to Lord Minto, February 14, 1810 in *Correspondence Regarding Ameer Khan and the Raja of Berar* (British Library, IOR/H/597, 99–103).
189 Ibid.
190 Ibid.
191 *Application from the Pindari Chief Amir Khan Requesting Employment*, Examiner's Office, December 1811 (British Library, IOR/F/4/335/7664, 4–9, 446).
192 "Minute of the Governor-General Lord Minto, 16th October 1809" in *Correspondence Regarding Ameer Khan and the Raja of Berar* (British Library, IOR/H/595A, 175–99).
193 Lord Minto to Jaswant Rao Holkar, February 23, 1810 in *Correspondence Regarding Ameer Khan and the Raja of Berar* (British Library, IOR/H/597, 243–4); H. T. Prinsep, *A Narrative of the Political and Military Transactions of British India Under the Marquess of Hastings, 1813–1818*, London: John Murray, 1820, 16.

194 Sarkar, *Daulat Rao Sindhia and North Indian Affairs, 1810–18*, 48; *Rough Notes on Ameer Khan* (British Library, IOR/H/511, 473).
195 "Minute of the Governor-General Lord Minto, 12 December 1809" in *Correspondence Regarding Ameer Khan and the Raja of Berar* (British Library, IOR/H/596, 125–34).
196 Graeme Mercer to Lord Minto, 3rd January 1810 in *Correspondence Regarding Ameer Khan and the Raja of Berar* (British Library, IOR/H/596, 587–91).
197 Batra, *The Relations of Jaipur State With East India Company,* 36–7.
198 Lal, *Memoirs of the Puthan Soldier of Fortune*, 359–60.
199 Tod, *Annals and Antiquities*, 204.
200 Raja Juggut Sing to Lord Moira, 28th March 1814 in *Correspondence Concerning the Pindaris* (British Library, IOR/H/598, 489–93).
201 Charles Metcalfe to N. B. Edmonstone, May 29, 1811 in *Papers on Political Matters in India, 1813* (British Library, IOR/H/519, 51–55); *Madras Courier*, January 28, 1812, 2; *Papers Regarding the Political Situation in Jaipur State*, Examiner's Office, May 1813 (British Library, IOR/F/4/394/10018, 1–5).
202 Sarkar, *Daulat Rao Sindhia and North Indian Affairs, 1810–18*, 71.
203 Upadhyay, *The Administration of Jodhpur State, 1800-1947 A.D.*, 29–30; Vyas, *Role of Nobility in Marwar*, 49–52.
204 *Madras Courier*, January 16, 1816, 4
205 Tod, *Annals and Antiquities*, 470; Ojha, *Udaipur Rajya Ka Itihas, Vol. 2*, 697–9.
206 Thompson, *The Making of the Indian Princes*, 154; James Tod, *Travels: Western India*, London: Wm. H. Allen & Co., 1839, xxxiv–vi.
207 *Madras Courier*, August 13, 1816, 3.
208 M. L. Sarma, *History of the Jaipur State*, Jaipur: Rajasthan Institute of Historical Research, 1969, 237.
209 Reginald Heber, *Narrative of a Journey Through the Upper Provinces of India, Vol. 2*, London: John Murray, 1828, 375; "Asiatic Intelligence," *Asiatic Journal and Monthly Register*, Vol. 3, No. 5, May, 1817, 507.
210 Lal, *Memoirs of the Puthan Soldier of Fortune*, 459–61. "Asiatic Intelligence," *Asiatic Journal and Monthly Register*, Vol. 3, No. 5, May, 1817, 509.
211 The Marchioness of Bute, ed., *The Private Journal of the Marquess of Hastings, Vol. 2*, London: Saunders and Otley, 1858, 127–8.
212 Lal, *Memoirs of the Puthan Soldier of Fortune*, 458–9.
213 "Memoirs of Ameer Khan," 267; Prinsep, *A Narrative of the Political and Military Transactions of British India Under the Marquess of Hastings*, 379, 390; Batra, *The Relations of Jaipur State With East India Company*, 43–4.
214 "Extract of a Letter Dated Madras, December 21, 1809," *The Evening Star*, July 6, 1810, 2.
215 *Madras Courier*, May 28, 1811, 2.
216 James Tod, *Several Short Accounts of Different States of Rajputana*, 87–108.
217 *Madras Courier*, January 27, 1815, 9; Bengal Proceedings (Secret), July 12, 1811 (British Library, IOR/P/BEN/SEC/234, No. 2).
218 J. Richardson to Lord Minto, June 27, 1810 in *Papers on Political Matters in India, 1813* (British Library, IOR/H/519, 39–49); Qeyamuddin Ahmad, *The Wahhabi Movement in India*, New York: Routledge, 2020, 40–4.
219 Kaye, *The Life and Correspondence of Charles, Lord Metcalfe, Vol.1*, 430–1.
220 A. F. M. Abdul Ali, "The Pindaris," *Islamic Culture*, Vol. 11, No. 3, July, 1937, 370–1.
221 "Origin of the Pindaries," *The Quarterly Review*, Vol. 18, No. 36, 1818, 475.
222 *Papers Respecting the Pindarry and Mahratta Wars*, London: G. L. Cox, 1824, 6.
223 An Officer, *Origin of the Pindaries*, 120; "Origin of the Pindaries," 466, 479–80.

224 "Speech of the Marquess of Hastings," *Monthly Magazine*, Vol. 47, No. 323, March, 1819, 173; "Secret Minute by the Earl of Moira" in *Political State of India, 1815–1816* (British Library, IOR/H/603, 29–5).
225 An Officer, *Origin of the Pindaries*, 120; "Origin of the Pindaries," 466, 479–80; *Asiatic Journal and Monthly Register*, Vol. 7, April, 1819, 418; K. M. Pannikar, *British Diplomacy in North India: A Study of the Delhi Residency, 1803–1857*, New Delhi: Associated Publishing House, 1968, 49–58; Kaye, *The Life and Correspondence of Charles, Lord Metcalfe, Vol.1*, 449–51.
226 Kaye, *The Life and Correspondence of Charles, Lord Metcalfe, Vol. 1*, 447.
227 The Marchioness of Bute, *The Private Journal of the Marquess of Hastings, Vol. 2*, 113–14.
228 An Officer, *Origin of the Pindaries*, 129.
229 Mesrob Vartavarian, "Pacification and Patronage in the Maratha Deccan, 1803–1818," *Modern Asian Studies*, Vol. 50, No. 6, 2016, 1761–2.
230 An Officer, *Origin of the Pindaries*, 122; James Grant, *Cassell's History of India*, London: Cassell, Petter and Galpin, 1880, 477.
231 Vartavarian, "Pacification and Patronage in the Maratha Deccan, 1803–1818," 1765–6.
232 Ali, "The Pindaris," 371; An Officer, *Origin of the Pindaries*, 129; The Marchioness of Bute, *The Private Journal of the Marquess of Hastings, Vol. 2*, 153; "Secret Minute by the Earl of Moira" in *Political State of India*, 52–3, 79.
233 An Officer, *Origin of the Pindaries*, 130–1.
234 Beveridge, *A Comprehensive History of India*, 114; An Officer, *Origin of the Pindaries*, 154–7, 162; Grant, *Cassell's History of India*, 162–4, 477; Blacker, *Memoir of the Operations of the British Army in India*, 27.
235 Beveridge, *A Comprehensive History of India*, 62–3; "The Government of Lord Hastings," *Encyclopedia Britannica*, May 3, 2023, https://www.britannica.com/place/India.
236 S. G. Vaidya, *Peshwa Bajirao II and Downfall of the Maratha Power*, Nagpur: Pragati Prakashan, 1976, 332; Birendra Kumar Sinha, *The Pindaris (1798–1818)*, Calcutta: Bookland, 1971, 30–1, 36–7.
237 Vartavarian, "Pacification and Patronage in the Maratha Deccan, 1803–1818," 1790.
238 Prinsep, *A Narrative of the Political and Military Transactions*, 218; Nida Arshi, "The East India Company, Rajput Chieftaincies and Pindaris: Changing Dynamics of a Triangular Relationship," *Proceedings of the Indian History Congress*, Vol. 72, Part I, 2011, 650.
239 An Officer, *Origin of the Pindaries*, 148.
240 Fraser, *Military Memoir of Lieut.-Col. James Skinner*, 140; Prinsep, *A Narrative of the Political and Military Transactions*, 229.
241 Prinsep, *A Narrative of the Political and Military Transactions*, 126; Fraser, *Military Memoir of Lieut.-Col. James Skinner*, 141–2; *Appendix in Support of the Claims of the Most Noble The Marquis of Hastings and all the Officers, Soldiers, and Others for Participation in the Booty Taken During the Pindarree and Mahratta War in the Years 1817 and 1818*, London, L. Thompson, 1822, 106–7; James Grant Duff, *A History of the Marathas, Vol. 3*, London: Longman, Rees, Orme, and Green, 1826, 461–2.
242 Prinsep, *A Narrative of the Political and Military Transactions*, 228–9.
243 Ibid., 334–5.
244 Prinsep, *A Narrative of the Political and Military Transactions*, 334–7; *Papers Respecting the Pindarry and Mahratta Wars*, 410–12.
245 "Mahommedan Chiefs," *Sun*, September 28, 1818, 4.
246 Malcolm, *A Memoir of Central India, Vol. 1*, 458–61.
247 Malavika Kasturi, *Embattled Identities: Rajput Lineages and the Colonial State in Nineteenth-century North India*, New Delhi, Oxford University Press, 2002, 33.

248 "Cursory Remarks on the British Government in India," *Kaleidoscope*, Vol. 2, No. 8, March, 1830, reprinted in Gautam Chattopadhyaya, ed., *Early Nineteenth Century Documents*, Calcutta: Research India, 1978, 109; "Mahommedan Chiefs," *Sun*, September 28, 1818, 4; J. F. Blumhardt, "Translation of Address Presented by the Leading Men of Calcutta to Francis Rawdon," in *Papers of Francis Rawdon-Hastings, 1817–1818* (British Library, Mss. Eur. C623). For a broader retrospective see "Speech by Kuvi Das Shyamal Das of Meywar," Foreign Department, Internal-A, July 1888, Nos. 18–24 (reprinted here as Appendix IV).
249 Tod, *Travels: Western India*, xxxviii; Mohan Singh Mehta, *Lord Hastings and the Indian States*, Bombay: D. B. Taraporevala Sons & Co., 1930, 145; Lokenath Ghose, *Modern History of the Indian Chiefs; Rajas, Zamindars, & C, Vol. 1*, Calcutta: J. N. Ghose & Co., 1879, 50–1; Upadhyay, *The Administration of Jodhpur State, 1800–1947 A.D.*, 32–3.
250 Mehta, *Lord Hastings and the Indian States*, 136; "From the Rana of Odeypoore to the Governor General," Bengal Proceedings (Political), June 26, 1819 (British Library, IOR/P/121/57); Fateh Lal Mehta, *Handbook of Meywar and Guide to its Principal Objects and Interests*, Bombay: Times of India Steam Press, 1888, 39.
251 "Pindaree Chiefs," *Asiatic Journal and Monthly Register*, Vol. 6, August, 1818, 208.
252 John Sutherland, *Sketches of the Relations Subsisting Between the British Government in India and the Different Native States,* Calcutta: G. H. Human, 1837, 146–7; Ahmad, *The Wahhabi Movement in India*, 7.
253 Prinsep, *A Narrative of the Political and Military Transactions of British India Under the Marquess of Hastings*, 399.
254 *Asiatic Journal and Monthly Register*, Vol. 7, February, 1819, 182.
255 Horace Hayman Wilson, *History of British India from 1805 to 1835, Vol. 3*, London: Madden and Malcolm, 1835, 105.
256 V. V. Gopal Row, *Life of Vennelacunty Soobrow*, Madras: C. Foster & Co., 1873, 108.
257 Hugh Pearson, *Memoirs of the Life and Correspondence of the Rev. Christian Frederick Swartz*, New York: Saxton and Miles, 1842, 102–11, 107, 115, 171.
258 Pearson, *Memoirs*, 240–1.
259 "Death of Soobrow," *The Bombay Times and Journal of Commerce*, February 19, 1848, 148.
260 Ibid.
261 Ibid.
262 F. R. Hemingway, *Madras District Gazetteers: Tanjore*, Madras: Government Press, 1906, 52; R. Jayaraman, *Sarasvati Mahal: A Short History and Guide*, Thanjavur: Sarasvati Mahal Library, 1981, 16.
263 For an overview see Savithri Preetha Nair, ". . . Of Real Use to the People: The Tanjore Printing Press and the Spread of Useful Knowledge," *The Indian Economic and Social History Review*, Vol. 48, No. 4, 2011, 500; T. J. Rama Rao and Major N. B. Gadre, "British Admirers of Maharaja Serfoji," *Journal of the Tanjore Sarasvati Mahal Library*, Vol. 14, No. 3, 1960; Savithri Preetha Nair, *Raja Serfoji II: Science, Medicine and Enlightenment in Tanjore*, New Delhi: Routledge, 2012. Also see "Raja of Tanjore," *Asiatic Journal and Monthly Register*, Vol. 13, 1834, 14.
264 Satyajit Das, *Selections from Indian Journals: Vol. 1*, Calcutta: K. L. Mukhopadhyay, 1963, 155.
265 William Blackburne to William Bentinck, June 7, 1806 (Tamil Nadu State Archives, Tanjore District Records, Bundle 3488, 161–5).
266 William Blackburne to William Bentinck, June 9, 1804 (Tamil Nadu State Archives, Tanjore District Records, Bundle 3480, 199–200).
267 Richard Jenkins to Barry Close, April 24, 1805 (Tamil Nadu State Archive, Tanjore District Records, Bundle 4354, 311–14).

268 William Blackburne to William Bentinck, January 3, 1806 (Bentinck Papers, Pw Jb 4/1–77, 30–4); Rajaram, "Educational Activities of H.H Rajah Serfoji Chattrapathy of Tanjore"; Sumathi Ramaswamy, *Terrestrial Lessons: The Conquest of the World as Globe*, Chicago: University of Chicago Press, 2017, 48–9.
269 [Subba Rao], *Balabodha Muktavali* [String of Pearls], 1809, 8 (British Library, Add Mss. 14139.g.7); Nair, ". . .Of Real Use to the People," 514–15.
270 Nair, ". . . Of Real Use to the People," 516; Peterson, "The Schools of Serfoji II of Tanjore," 36.
271 Rama Rao and Gadre, "British Admirers of Maharaja Serfoji," 1.
272 "Raja of Tanjore," *Asiatic Journal and Monthly Register*, Vol. 13, 1834, 14.
273 Madras Proceedings (Political), March 26, 1830, (British Library, IOR/P/318/107, 262).
274 S. Venkitasubramonia Iyer, *Swati Tirunal and his Music*, Trivandrum: College Book House, 1975, 6–7.
275 S. Venkitasubramonia Iyer, "Some Compositions of Sri Swati Tirunal: Some Firsts in Karnatak Music," *Sangeet Natak*, Vol. 19, 1971, 34.
276 S. Venkitasubramonia Iyer, "Maharaja Svati Tirunal and His Times," *Journal of the Music Academy*, Vol. 22, 1951, 155.
277 *Ibid.*, 155.
278 P. Shungoonny Menon, *A History of Travancore from the Earliest Times*, Madras: Higginbotham and Co, 1878, 394–5.
279 James Welsh, *Military Reminiscences Extracted from a Journal of Nearly Forty Years' Active Service in the East Indies, Vol. 2*, London: Smith, Elder and Co., 1830, 235–6.
280 Welsh, *Military Reminiscences*, 235–6; David Newall to Thomas Munro, March 25, 1827 (British Library, Mss. Eur F151/67, 69–70).
281 Hastings Fraser, *Memoir and Correspondence of General James Stuart Fraser*, London: Whiting & Co., 1885, 111.
282 Madras Proceedings (Political), February 26, 1830, 152–3 (British Library, IOR/P/318/107).
283 [Subba Rao], *Balabodha Muktavali*, 5. I am deeply grateful to Sajid Inamdar for translating these extracts from Marathi into English.
284 Ibid., 2–3.
285 A valuable description of the traditional course can be found in W.B. Addis to Alexander Campbell, 1827 (Council for World Mission Archive, School of Oriental and African Studies, CWM/LMS/10/02/05/002).
286 [Subba Rao], *Balabodha Muktavali*, 7.
287 Ibid., 7–8.
288 Ibid., 5.
289 Ibid., 6.
290 Ian Raeside, "Early Prose Fiction in Marathi, 1828–1885," *The Journal of Asian Studies*, Vol. 27, No. 4, 1968, 794.
291 M. Sadasivam, ed., *A Catalogue of Serfoji's Personal Collection and Other Rare Books*, Thanjavur: TMSSM Library Society, 1989, 38–48.
292 Swati Tirunal to William Morison, March 5, 1828 (Bentinck Papers, Pw Jf 1814 2). The reference was to Charles Rollin, *The Ancient History of the Egyptians, Carthaginians, &c, Vol. 2*, Boston: Munroe & Francis, 1805, Bk. 4.
293 Rajah of Tanjore to [Benjamin Torin?], January 25, 1806 (British Library, Mss. Eur C887).
294 John Malcolm, *A Memoir of Central India, Vol. 1*, London: S. R. Bentley, 1823, iv.
295 Serfoji Rajah, *Devendra Kuravanji: A Drama in Marathi Giving the Geography of the World in Songs*, ed., T. L. Thyagaraja Jatavallabhar, Kumbakonam: Sri Mahabharatam

Press, 1950, Preface; Radha Krishnamurthy, "World-Geography in Marathi Dance-Drama," *Quarterly Journal of the Mythic Society*, Vols 78–9, 1987, 155–7; Ramaswamy, *Terrestrial Lessons*, 48–9; Peterson, "Tanjore, Tranquebar and Halle," 117–19. On *kuravanji* more generally, see Indira Viswanathan Peterson, "The Evolution of the Kuravanci Dance Drama in Tamil Nadu: Negotiating the 'Folk' and the 'Classical' in the Bharata Natyam Canon," *South Asia Research*, Vol. 18, No. 1, 1998, 39–72; Radhika Seshan, "From Folk Culture to Court Culture: The 'Kuravanji' in the Tanjore Court," *Proceedings of the Indian History Congress*, Vol. 65, 2004, 334.

296 Subba Rao, *Krishna Kumari: The Tragedy of India*, ed. Rahul Sagar, London: Bloomsbury, 2024, 72.

297 Ibid.

298 Lal, *Memoirs of the Puthan Soldier of Fortune*, 399; D. C., "Some Account of Abdool Messee, 84–6.

299 Subba Rao, *Krishna Kumari*, 117.

300 Madras Proceedings (Political), March 26, 1830, (British Library, IOR/P/318/107, 265–6).

301 Ibid.

302 Subba Rao, *Krishna Kumari*, 72.

303 John Malcolm, *A Memoir of Central India, Vol. 2,* London: S. R. Bentley, 1823, 268.

304 [Subba Rao], *Balabodha Muktavali*, 4.

305 Subba Rao, *Krishna Kumari*, Preface.

306 "Original Correspondence," *Literary Gazette & Journal of the Belles, Lettres, Arts, Sciences &c.*, October 22, 1842, 370; "Asiatic Society," *Literary Gazette and Journal of Belles Lettres, Arts, Sciences &C.*, June 11, 1842, 407.

307 "Education in India," *Literary Gazette and Journal of the Belles Lettres, Arts, Sciences, &c.*, October 22, 1842, Vol. 26, No. 1344, 730; "Soob Row," *Sun*, November 6, 1841, 7.

308 Madras Proceedings (Political), April 21, 1810 (British Library, IOR/P/317/34, 1154–7).

309 Otto G. Trevelyan, *The Life and Letters of Lord Macaulay, Vol. I*, New York: Harper & Brothers, 1877, 232.

310 "Death of Soobrow," 148.

311 *Official and Descriptive Catalogue of the Madras Exhibition of 1855*, Madras, 1855 (see 'Travancore').

312 "Kishan Kower: An Oriental Tale," *Court Journal*, Vol. 7, 1835, 52–3; "The Bengal Annual for 1834," *The Atheneum*, August 23, 1834, 620; *The Hindoos, Vol.1*, London: Charles Knight, 1834, 298.

313 G. G. Richardson [Catherine Eliza Richardson], "Kishen Kower: A Fragment" in *Poems by G.G. Richardson*, Edinburgh: Cadin & Co., 1828, 109–12.

314 Elizabeth B. E. Smith, "Three Moons," in *The East India Sketch-Book Vol. 2*, London: Richard Bentley, 1832, 193–217.

315 J. L. Mowatt, "Kishen Kowur" in David L. Richardson, *The Bengal Annual: A Literary Keepsake 1834*, Calcutta: Samuel Smith & Co., 1834, 366.

316 [Robert Grenville Wallace], *Forty Years in the World; or, Sketches and Tales of a Soldier's Life, Vol. 1*, London: George Whittaker, 1825, 278.

317 [Henry Lawrence and Honoria Lawrence] "Romance and Reality of Indian Life," *Calcutta Review*, Vol. 2, 1844, 426–7.

318 Letitia Elizabeth Landon, "Kishen Kower," in *The Complete Works of L. E. Landon*, Boston: Crosby, Nichols, Lee & Co., 1860, 267–70; P. T. H [Prinsep, Henry Thoby], "Kishen Koomaree, Princess of Oodeepoor: A True Tale of Rajwara, A. D., 1810," in *Ballads of the East and Other Poems*, London, 1846, 73. Also see Ulloor S. Parameswara Iyer, "Letitia Elizabeth Landon" in N. Viswanathan, ed., *English Essays and Poems of Mahakavi Ulloor*, Trivandrum: University of Kerala, 1978, 30–3.

319 Mill and Wilson, *History of British India from 1805 to 1835, Vol. 1*, 83–95.

320 George Poulett Cameron, "Kishen Kower; or, the Maid of Odeypoor" in *The Romance of Military Life: Being Souvenirs Connected with Thirty Years' Service*, London: G. Cox, 1858, 1–23.

321 Malleson, *An Historical Sketch of the Native States of India*, 24; "The Native States of India by Colonel Malleson," *Friend of India*, July 17, 1875, 666.

322 "India," *Evening Mail*, January 1, 1877, 2.

323 Ibid.

324 George Herbert Trevor, *Rhymes of Rajputana*, London: Macmillan and Co., 1894, 51. Also see *Madras Weekly Mail*, February 25, 1904, 202; "Viceroy's Speech," *Homeward Mail*, November 20, 1909, 1479.

325 Trevor, *Rhymes of Rajputana*, v; *Tales of Rajput Chivalry*, Calcutta: University of Calcutta, 1938.

326 [Margaret Elizabeth Noble], *The Complete Works of Sister Nivedita, Vol. 1*, Calcutta: Sister Nivedita Girl's School, 1967, 358.

327 "Kishen Koomaree," *Bombay Quarterly Review*, Vol. 3, No. 5, 1856, 88.

328 Jogindranath Basu, *Michael Madhusudan Dutter Jibancharit*, Calcutta: Chakraborty, Chatterjee & Co., 1907, 442; Kshetra Gupta, ed., *Kabi Madhusudan O Tar Patrabali*, Calcutta: Nabashakti Press, 1933, No. 73.

329 Gupta, *Kabi Madhusudan O Tar Patrabali*, No. 67.

330 Gupta, *Kabi Madhusudan O Tar Patrabali*, Nos. 77, 83, 84; Gour Das Bysack, "Reminiscence of Michael M. S. Datta," in Basu, *Michael Madhusudan Dutter Jibancharit*, 649.

331 Gupta, *Kabi Madhusudan O Tar Patrabali*, No. 83; Basu, *Michael Madhusudan Dutter Jibancharit*, 491–2.

332 Michael Madhusudan Dutt, *Krishnakumari Nataka*, Calcutta: Isvar Chandra Vasu, 1861.

333 Susila Mukhopadhyay, *The Story of the Calcutta Theatres, 1753–1980*, Calcutta: K.P. Bagchi, 1982, 35–42, 626.

334 *Amrita Bazar Patrika*, July 10, 1873, 172; *Pioneer*, July 23, 1873, 2–3.

335 Shoshee Chunder Dutt, "Krishna Koomari; or The Flower of Rajasthan" in *Stray Leaves; or Essays, Poems and Tales*, Calcutta: D'Rozario & Co., 1864, 259–61; Mahadev Govind Ranade, "The Growth of Marathi Literature" in *Miscellaneous Writings of Mr. Justice M. G. Ranade*, New Delhi: Sahitya Akademi, 1992, 25; J. F. Blumhardt, *Catalogue of the Library of the India Office: Marathi and Gujarati Books*, London: Eyre and Spottiswoode, 1908, 201; "Literary Activity in Bombay," *Madras Weekly Mail*, December 29, 1892, 17.

336 "Tod's Annals of Rajasthan," *Madras Mail*, June 16, 1873.

337 *Report of the Director of Public Instruction in the Bombay Presidency for the Year 1875–76*, Bombay: Bombay Education Society's Press, 1876, 112; Richard J. Meade, *Report on the Administration of the Hyderabad Assigned Districts for the Year 1878–79*, Hyderabad: Residency Press, 1880, 60; *Reports on Publications Issued and Registered in the Several Provinces of British India, During the Year 1883*, Calcutta: Superintendent of Government Printing, 1885, 84; G. U. Pope, *Textbook of Indian History*, London: W. H. Allen & Co, 1880, 227; *Pioneer*, August 8, 1873, 3; *Selections from the Records of the Government of India, Vol. 85*, Calcutta: Office of the Superintendent of Government Printing, 1882, 155; Emilia Alymer Blake, "My Own Love," *Victoria Magazine*, Vol. 32, 1878, 435.

338 Manmatha Nath Dutt, ed., *Gleanings From Indian Classics, Vol. 2: Heroines of Ind*, Calcutta: G. C. Chackravarti, 1893, 135–43; "Hindoo Female Celebrities," *Calcutta Review*, Vol. 48, No. 96, 1869, 31–3; Edward Balfour, *The Cyclopædia of India and of Eastern and Southern India, Vol. 2*, London: B. Quaritch, 1885, 578; 60–8; Louisa Bigg, "Krishna Kumari's Bridal," *Women's Penny Paper*, February 23, 1889, 2.

339 Alfred C. Lyall, *Asiatic Studies, Religious and Social*, London: John Murray, 1884, 193; H. L, "The Sacrifice of Krishna Kumari Bhaie," *Indian Female Evangelist*, Vol. 7, No. 47, 1883, 119–21.

340 Rajanikanta Gupta, "Abalar Atymatyaga" in *Arya Kirti, Vol. 3*, Calcutta: Medical Library, 1883, 36–41.

341 L. D. Barnett, ed., *A Catalogue of Kannada, Badaga, and Kurg Books in the Library of the British Museum*, London: British Museum, 1910, 3, 182; K. M. George, ed., *Modern Indian Literature: An Anthology, Vol. 1*, New Delhi: Sahitya Akademi, 1992, 171–2.

342 [Margaret Elizabeth Noble], *The Complete Works of Sister Nivedita, Vol. 1*, 356.

343 Flora Annie Webster Steel, *India Through the Ages: A Popular and Picturesque History of Hindustan*, London: George Routledge & Sons, 1909, 329. Also see "The Maharana's Ancestry," *Indian Daily News*, November 23, 1905, 13.

344 "The Census of Rajputana," *Englishman's Overland Mail*, December 26, 1912, 2.

345 Douglas Sladen, "Preface" in James Tod, *Annals and Antiquities of Rajasthan Vol. 1*, London: George Routledge & Sons, 1914.

346 "Romance of an Indian Princess," *Western Times*, August 4, 1902, 6; "An Indian Maid's Romance," *Philadelphia Inquirer*, July 24, 1902; Walter Roper Lawrence, *The India We Served*, London: Cassell and Co., 1928, 218.

347 "Krishna Kumari: by Edward Thompson," *The Modern Review*, Vol. 36, 1924, 312; "Krishna Kumari," *Western Daily News*, May 2, 1924; *The Nation and Athenaeum*, Vol. 35, No. 8, 1924, 252.

348 Sitaram Shastri, *Krishna Kumari Nataka*, Madras: Progressive Press, 1913; P. Seshadri, "Krishnakumari" in *Champak Leaves*, Allahabad: Indian Press, 1923, 34–5; C. C. Mehta, *Bibliography of Stageable Plays in Indian Languages: Part I*, Baroda: The Maharaja Sayajirao University of Baroda Press, 1963, 209.

349 *Leader*, August 12, 1922; *Leader*, September 29, 1922.

350 *Bombay Chronicle*, July 11, 1931, 14.

351 Basu, *Michael Madhusudan Dutter Jibancharit*, 453; Michael Madhusudan Datta, *Krishna Kumari*, ed., Bijanbihari Bhattacharya, Calcutta: Brindaban Dhar and Sons, 1948, Preface.

352 Farley Richmond, "The Political Role of Theatre in India," *Educational Theatre Journal*, Vol. 25, No. 3, 1973, 322–33.

353 Bhupendra Hooja, ed., *A Life Dedicated: Biography of Govind Das*, Delhi: Seth Govind Das Diamond Jubilee Celebrations Committee, 1956, 156; S. Balakrishnan, *Krishna Kumari: Princess of India*, Madras: Minerva Press, 1964.

354 C. Vasudevaiah, *Aryakirti*, Mysore: Kavyalaya, 1954; G. S. Amur, *Dattatreya Ramachandra Bendre*, New Delhi: Sahitya Akademi, 1994, 26; Ullattil Sankarankutti Menon, *Krishnakumari*, Trichur: Kerala Sahitya Akademi, 1993.

355 Alok Ray, ed., *Krishna Kumari Natak*, Kolkata: Dey's Publishing, 2018.

356 Gauri Viswanathan, "Currying Favour: The Politics of British Educational and Cultural Policy in India, 1813–1854," *Social Text*, Nos. 19–20, 1988, 85–104.

357 Viswanathan, "Currying Favour," 85–104.

358 Vinay Dharwadker, "The Historical Formation of Indian-English Literature," in Sheldon Pollock, ed., *Literary Cultures in History: Reconstructions from South Asia*, Berkeley: University of California Press, 2003, 220–2.

359 Suddhaseel Sen, *Shakespeare in the World: Cross-Cultural Adaptation in Europe and Colonial India, 1850–1990*, New York: Routledge, 2020, 5–8.

360 Dharwadker, "The Historical Formation of Indian-English Literature," 220–2; Sadana, Rashmi, "Writing in English" in Vasudha Dalmia and Rashmi Sadana, eds., *The Cambridge Companion to Modern Indian Culture*, Cambridge: Cambridge University Press, 2022, 126.

361 Dharwadker, "The Historical Formation of Indian-English Literature," 222.
362 K. R. Srinivasa Iyengar, *The Indian Contribution to English Literature*, Bombay: Karnatak Publishing House, 1945, 4.
363 Jesse Page, *Schwartz of Tanjore*, London: Society for Promoting Christian Knowledge, 1921, 90. Also see S. Seetha, *Tanjore as a Seat of Music During the Seventeenth, Eighteenth and Nineteenth Centuries*, PhD dissertation, University of Madras, 1981, 109–15.
364 Tapan Raychaudhuri, *Europe Reconsidered: Perceptions of the West in Nineteenth-century Bengal*, Delhi: Oxford University Press, 1988, 2; Edward Charles Buck, *Indo-Anglian Literature, Vol. 2*, Calcutta: Thacker, Spink and Co., 1887, 4.
365 *Papers Regarding the Administration of Travancore State, Vol. 1*, Board's Collections Vol. 1268, 179–81 (British Library, IOR/F/4/1268/50913). For a broader survey see Robin Jeffrey, *Politics, Women and Well-Being: How Kerala Became "a Model"*, London: Palgrave, 2016.
366 R. K. Yajnik, *The Indian Theatre: Its Origins and Later Developments Under European Influence with Special Reference to Western India*, London: George Allen and Unwin Ltd, 1933, 83–7; Meera Kosambi, *Gender, Culture, and Performance: Marathi Theatre and Cinema before Independence*, New Delhi: Routledge, 2015, 23–5.
367 Yajnik, *The Indian Theatre*, 83–7.
368 Nandi Bhatia, *Acts of Authority/Acts of Resistance: Theatre and Politics in Colonial and Postcolonial India*, Ann Arbor: University of Michigan Press, 2004, 15–17.
369 Sudipto Chatterjee, "Mise-en-(Colonial-)Scene: The Theatre of the Bengal Renaissance," in J. Ellen Gainor, ed., *Imperialism and Theatre: Essays on World Theatre, Drama and Performance 1795–1995*, London: Routledge, 1995, 21–3; P. Guha Thakurta, *The Bengali Drama: Its Origin and Development*, London: Trench, Trubner & Co., 1930, 50.
370 Sharmistha Saha, *Theatre and National Identity in Colonial India: Formation of a Community through Cultural Practice*, Singapore: Springer, 2018, 35–6.
371 Ananda Lal, *Indian Drama in English: The Beginnings*, Kolkata: Jadavpur University Press, 2019, 11.
372 Lal, *Indian Drama in English*, 11, 29.
373 Kosambi, *Gender, Culture, and Performance*, 10–12; M. M., "Drama (Marathi)," in Amaresh Dutta, ed., *Encyclopaedia of Indian Literature, Vol. 2*, New Delhi: Sahitya Akademi, 1988, 1087–8; Seetha, *Tanjore as a Seat of Music*, 95–125; C. G. Usha, "Contribution of Travancore Royal Family to Kathakali Art" in K. R. Basavaraja, ed., *Proceedings of 8th Annual Session of the South India Historical Congress*, Hyderabad: *South India Historical Congress*, 1991, 186, 190–1.
374 Jyotsna Singh, *Colonial Narratives, Cultural Dialogues: Discoveries of India in the Language of Colonialism*, London: Routledge, 1996, 110–12.
375 Ibid., 110–12.
376 Ibid., 104.
377 Jasodhara Bagchi, "Shakespeare in Loin Cloths: English Literature and the Early Nationalist Consciousness in Bengal" in Svati Joshi, ed., *Rethinking English: Essays in Literature, Language, History*, Delhi: Trianka, 1991, 146–59.
378 Sisir Das, "Shakespeare in Indian Languages" in Poonam Trivedi and Dennis Bartholomeusz, eds., *India's Shakespeare: Translation, Interpretation, and Performance*, New Delhi: Pearson, 2005, 47–53.
379 Poonam Trivedi, "Folk Shakespeare: The Performance of Shakespeare in Traditional Indian Theatre Forms" in Trivedi and Bartholomeusz, *India's Shakespeare*, 154.
380 G. K. Bhat, *Tragedy and Sanskrit Drama*, Bombay: Popular Prakashan, 1974, 89–90, 105–7; V. Raghavan, "The Aesthetics of Ancient Indian Drama," *Indian Literature*, Vol. 1, No. 2, 1958, 68.

381 Bihani Sarkar, *Classical Sanskrit Tragedy: The Concept of Suffering and Pathos in Medieval India*, London: I.B. Tauris, 2021, 2–5; Virginia Saunders, "Some Literary Aspects of the Absence of Tragedy in the Classical Sanskrit Drama," *Journal of the American Oriental Society*, Vol. 41, 1921, 152.

382 Raghavan, "The Aesthetics of Ancient Indian Drama," 70.

383 Bhat, *Tragedy and Sanskrit Drama*, 107.

384 Subba Rao, *Krishna Kumari*, 111.

385 Bankim Chandra Chatterjee, "Imitation" in Sen, *Shakespeare in the World*, Appendix I; Aparna Bhargava Dharwadker, "Michael Madhusudan Dutt," in *Poetics of Modernity: Indian Theatre Theory, 1850 to the Present*, New Delhi: Oxford University Press, 2019, 11; Singh, *Colonial Narratives, Cultural Dialogues*, 111.

386 Dharwadker, "Michael Madhusudan Dutt," 16.

387 The same fate has befallen the other pioneering tragedy of the era, Vinayak Janardhan Kirtane's *Thorle Madhavrao Peshwa* (1861), which lays bare the factionalism that weakened the Maratha Empire. *Thorle Madhavrao Peshwa*, which "borrowed" from Shakespeare, was critically praised as "a radical departure" from traditional Marathi *sangeet-natak* (musical play). Though it had the double honor of being first prose play in Marathi and the first tragedy in that language, it was never translated into English and therefore continues to be unknown outside Maharashtra. (On this see Rakesh H. Solomon, ed., *Globalization, Nationalism and the Text of 'Kichaka-Vadha'*, London: Anthem Press, 2014, 16; Kosambi, *Gender, Culture, and Performance*, 79–80; Pramod Kale, "Epic to Polemic: Social Change in Marathi Drama, 1843–1879," *Sangeet Natak Academy*, January–March, 1972, 39–40; Shanta Gokhale, *Playwright at the Centre: Marathi Drama from 1843 to the Present*, Calcutta: Seagull Books, 2000, 11–15; Kedar A. Kulkarni, *Theatre and the Making of the Modern Indian Subject in Late Nineteenth Century India*, PhD dissertation, San Diego: University of California, 2013, 64–70; Kedar Arun Kulkarni, *World Literature and the Question of Genre in Colonial India*, New Delhi: Bloomsbury, 2022.).

388 K. Swaminathan, "Introduction" in Balakrishnan, *Krishna Kumari: Princess of India*, ix.

389 Ibid., ix.

390 Subba Rao, *Krishna Kumari*, 89.

391 Ibid., 84.

392 Ibid., 108.

393 On nationalist theatre in the latter part of the nineteenth century see Rustom Bharucha, *Rehearsals of Revolution: The Political Theater of Bengal*, Honolulu: University of Hawaii Press, 1983, 21–3; Rakesh H. Solomon, "Culture, Imperialism, and Nationalist Resistance: Performance in Colonial India," *Theatre Journal*, Vol. 46, No. 3, October, 1994, 324–7; Bhatia, *Acts of Authority/Acts of Resistance*, 35–9; Nirmal K.R., Bandyopadhyay, "Hindu Revivalism in Late Nineteenth Century Bengali Theatre," *Proceedings of the Indian History Congress*, Vol. 57, 1996, 606–11.

394 It foreshadows, in this sense, Munshi Premchand's celebrated short story, *Shatranj Ke Khilari* which was published in 1924 (Munshi Premchand, "A Game of Chess," trans. Saeed Jaffrey, in Andrew Robinson, ed., *The Chess Players and Other Screenplays*, London: Faber & Faber, 1989, 62–76).

A Note on the Text

This edition of *Krishna Kumari* is based on the edition printed by the Government Press in Trivandrum in 1840. It has been checked against copies held by the British Library in London, the Government Museum Library in Chennai, and the University of Washington Library in Seattle, as well as the microfilmed copy collated in Allardyce Nicoll and George Freedley's *English and American Drama of the Nineteenth Century*.* There are no material differences between these copies, excepting a few variations in punctuation marks caused by printing inconsistencies. There are two interesting differences in presentation: the University of Washington's copy features an elegant frontispiece, likely added by a later binder, while the microfilmed copy features Subba Rao's signature and compliments to a British friend in Travancore. The original manuscript remains untraced.

The original edition is modified here in two respects. The most important change is to the title of the play. The 1840 edition bears the title *Kishun Koovur: A Tragedy in Five Acts*. This title owes to John Malcolm, who rendered the Udaipur princess's name as "Kishen Kower," which Subba Rao then corrected to "Kishun Koovur." It has since been established that the princess's name was not Kishen (or hence Kishun) but Krishna. The suffix employed by Malcolm (and hence by Subba Rao) is problematic as well. Kower (or Koovur) are meant to be transliterations of *Kunwar*, the suffix applied in Rajasthan to an unmarried or underage child. Unfortunately, these transliterations are jarring to the eye. To further complicate matters, James Tod's *Annals and Antiquities of Rajasthan* gives the princess the suffix *Kumari*, meaning maiden. Given how influential Tod's *Annals* has been, subsequent accounts have invariably referred to the princess as Krishna Kumari. Thus, to bring Subba Rao's work in line with prevailing usage, I have retitled it *Krishna Kumari*.

The spelling of Subba Rao's own name has been modernized as well. Initially, the East India Company's correspondence transliterated Subba Rao as Soobrow (where row is pronounced as in "having a row"). Once his name acquired cachet, Subba Rao had little reason to change how it was spelt. Thus, even his official obituary, published by the Travancore *darbar*, renders his name as Soobrow. Over time, however, as the British consciously modernized how they transliterated Indian names, references to him in official correspondence changed to Soob Row, then Subba Row, and finally to Subba Rao. I have therefore, accordingly, rendered his name as Subba Rao, making it more familiar and accessible to contemporary audiences.

---

* Soobrow, *Kishun Koovur: A Tragedy in Five Acts*, Trivandrum: Government Press, 1840 (British Library, 841.b.62; University of Washington Library, 891.2 Su15k; Government Museum Library, D623); Soobrow, *Kishun Koovur: A Tragedy in Five Acts*, Trivandrum: Government Press, 1840 in Allardyce Nicoll and George Freedley, eds., *English and American Drama of the Nineteenth Century*, New York: Readex Microprint, 1965 (New York University, MP 7, Boxes 34–38, Se-Vz). I am indebted to Allee Monheim and Shaye Anis at the University of Washington Library for access to the unique copy held by the Special Collections division.

The text of the original has been edited carefully and sparingly. The most important change is to spellings, which have been modernized. For instance, "out-witting" and "master-piece" are now rendered as "outwitting" and "masterpiece." Similarly, a place name like "Nagore" has been changed to the more recognizable "Nagaur." The same goes for names: "Maun" is rendered as "Man," "Ameer" as "Amir," and so on. Transliterations have been modernized too: "*durbar*" has been changed to "*darbar*," "*Boi*" to "*Bai*," etc. Such transliterated terms have been italicized except in cases where their usage is common. Thus, for example, Maharaja is not italicized, but *dak* and *musnud* are. The extensive use of capitalization, which was the norm in the nineteenth century, has been reined in here. Thus, "Prince" becomes "prince" and "Princess" becomes "princess," and so on. Capitalization has been retained only in instances where Subba Rao means to emphasize a term, e.g. "Science of Politics."

Finally, to aid the contemporary reader, brief footnotes have been added to shed light on key characters or to define transliterated terms. These definitions can be found in the Glossary as well. The original edition featured a small number of typographical errors. These errors have now been corrected, with all such changes noted. In no instance has the meaning of the original text been altered. No changes have been made to the punctuation or stage directions, so as to retain the punchy, theatrical style of the original prose.

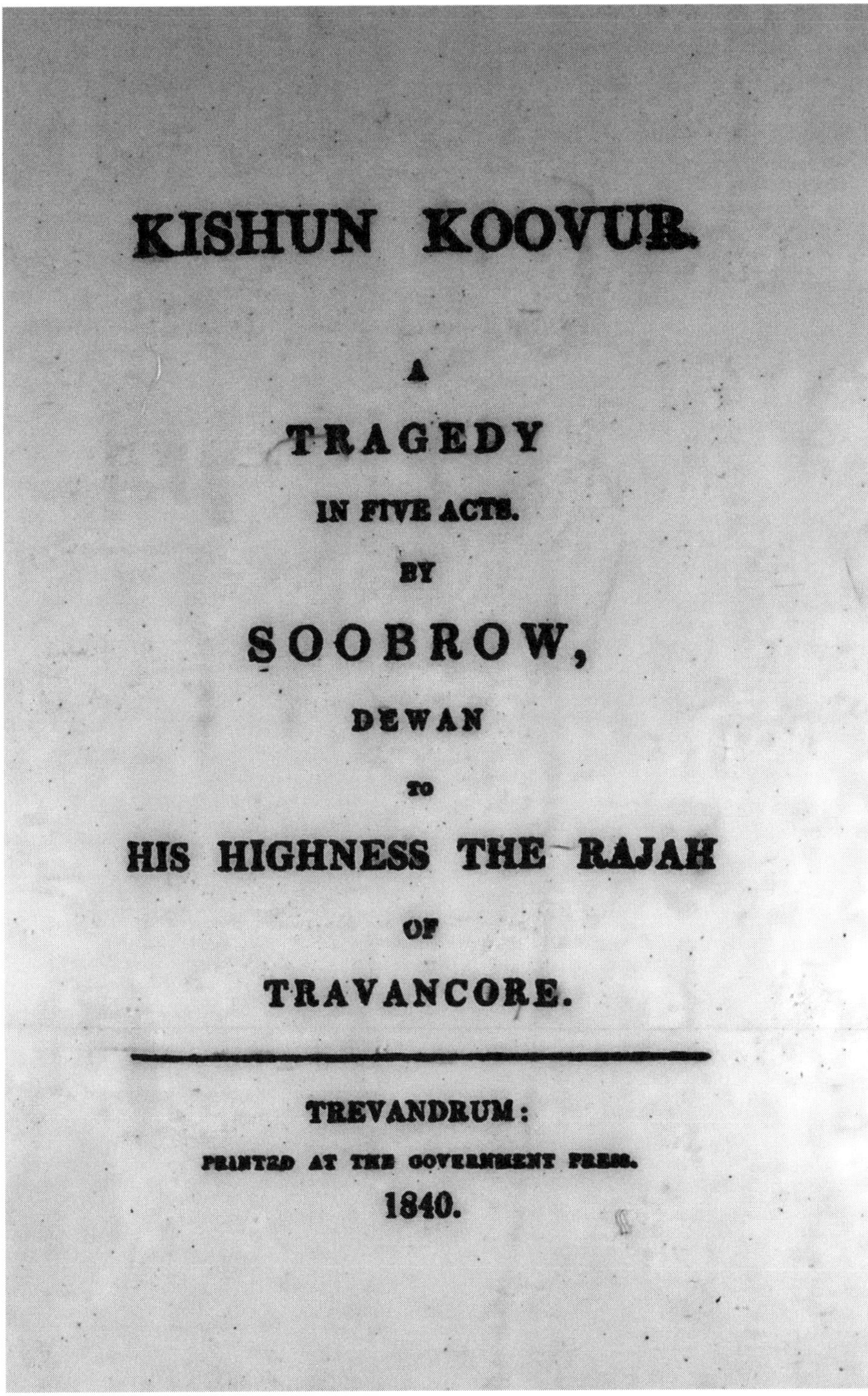

KISHUN KOOVUR.

A

TRAGEDY

IN FIVE ACTS.

BY

SOOBROW,

DEWAN

TO

HIS HIGHNESS THE RAJAH

OF

TRAVANCORE.

TREVANDRUM:

PRINTED AT THE GOVERNMENT PRESS.

1840.

Title page of the original 1840 edition.

KRISHNA KUMARI

PREFACE

A perusal of the train of events, which led to the tragical fate of the princess Krishna Kumari of Udaipur, as given in Sir John Malcolm's *Central India,*[*] having made a deep impression on the author's mind, and suggested the idea, that the subject might be formed into a dramatic piece, in the shape of a Tragedy, the author commenced writing it several years ago, more as a recreation in his leisure hours, and to comply with the wishes of some his friends, than with any intention of printing and publishing the production.

Since the work has been finished, several English gentlemen have perused it, and some of them being the author's friends, were kind enough to express favorable opinions regarding it. Such encomiums the author entirely attributes to their friendly partiality and indulgence, rather than to any intrinsic merits of the composition itself, which, he knows, it does not possess. Latterly, His Highness the Raja[†], the master of the author, having expressed a wish, that this work should be printed in his press, which the Travancore government had lately established at this place, it was done so, in obedience to the wishes of His Highness, who, it is needless to mention, stands so highly distinguished among the princes of Hindustan for enlightened views and munificence in encouraging all sorts of literary pursuits, as well as scientific researches.

Thus, a piece, merely written for private amusement, is become at once an object of public gaze, and its errors, which privacy had thrown a friendly shade upon, stand now prominently forth in the glaring light of publicity. Under these circumstances, the author, being well aware of his utter insufficiency, to produce a literary work of this kind, and of the manifold demerits of the present production, has nothing left him but humbly to apologize to the public for his having assumed the responsible character of an author, and to crave their utmost indulgence in their judgements upon the drama in question. To the British critic the author has only to observe, that this is the production of a *Native* of Hindustan, and this simple statement, it is hoped, will not only be sufficient to blunt his shafts of justly merited censure, but also calculated to make him view, with a favorable eye, this puny attempt at an English dramatic composition by a foreigner.

THE AUTHOR

Trivandrum
29th February 1840

---

[*] John Malcolm, *A Memoir of Central India, Vol. I,* London: Kingsbury, Parbury & Allen, 1824.

[†] Swati Tirunal, the Maharaja of Travancore (1813–46).

DRAMATIS PERSONAE

Men

Man Singh, Raja of Jodhpur
Sawai Singh, his Pradhan
His Munshi
His General

Jagat Singh, the Raja of Jaipur
His Bakshi
His Sycophant

Maharana, the Raja of Udaipur
Ajit Singh, his favorite
Sangram Singh, the Chief of Sardargarh
and a relation of the Maharana
Officers, Servants, &c.

Holkar
His Minister

Amir Khan, Holkar's General
His Jamadar
His Brother-in-law
His Khansama

Women

Queen of Udaipur
Krishna Kumari, her daughter
Chand Bai, sister of the Maharana
Maid of Krishna Kumari

KRISHNA KUMARI

ACT THE FIRST

SCENE I.
A MAGNIFICENT HALL IN THE PALACE OF JODHPUR, EARLY IN THE MORNING

Enter Man Singh the Raja

Man. I am in a strange dilemma, indeed: I know, my Pradhan* Sawai Singh is a dangerous man; can I get rid of him by dismissing him at once from his office? No! It is hazardous; for he will surely instigate all the malcontent *sardars*† of my *darbar*‡, and raise conspiracies against me. And how can I retain him, who would have Dhonkal Singh§ to be placed on the throne? He is naturally very obstinate, and always violently bent on whatever becomes the object of his pursuit. — But here he comes.

Enter Sawai Singh

Sawai. Sir, the tranquility and the peace of this kingdom require, that I should be positive in urging the necessity of admitting the claims of Dhonkal Singh to the throne: the general voice of the people must convince you fully, how dangerous it is to withhold it from its lawful owner.

Man. Do you suppose, Pradhan, that I am ignorant of my duty towards our deceased sovereign, my brother, Bhim Singh? Am I so ungrateful as to deprive his only son, the amiable prince Dhonkal Singh, of his right? No! God forbid, that I myself should become my own bitterest enemy, by acting against the reasonable dictates of my

---

* The original text describes Sawai Singh as Man Singh's *dewan* (prime minister). He was in fact *pradhan* (literally, foremost). This was a political office, occupied by one of the principal *rawats* (lords). Sawai Singh, the *rawat* of Pokhran, had also served as *pradhan* under Man Singh's predecessor, Bhim Singh. The *pradhan* represented the landed classes, and could marshal them to support (or oppose) the Maharaja. By contrast, the *dewan* was typically not a Rajput and was responsible for civil administration.

† A common term in Northern and Western India for feudal lords who were entitled to collect revenue and raise troops from assigned territories, but were supposed to be subordinate to, and owe fealty to, the Maharaja.

‡ The royal court.

§ The son of Man Singh's cousin and predecessor, Bhim Singh. Dhonkal Singh was apparently *in utero* when Bhim Singh expired, allowing Man Singh to ascend to the throne. At the time of his ascension, Man Singh had pledged to step down should Bhim Singh's unborn child prove to be a male. Later, he declined to follow through, questioning the child's paternity, to the chagrin of Sawai Singh, whose sister was Dhonkal Singh's mother.

conscience! But be not hasty; I will in the first place make some needful arrangements in all the important affairs of the realm, and then shall lose no time in placing the prince upon the *musnud*[*] of his father; do you understand me?

Sawai. Aye, perfectly Sir! (*Aside)* His lust of power is too strongly rooted in him to be subdued by the ordinary means of persuasion; but the stratagem which I have already devised has a great chance of success in this affair. (to *Man Singh)* Your reasons on this point are very excellent; but to apprise you of some other important matter was the chief errand of my coming to you so early in the morning.

Man. What is it, Pradhan?

Sawai. Why, Sir, it is about Krishna Kumari, the most beautiful and accomplished princess of Udaipur, who, you know, had been already betrothed to our deceased monarch, Bhim Singh.

Man. Well, this being a matter of great consequence, I wish to have a long conference with you about it; but an urgent business requires that I should leave you for a little while. (*Exit)*

Sawai. *(to himself)* A considerable time ago I have written a letter to my friend[†] at Jaipur: it must certainly have excited in the heart of Jagat Singh the desire of obtaining the hand of Krishna Kumari. I cannot comprehend, why the answer is delayed so long. — But here comes the Munshi[‡]!

Enter Munshi, with a letter in his hand

Munshi. Sir, I have just received this letter express by *dak*[§] of Jaipur, which according to your order I have brought to you immediately.

Sawai. Well done! Come open and read it to me.

Munshi. *(opens and reads)* "I received your favor of the 15th *ultimo*[**], and when I had read it to the Raja, it kindled in him the fire of love to a degree beyond belief, in consequence of which, he immediately dispatched his letters to Udaipur, and has lately received a satisfactory answer from Maharana, who having accepted his suit, expresses his particular pleasure in having him for his son-in-law, in preference to all the other princes of Rajputana."

Sawai. This is very unfortunate, indeed; his success seems to be certain; but I did not expect that it would so soon come to that point. Munshi, we must prevent this from taking place at all events.

Munshi. Do you mean the marriage between Jagat Singh and the princess of Udaipur?

---

[*] The throne. Literally, it refers to the cushioned bolster upon which the Maharaja leaned. Derives from the Arabic word *sanad* (to lean upon).

[†] This would have been Rai Chand, the *dewan* of Jaipur.

[‡] A secretary or scribe. A *munshi* would handle confidential correspondence. Man Singh's *munshi* was Jeet Mal Singhvi, whom the Raja frequently entrusted with delicate diplomatic missions.

[§] A courier or mail carrier.

[**] The preceding month.

Sawai. Aye, to be sure, the same.

Munshi. Why, Sir, was it not yourself who incited Jagat Singh to sue for this matrimonial alliance?

Sawai. Yes, what then? I did it for no other purpose than to raise commotions and bloodshed in the states of Rajputana, and thereby to attain the object I have in view.

Munshi. Surely, this is an impenetrable mystery! But Sir, how can you prevent it now, after the matter is gone so far?

Sawai. Aye, to prevent it? Nothing is easier — But here the Raja comes, withdraw to the next room and come back again when I am alone. (*Exit Munshi*)

Enter Man Singh

Man. Well, Pradhan, you seem to be very pensive; pray what have you to tell me about Krishna Kumari?

Sawai. Why, Sir, the subject is too serious to be disregarded, because, when the honor of this court is at stake, I cannot help being restless. You know already, Sir, that the hand of this princess had been long ago promised to our deceased monarch.

Man. I do; but what then?

Sawai. Why, Sir, shall we tamely suffer the prize to be borne away by Jagat Singh, the Raja of Jaipur?

Man. By no means! Is anything stirring now about a nuptial treaty between the courts of Jaipur and Udaipur?

Sawai. Oh, Sir, the business is almost finished; I am disgusted at the very thought of it: this infatuated Maharana of Udaipur has already fixed his choice upon Jagat Singh, as his son-in-law, and the marriage is likely to be celebrated within a very short time.

Man. This is too bad! We must support our claims, and preserve our honor at all hazards.

Sawai. Yes, you are in the right; but how can we effect it, unless we go to war with your rival Jagat Singh?

Man. Aye, it is impossible; let us then, with all possible expedition, procure first the alliance of Sindhia*, and then let us try to get succor from the British Government through the means of Sir John Malcolm†, who resides now at Delhi.

---

* Daulat Rao Sindhia, the leading Maratha *sardar* (chieftain) in Central India. The territories under his control eventually came to known as Gwalior State.

† The British military officer and diplomat who had negotiated the East India Company's treaties with Daulat Rao Sindhia and Jaswant Rao Holkar following the recently concluded Second Anglo-Maratha War (1803–5).

Sawai. I shall lose no time in doing everything that is practicable in this weighty affair, and God will doubtless grant us success in this our just undertaking.

Exit Man Singh

Sawai. *(to himself)* Ha, he is completely caught; now I will teach him to bow to my superior wisdom; I will, by my magic, render his crown more ponderous to him, than he ever thought it would be, and then reduce him to the necessity of divesting himself of that burden, which he will of course be very glad to put upon the head of Dhonkal Singh.

Enter Munshi

Munshi. I am ready at your service; have you any commands for me?

Sawai. Yes, I would have you write two letters, one to Sindhia, and the other to Sir John Malcolm, requesting their assistance in the war, which we are going to wage against Jagat Singh.

Munshi. I will write them both presently (*sits down to write)*.

Sawai. *(traverses the room in deep meditation, and after a pause addresses the Munshi)* Well, have you done?

Munshi. Yes, Sir, here are the letters; please to sign them.

Sawai. *(signs and delivers them again to the Munshi)* Here, take them, and send them immediately by the *dak* of this day; but stop, write another to Jagat Singh, in which apprize him fully and faithfully of what is going on here against him; and let him know likewise, that he shall have reason to repent, if he should not exert himself in making vigorous preparations to support his claim to Krishna Kumari, whom her father has already promised him in marriage. Do you understand my meaning?

Munshi. Aye, as clearly as there is a sun in the sky (*writes and gives the letters)*.

Sawai. *(returns it after signing)* Come, make all possible haste and send this letter to Jaipur, that it may reach there in proper time.

Munshi. Very well, Sir, I will obey your commands punctually; but pray, Sir, why do you excite and encourage both Man Singh and his rival at once? I am entirely at a loss to account for this glaring inconsistency in your conduct.

Sawai. This is nothing but a common political maneuver; do you understand?

Munshi. Not so clearly, Sir; will you be so kind as to explain to me the meaning of that mysterious word *political*?

Sawai. Aye, it refers to an abstruse science, in which are laid down certain rules, whereby the most detestable vices are made to pass for exalted virtues, and man is taught to change like the chameleon according to circumstances; but none but those, who have any talents for it, can learn this science to any advantage and perfection.

Munshi. Thank God, I have no talents for such an abominable science! But why do you trouble your head about it, and what profit do you expect to reap from it?

Sawai. You empty-headed simpletons are but very poor judges of the noble deeds of us, statesmen. My head, you know, is well stocked with many devices, contrivances, systems, and plans of all descriptions. I should be wanting in my duty towards society, if I would not make use of some of them in this critical juncture, in establishing the public tranquility of this state, which is now sadly disturbed by this usurper.

Munshi. Very true, Sir; but remember also, you may be wanting in your duty towards yourself, if you do not preserve that head—or as you would have it, that storehouse—from external injury; because, I know, either the brains are knocked out of such heads, as you represent yours to be, or sometimes they are severed entirely from the seat; but God preserve yours, which I hope you will carry safe on your shoulders.

Sawai. Pshaw! Pusillanimity is undoubtedly the cause of many groundless fears and gloomy anticipations; but enough now! *(Exeunt)*[*]

SCENE II.

A SUPERB SALOON IN THE PALACE OF JAIPUR

Enter Jagat Singh, the Raja, his Bakshi[†]*, and a Sycophant*

Jagat. So, by the last letter, Man Singh seems determined to wage war with me, on account of Krishna Kumari. Well, Bakshi, what answer have you received from Sir John Malcolm, about the alliance of the British Government, which we have solicited through his means?

Bakshi. Sir, the answer unfortunately is negative; but luckily the same reply, I am told, was given to our enemy; of course, the English will remain neutral in our present contest.

Jagat. So much the better—then let us apply to Holkar[‡] for his aid; he will I dare say be very glad to assist me in this affair; because I am informed that Sindhia, in compliance with the request of Man Singh, has already dispatched part of his army to Jodhpur, under the command of his *sardars* to assist him.

Bakshi. Very true: Holkar will send us a large army, but it will cost us very dear, on account of the enormous expenses, which these auxiliaries will oblige us to undergo.

Jagat. Aye, to be sure, that is a serious business.

Sycophant. But the inestimable beauty of Krishna Kumari is worth all the gold of the world: and show me, who but our Raja is worthy to possess her?

---

[*] A stage direction instructing a group of actors to leave the stage.

[†] The officer charged with managing the military payroll, a responsibility that could include mustering and commanding troops. Jagat Singh's *bakshi* was Shiv Lal.

[‡] Jaswant Rao Holkar, the second-most powerful Maratha *sardar* (chieftain) in Central India. The territories under his control eventually came to be known as Indore State.

Bakshi. None, indeed: but the just prince must always disregard his personal happiness, when he is sure that the public welfare of his country is to be affected thereby.

Jagat. Aye, but you are wrong there: will not the reputation of Jaipur be eclipsed, if the Raja of Jodhpur marry the princess of Udaipur? What think you of that?

Bakshi. Oh! That is a different case altogether, which certainly requires our particular attention.

Sycophant. *(to the Raja)* Your Highness' argument is incontrovertible. *(to Bakshi)* Are you now fully convinced of the propriety and necessity of undertaking this war, be its expenses what they may?

Bakshi. Yes, I am. *(Aside)* Moreover, I am well convinced of the strength of the argument, which flatterers adduce in support of their credulous masters. *(to the Raja)* Then I shall immediately write a letter to Holkar upon this subject *(sits down to write)*.

Jagat. *(to Sycophant)* Well, my friend, what is your opinion about the advantages of our sublunary* state?

Sycophant. Why, Sir, I value it only on account of the riches and pleasures which it contains.

Jagat. I am of the same opinion with you: but many, I know, are not satisfied with my conduct; and you know already there are murmurs against me in the city.

Sycophant. Aye, some wretches, who are ignorant of the true nature of things, and being deluded by some old books, are foolish enough, to desire the world to be newly modelled according to their chimerical plans: let us leave them to themselves, and follow quietly the dictates of our reason.

Jagat. But they say, and maintain, that love of women, wine and all other luxuries of the kind, are so many vices, which are surely to be punished in the next world! I myself cannot help shuddering at the very thought of hell.

Sycophant. Aye, the essential part of priestcraft consists in keeping the credulous constantly in awe of future punishment.

Jagat. Are there any arguments, to annihilate their fantastical notions?

Sycophant. Oh! The best ones, Sir—The strong instinctive impulses of the five senses, the fascinating power of the fair sex, and the other enjoyments, are not human inventions; and since they are the works of God, whom they allow to be just and merciful, I do not think, that these temptations were created by Him as so many traps, merely to ensnare his poor creatures, in order that He may torment them afterwards in hell, and feast his divine eyes and ears with their misery and groans!

Jagat. Surely, you have completely reasoned me out of my fears; *(to Bakshi)* what say you about these arguments, which seem to be unanswerable?

---

* The earthly or the mundane. Literally, that which is beneath the moon.

Bakshi. Why, Sir, Your Highness may, if you please, honor his frenzy with the name of arguments; but my humble opinion is, that the noble theme of future reward and punishment, for our good and bad deeds, is so clearly demonstrated, that it is too bright to be obscured by the gloom of sophistry; and the reasons upon which it is founded, are already sanctioned by divine injunctions—consequently, they are like so many immoveable rocks, which cannot be overturned by the hands of the children of ignorance. But be that as it may, my letter to Holkar is finished; will you be pleased to sign and seal it, Sir?

Jagat. Aye, give it to me; *(reads)* it is very well written; *(signs, seals and returns it to Bakshi),* come, take it, and let it be dispatched forthwith.

Bakshi. I will send it away immediately. *(Exit)*

Jagat. Well, my friend, you see my Bakshi entirely differs from our opinion; of course, he may view my present preparations of war in a different light from what we see them in.

Sycophant. Perhaps he may; but what is it to us? We must not lose sight of Krishna Kumari.

Jagat. No, that we never shall! *(Exeunt)*

SCENE III.

A SPACIOUS HALL IN A BUNGALOW NEAR THE FORT OF BHANPURA

Enter Jaswant Rao Holkar, his Minister, and Amir Khan his General*

Holkar. In chimerical hopes of extirpating the English from Hindustan, we have in vain exhausted all our resources, and strained every nerve, in this unhappy war† with the English Government, and which at last has thus terminated in our disgrace and ruin, and left us the shameful experience of our folly, as well as their superiority over us, in every respect.

Amir. Yes, but I am at a loss to account for the blindness of the divine decree, which has ordained that these barbarians, the most detestable *kafirs*‡, the wearers of hats, should become masters of Hindustan.

---

* Holkar's *dewan* was Ganpat Rao. But the character of the Minister seems to be based on his successor, Tantia Jog, who is portrayed warmly in Malcolm's *Central India*. Jog started out as as a *sowkar* (financier) to Holkar. After Holkar went insane and Tulsi Bai assumed the Regency, Jog was promoted to *bakshi* (paymaster). He and Ganpat Rao then led the Maratha faction in the Holkar *darbar* that opposed Amir Khan's Pathan faction. After the Third Anglo-Maratha War, Jog was deputed to negotiate with the East India Company. The resulting Treaty of Mandsaur (1818) saw Holkar accept British paramountcy and cede vast territories including those the Company had promised Amir Khan. With Malcolm's support, Jog was then appointed *dewan* of Holkar's much-shrunken state whose finances he subsequently repaired.

† The recently concluded Second Anglo-Maratha War (1803–5) in which Holkar had been humbled by the East India Company.

‡ A person who disbelieves or denies the tents of Islam.

Minister. It is the will of our Gods! And it has already been foretold in our Puranas*, that this our holy land should be overrun by barbarians, of what description soever they may be, whether Mussalmans, Europeans, or any other foreigners.

Amir. Then you seem to make no distinction between true believers, and those the very meanest of the Nazarenes†, the English? *(Laughs)*

Minister. Oh, Sir, the distinction is too striking to escape even the eye of a superficial beholder; but it is unquestionably in favour of the English nation.

Amir. Then you will prefer the English Government to that of the Mussalmans in this country, will you?

Minister. I do not understand you well, Sir; I think you would have me allow, that Mussalmans had at one time discharged the duties of Government in this country; is that your meaning?

Amir. My meaning! Strange folly indeed. Is there any doubt that Mussalmans have been in possession of Hindustan for a long time?

Minister. Who is doubting of that? But, now I perceive our mistake: it lies in the meaning of the term *Government*. If you suppose this word to be synonymous with brutish tyranny, our controversy is at an end; because, I grant, the Mughals have tyrannized over us, for six or seven centuries, and treated us rather like slaves, than lawful subjects.

Amir. *(Laughs)* Pray, Sir, what is *your* definition then of the word Government.

Minister. Government is nothing else but the establishment of a legal authority, to make proper use of the united power of the whole society, in securing the reasonable liberty and privileges of every one of its members, and checking each individual from encroaching upon the rights of others, and thus preserving the community from mischiefs of every description.

Amir. Keep your Brahmanical subtleties to yourself; mere play of words! I have not philosophy enough to trouble my head about them. But, be that as it may, was not our Government very liberal, and consequently favorable to all classes of Hindus?

Minister. Yes, it was so, to those who had chosen abject slavery as the only means of preserving their lives and property; but to all others it was rather a scourge than a Government, because nothing was safe under it. There is scarce any town, village, pagoda, or any sacred place whatever, in Hindustan, which does not exhibit some marks of your rapacity, depredations, and the violence of your religious bigotry.

Amir. I know very well, that you idolaters always hate our pure religion. The English are not superstitious pagans like you, but we consider them infidels, because, they brand our Prophet with the epithet of *Imposter*; and call theirs the *Son of God*. However both of us, Christians and Mahomedans, being your natural enemies, what reason have you to prefer one to the other?

---

* The sacred, mythical literature of the Hindus. Literally, in Sanskrit, the term means old or ancient.

† A derivative of the Arabic word *nasara*, the term used in the Koran to describes Christians.

Minister. My reasons are quite obvious; in the first place, the Christian religion is as mild as that of the Brahmins; they propagate it by gentle means of persuasion. The very suffering of their prophet corroborates fully their assurance, that divine blessings are not to be gained by slaughter and rapine, but by humility alone. And I need not say, that your religion owes its success to sword and fire.

Amir. Pray, let me know, what you think about your own religion.

Minister. As to our religion, it is as old as the world itself; and in consequence, I allow, it is full of absurd ceremonies, mysteries, and superstition; but then it contains also the best percepts founded on solid virtue and wisdom.

Amir. *(Laughs)* Well, if so, does it not appear the work of the devil rather than the revelation from God, because, you yourself allow, that it is full of superstitions and absurdities; don't you?

Minister. Yes, I do; but show me, if there is any religion, which is destitute of superstition of one kind or other; because I know, the emissaries of the devil, who are as busy in India as in Arabia, and who always become the commentators of many of the abstruse and ambiguous passages of the sacred books, convert many to their own fraternity, and thus make use of the same divine instrument, to corrupt mankind. This instance is fully corroborated everywhere, by the formation of many divisions among the followers of the same religion. But be that as it may, show me if you can, whether there be any such mild and just government as that of the English, wherein the rights and liberties of the subject are so much respected, and all religions not only tolerated, but even encouraged in a great degree?

Amir. This shameful tameness of the cowardly race of the Hindus has rendered them slaves to all the invaders. *(to Holkar)* Is not your defeat owing to the cowardice of your courtiers, who do not hesitate to praise our foe, even in your presence?

Minister. Oh! Not in the least, Sir; we have done all that was practicable in the war against the English; but it is true as our Maharaja observed, that we are at last fully convinced of our inferiority to them in wisdom and courage; and I dare say, all these disasters are the fruits of your rashness in undervaluing the merits of the great English nation.

Holkar. *(interrupts them)* These foolish controversies are of no avail. *(to Amir)* I would have you march at the head of part of the army, with all the possible expedition to Jaipur, to assist Jagat Singh, who has applied for my aid in the war, which he has lately declared against his rival Man Singh.

Amir. I will lose no time in obeying your commands. *(Exit)*

Holkar. *(to the Minister)* I employ these Pathans on account of their bravery; but as to their religion and government, they are by no means favorable to any other nation but their own. But our prudence requires that we should not attempt to interfere with or oppose their strong rooted prejudices. Mind that!

(Exeunt)

ACT THE SECOND

SCENE I.

A ROYAL PAVILION PITCHED ON A PLAIN; AN IVORY THRONE IN THE MIDDLE OF IT, WITH SEVERAL CHAIRS AROUND; A DISTANT VIEW OF A RIVER AND HILLS

Enter Jagat Singh and sits down on the throne

Jagat. *(to himself)* Indeed, this is a very critical juncture. I have already taken the field in person; Amir Khan, though hourly expected, is not yet arrived; shall I hazard the battle with my own troops alone, unassisted? No! It would be a rash step surely; but here comes my Bakshi; I know he has a very wise head, though his prudence makes him now and then a little too slow in his proceedings.

Enter Bakshi

Bakshi. God be praised! I came to inform you, that Amir Khan is just arrived with his headquarters, and is ready to wait upon Your Highness; shall I bring him in?

Jagat. Bring him, to be sure; I am all impatience to see him.

Bakshi. Very well, Sir. *(Goes and returns with Amir Khan, who salutes the Raja with salaams*, presents him with eleven mohurs†, and stands before him with profound respect and downcast eyes).*

Jagat. *(returns his salaam, and permits him to sit down on a chair at his right side)‡*. How is your health, Sir? You seem fatigued by your forced marches from Bhanpura.

Amir. I am quite well, and ready to your service; my fatigue is nothing, when I consider the noble errand of coming here, to have the honor of paying my homage personally at your feet, and of serving Your Highness in the cause, which I know is just.

Jagat. Are you then convinced of the propriety of my claim to the hand of Krishna Kumari, and of the necessity of my taking hostile measures against Man Singh, my rival?

Amir. Aye, perfectly well, Sir; her father was very right in choosing you for his son-in-law; who can doubt the right of a father to dispose of his daughter?

Jagat. Though you are a Mussalman, you seem to have a competent knowledge of our laws.

---

* A respectful greeting performed by slightly bowing the head and raising the right hand to the forehead.

† A gold coin, containing 190 grams of gold, and equivalent to fifteen rupees, issued by the Bengal Presidency of the East India Company.

‡ To be seated on a Maharaja's right side was a mark of high honor.

Amir. Aye, Hindustan being my native country, I am in some degree acquainted with your customs and manners, and I cannot help admiring your *shastras*[*], for the beauty of their wise percepts, which I dare say, are quite similar to the divine injunctions of our holy Koran.

Jagat. Your wisdom is proportionate to the reputation, which you have justly acquired by your splendid exploits in Hindustan; but now go and take rest. I have already preconcerted the plan of attack; let us commence it tomorrow at a convenient hour. Here, receive this from me, as a token of my particular regard for you *(presents him with khilat*[†] *and jewels).*

Amir. I cannot be sufficiently thankful for this kindness *(receives the khilat with a good grace).* I will order my troops to be in readiness: Your Highness may dispose of your servant in any way you please. *(Exit)*

Jagat. Well, Bakshi, this brave Pathan chief is very polite; and seems to be sincerely determined to afford me every assistance in his power.

Bakshi. I hope he will be what he appears to be; but deeds rather than words are the best proofs of one's sincerity.

Jagat. To be sure they are; but what private information have you received from the camp of Man Singh?

Bakshi. A very satisfactory one indeed: a spy tells me, that some of his *sardars* are dissatisfied, but the cause of it is not well known.

Jagat. What was the result of the skirmish, which our advanced guard has had with one of their foraging parties?

Bakshi. It was entirely in our favour, Sir; some prisoners, who were taken in this affair, assure me, that their army, being divided in parties and factions, is not in a condition to fight.

Jagat. It is very lucky; let us make haste then, to take advantage of this circumstance, and attack them at once with our united forces.

Bakshi. Aye, that is the best plan: but Amir Khan being a Mussalman, and a soldier of fortune by rank, enterprising, unsteady, and subtle, he can assume any character, and put it off at pleasure; therefore, I would have Your Highness be upon your guard, that it may not be in his power to abuse your confidence.

Jagat. Oh! There is no fear of that; he can have no other object in view but our interest; let us proceed to operations. *(Exeunt)*

---

[*] The law books, descending from antiquity, that detail how Hindu society ought to be governed.

[†] A ceremonial gift of dress or expensive cloth.

SCENE II.
A GREEN VELVET TENT

Enter Man Singh, pensive

Man. *(to himself)* Alas! I am very unfortunate! What is to be done now? Both Bapuji Sindhia* and Sarjerao Ghatge†, who are sent by Sindhia to assist me, are actually ravaging my country! The disgraceful defeat of this day is certainly owing to the disloyalty of some of my *sardars*, who are ill-advised by this scoundrel, my Pradhan, Sawai Singh. But here he comes.

Enter Sawai Singh

Sawai. My duty obliges me to inform you sincerely, that our entire overthrow is inevitable; the *sardars* will not do their duty punctually, unless they behold their lawful sovereign Dhonkal Singh on the *musnud*; my persuading and exhorting them, on your behalf, is of no avail.

Man. Aye, on my behalf? A monstrous lie! I know, you have made use of your persuasions and exhortations, but in a quite different way.

Sawai. *(Aside)* He seems to have smelled the rat; no matter, he is entirely ensnared—I may bring him to any terms I like. *(to Man Singh)* I do not understand you well, Sir.

Man. Don't understand me? So much the better; but do you know whom you are speaking to?

Sawai. Aye, perfectly well; to the usurper of Jodhpur; your menacing looks and your authoritative tone will not avail you anything; I will henceforward consider myself to be my own master, and will do my duty to my king and country, according to the dictates of my own conscience. *(Exit; meets the Munshi and addresses him)* Will you walk with me to my tent, Munshi?

Munshi. Aye, with all my heart; any news, Sir?

Sawai. A very pleasant one; Man Singh shall soon meet the fate which he deserves: many of our *sardars* are ready to assist me in my designs against him. Amir Khan is to join our party, I will raise Dhonkal Singh to the throne without any delay; thus you see my triumph is complete. These are the glorious deeds, which I have premeditated, and which my head has achieved within a very short time.

Munshi. Aye, very true; but —

Sawai. There is no need for your Buts, you know.

---

* A key lieutenant and relative of Daulat Rao Sindhia.

† A strong-willed Maratha chieftain and father-in-law to Daulat Rao Sindhia.

Munshi. I know, Sir; but, what do you expect from all these your achievements?

Sawai. Why, Dhonkal Singh shall have the name, and I, the power of the Raja; do you understand?

Munshi. Yes, I do; your proficiency in the Science of Politics is admirable, indeed; but have a care, lest the indiscreet practice of it cost you your life, as it has done to many of its professors.

Sawai. Don't fear, I have enough of prudence: I am guided by it like yourself in every circumstance; but *you* suffer timidity to pass for that virtue, which *I* would not. The difference between you and me is that, which consists between the timid and the brave. *(Exeunt)*

Man. *(alone in his tent)* Yes, my misfortune is complete; I have now two formidable enemies to contend with: Sawai Singh at home, and Jagat Singh abroad! But here comes my brave General[*], who is my only confidant now.

Enter General

General. We are undone! Another attack, which is very likely to be made by the enemy, will certainly decide our fate. The whole of our artillery and ammunition fell into the hands of the enemy—if we do not reach soon our capital, all of us will be taken prisoners, and perhaps fall a sacrifice to the rage of Sawai Singh, who bestirs himself with great diligence, and rides from tent to tent, in order to execute his black designs against Your Highness.

Man. *(after a long pause)* What has become of my private letter to Amir Khan, which you have already sent him by your confidential servant? Can he be gained over from our enemies?

General. I have just received a very favorable intimation on that subject; this private intercourse will I hope, be of very great use to us; but I will tell you all, after our safe arrival at Jodhpur; now let us fly from this dangerous situation, and make the best of our way to the capital.[†]

Man. If we must, we must; come, then, let us escape with those few faithful troops of our household.[‡] *(Exeunt)*

---

* This was Man Singh's *bakshi* Inder Raj Singhvi, who later became *dewan*. He was murdered in 1815 on Amir Khan's orders after he advised Man Singh to counter the Pathan by allying with Sindhia.

† The advice to mount a retreat was actually given by Shivnath Singh, the *thakur* (chieftain) of Kuchaman, one of the few Jodhpur nobles to ally with Man Singh.

‡ Man Singh's household troops comprised 3,500 troops, 1,500 cavalry, and 25 guns under the command of Hindal Khan, a Rohilla from Panipat.

SCENE III.
AN OLD CHOULTRY* ON THE BANK OF A LARGE TANK, NEAR VILLAGE

Enter Jagat Singh and his Sycophant

Jagat. God be praised! I have gained a signal victory over my enemy; his army is completely routed; Man Singh, with the remainder of his troops, has shut himself up in the fort of Jodhpur, which he will be obliged to surrender at last.

Sycophant. This event I had already anticipated. The beautiful Krishna Kumari shall be yours, because Heaven is always just, in rewarding merit. Did not I urge, the other day, the necessity of undertaking war, on this score?

Jagat. Yes, but the overcautious policy of my Bakshi would not easily yield to our preconcerted measure.

Sycophant. Thus, the excess of prudence, as I have very often told you, prevents people from taking advantage of the favorable circumstances, which present themselves; but, here he comes, let us drop the subject.

Enter Bakshi in great agitation

Jagat. You seem to be almost breathless! Pray, what is the matter? What has happened to you?

Bakshi. The worst, Sir, not to me alone, but to Your Highness, and to the kingdom of Jaipur.

Jagat. Why, in the name of wonder, what do you mean?

Bakshi. We are betrayed, undone, ruined! What I had anticipated is come to pass at last. Amir Khan, by the instigation of Man Singh, is now become our open enemy. He, in conjunction with some *sardars* of Jodhpur, has already defeated several divisions of our army, and taken from them all the ordnance and other trophies, which we have lately captured, and has restored them to our enemy.

Jagat. This is most unfortunate indeed! But what inducements had he for doing so?

Bakshi. None, that I can see, Sir; but, under pretense of want of provisions, a party of his lawless Pathans were pillaging one of our fertile districts; and the troops that were stationed there, were obliged to drive them out of it by force of arms. This unforeseen circumstance is said to have exasperated this unprincipled Mussalman chief; but the fact is, that a private understanding exists between him and Man Singh.

Jagat. Oh! this my disaster is too heavy to be borne! What to do, I know not!

---

* A South Indian term that describes a building or sheltered space, such as a detached pillared hall or temple porch used as a resting or meeting place by travelers and locals. In the context of Western India, the more fitting term would have been *chawri* or *dharmshala*.

Bakshi. I think it advisable, that we should decamp immediately, and march straight to our capital, which will undoubtedly be ransacked, should we not reach it in proper time.

Jagat. Thus, our triumph is changed into disgrace!

Sycophant. Aye, thus the wheel of fortune, which already lifted us to the sky, has brought us to the ground by one single rotation.

Jagat. Really, I now think, we mortals are doomed to suffer all sorts of reverses.

Sycophant. Nay, many disappointments, crosses and privations of all descriptions.

Jagat. Ah! What are our conjectures, discussions and debates about the probabilities of the future? Nothing but the prattling of children.

Sycophant. Aye, rather the chirping of birds; or, if you please, the howling of jackals, and barking of dogs.

Jagat. My motives and reasons for undertaking this war, were just.

Sycophant. So they were, but the result of it —

Bakshi. Clearly points out, that our motives were wrong, and our reasons erroneous. *(Aside)* The tongue of the Sycophant forms an admirable echo, to confirm our poor prince in his delusion. *(to the Raja aloud)* But we have no time to lose, let us hasten to Jaipur.

Jagat. Wait here a little while; I will go and give the necessary orders for the dispatch of my *zenana*[*]. I will be back presently. *(Exit)*

Bakshi. Is it not extraordinary, that barefaced flattery, consisting of downright falsehood and absurdity, should pass for sincerity with princes?

Sycophant. Aye, it is from this circumstance alone, that this great art has become a sort of current coin in all *darbars*; and I think, it is chiefly upon this that the safety and success of the courtier depend.

Bakshi. How? Show me; where is your safety, if the Raja should recollect what you have asserted before, and then compare it with what you have said afterwards, upon the same subject?

Sycophant. There is no fear of that; because, from time immemorial up to this present moment, princes are uniformly the same inconsiderate beings; and of course, the success of our profession depends partly upon their forgetfulness, and partly upon their humor, which requires to be tickled always by sweet words.

---

* The quarters in which the women of the household were secluded. It is unclear whether Jagat Singh brought women from his *zenana* to the front. This line may have been intended to dramatize Malcolm's description of Jagat Singh as "dissolute" and devoted to "sensual pleasures" (see Appendix I).

Bakshi. Well, then, if deluding credulous princes, and thereby ruining the community, and of consequence, sinning against God, are the advantages, which are to be reaped from this art, I detest it as a diabolical vice, or as a kind of sweet poison; but I wish you will henceforward mend your conduct; will you?

Sycophant. No, you cannot reason me out of the course, which I pursue entirely for the sake of my self-interest. I acquire the same fortune, and influence by my adulations, fawning, and cringing, which you do by your rigid philosophy and virtuous career; but the difference is, that my way is short, easy and pleasant: whereas yours is long, difficult and dangerous: do you know?

Bakshi. Yes, perfectly. *(Aside)* These fellows, have no principles; of course, they will always cling to their vices because they find their profit by it. *(Aloud)* But here comes the Raja.

Enter Jagat Singh

Jagat. Bakshi, order my tents to be struck, let the cavalry proceed before, and as to my bodyguard, let it march with my palanquin. Are your followers and palanquin ready? I would have you command my rear guard which shall consist of my infantry. *(to Sycophant)* Make haste, will you? Mount your horse, and come along with me, that we may converse together on our way. *(Exeunt)*

SCENE IV.

A ROOM IN A COUNTRY HOUSE, POORLY FURNISHED, WITH A SMALL GARDEN IN THE FRONT

Enter Sawai Singh, dejected

Sawai. *(to himself)* My hopes are frustrated! Amir Khan has changed sides! He has defeated Jagat Singh's army, in consequence of which the revolted *sardars*, on whom I relied for succor, have joined the standard of Man Singh! What is to be done now? But, here comes Munshi, he may perhaps be of some use to me.

Enter Munshi with a melancholy air

Sawai. Munshi, the smiles of fortune in our favor are at an end; our affairs, you know, have begun, all of a sudden, to wear a gloomy aspect; these are the works of our unpropitious stars.

Munshi. Nay, I say, these are the evils, produced by your intriguing head, which I know is now as empty as an exhausted receiver of the air-pump; because, you have already drained it of all its contents, in these your glorious achievements.

Sawai. Your ill-timed raillery is as insupportable as the sensation, which is felt when the wound is touched by a firebrand.

Munshi. Yes, I know; your disappointment and guilty conscience makes your grief more poignant.

Sawai. Aye, but my motives were just in this affair, you know!

Munshi. They may have been so; but your deeds were not.

Sawai. How so?

Munshi. Why, a moment's retrospection of your past treacherous conduct will convince you fully, that you were hurried on by blind ambition, and that you have disregarded the dictates of your conscience.

Sawai. Ah! what is the use of our ruminating thus on what is past? Let us now consider, whether it is entirely impossible to secure the rights of the prince.

Munshi. Nay, let us rather consider, whether we can secure your natural right to your own head; do you understand me?

Sawai. Not quite clearly: am I now exposed to any immediate danger?

Munshi. Aye, to an imminent one, Sir; you must be well aware that Man Singh, being freed from all his dangers from abroad, will not fail to employ all his resources for the extinction of your life, which alone he thinks is wanting to consummate his worldly bliss.

Sawai. How came you to think thus?

Munshi. It is not guessing, Sir, but I have been well informed that Man Singh is actually concerting a plan to attain this object, which he has always in view, through the instrumentality of Amir Khan; who, I doubt not, will forward all his designs with great readiness.

Sawai. If so, I am undone; whether I may strive to better my condition by residing here, or whether it will be prudent to save my life by flight, I am at a loss to determine.

Munshi. I think, the second method is preferable, because of its practicality in this critical juncture.

Sawai. It is a very disagreeable alternative, indeed.

Munshi. But, it is become a necessary one, on account of many untoward circumstances of your own creating.

Sawai. Aye, but what will people say about me, when they come to know, that I am obliged to run away to save my life?

Munshi. Why, they will be very glad to honor you with the title of an imprudent adventurer, a villain, a scoundrel, or at least, that of a stupid blockhead.

Sawai. Shame! But, suppose I should have succeeded in my undertakings?

Munshi. Then, you would have been considered as a skillful System-monger, a famous Raja-maker, an able Politician, or the most capital Statesman the world ever has produced.

Sawai. Then according to your maxim, howsoever bad the character of a man may be, his riches, his influence, and after all, his success in the affairs of the world (no matter, whether he owes it to just or fraudulent means, or to mere chance), will infallibly raise him to the highest pitch of esteem among mankind; will it not?

Munshi. Yes, it will; but the thinking part of mankind will expose to the world the bad motives of the successful wicked man.

Sawai. But the thinking part is very small in comparison with the great mass of unthinking people.

Munshi. You are in the right: it is undoubtedly; but this inequality in numbers seems to be sanctioned by divine wisdom for some good end.

Sawai. Then, my mistake lies in being dazzled by the esteem of the greater number, and proceeding to gain it by the meanest artifices; does it not?

Munshi. Aye, it does; but, I wish you had made this seasonable conclusion before you had brought the matter to this crisis; but, then, your spirits were in continual ferment, occasioned by your violent thirst for power.

Sawai. Alas! what is past, is past: shall I flee to the city of Nagaur for refuge?

Munshi. Aye, that fort I think, is the best shelter for you, because it is beyond the reach of your foes.

Sawai. Will you be so kind as to follow me thither?

Munshi. No, I beg your pardon. Being a man of a great family, and in the service of Man Singh, my duty as well as prudence does not permit me to involve myself in your misfortunes.

Sawai. Well, will you permit me, then to proceed to Nagaur?

Munshi. Aye, with all my heart, make haste, I wish you success, and request you will henceforward abstain from the course you have hitherto pursued, and tread in the safe path of virtue. So may God be with you.

Sawai. Thanks for your good wishes; So good, bye.

(Exeunt severally)

ACT THE THIRD

SCENE I.

A SALOON IN THE PALACE OF JODHPUR, EVENING TIME

Enter Man Singh and his General

Man. Praise to God! Jagat Singh is completely defeated, and driven back to Jaipur; but still the work is only half done, because I have yet much to dread from the machination of Sawai Singh: have you communicated my designs to Amir Khan?

General. Yes, Sir; I have assured him of your heartfelt gratitude for the services, he has rendered this *darbar*, adding also that your success in this case cannot be complete, unless you get rid of Sawai Singh and his party; and in consequence, that you will be much obliged, if he will seize and deliver them into your hands by any means whatever.

Man. And what did he say to that?

General. He hesitated for some time to give me any satisfactory answer, as is always the case with him, when pecuniary emoluments are not offered to him in a distinct manner; and then I gave in his hands your written agreement, which he read over and over again, with great attention, seemed to be quite pleased and said with a smile, that he would undertake the difficult task of apprehending Sawai Singh within a very short period.

Man. Do you know what that agreement contains?

General. Perfectly well, Sir, you have offered him thc sum of two lakhs[*] of *sicca*[†] rupees, and a fine *jagir*[‡] in to the bargain, if he would undertake the seizure of Sawai Singh. Is it not?

Man. Aye, that is it; but what think you about the propriety of this scheme?

General. Surely, it is the best that can be devised; because, the ruin of our implacable enemy is our only safety, and thc thing we must chiefly aim at, cost what it will.

Man. The people will perhaps complain against me for being so lavish of the public property.

General. Oh, no; perhaps those, who are regardless of Your Highness' happiness, may murmur a little, but it is of no consequence; because, you know the people are no more than slaves of the king; *he* is the sole proprietor of their lives, honor and property; this I know is the law sanctioned by divine injunctions.

---

* A lakh denominates a hundred thousand.

† A *sicca* rupee was a newly coined rupee, containing 176 grams of silver, issued by the Bengal Presidency of the East India Company.

‡ A grant of land and the rent accruing from it.

Man. Aye, you are the only man, that is sincerely attached to me; and since the plan has met with your approbation, I care not about the murmurings of the people. But pray, do you know, where Sawai Singh is now?

General. Yes, Sir, it was reported by my spies last night, that he fled to Nagaur with a few of his wretched adherents.

Man. Oh, did he escape then?

General. No matter: Amir Khan will pursue him wherever he goes, and effect his seizure at all events; because this Mussalman's expertness and ingenuity in these matters are so amazing, and his endowments, both bodily and mental, so wonderful, that they almost approach to magical power.

Man. Sawai, quite elated with the smiles of deceitful fortune, almost fancied himself amongst the Gods; but now he is no more than a poor fugitive in the fortress of Nagaur.

General. Yes, what else can he expect when he has entirely forgotten his duty towards his king, who according to our *shastras*, is God upon earth?

Man. Your extensive knowledge cannot sufficiently be admired, but it is growing rather late; let us break off our conference. Tomorrow you go to Amir Khan, and ascertain from him what measures he intends to take in order to apprehend Sawai Singh. *(Exeunt)*

SCENE II.

A PARLOUR IN A BUNGALOW, SITUATED IN AN EXTENSIVE GARDEN, IN THE VICINITY OF JODHPUR

Enter Amir Khan, attentively looking at his watch

Amir. *(to himself)* It is past nine: I must reach Nagaur as soon as possible: the Raja is very liberal; he promises me *jagir*, besides two lakhs of rupees; surely, it is a very good bargain; but how can I execute his commission? By open force against the fort of Nagaur? No! That is impossible; but, here comes my confidential Jamadar[*].

Enter Jamadar

Jamadar. In obedience to your commands, I have given the necessary orders to our troops, to be in readiness to march to Nagaur, shall we have any occasion for some fieldpieces[†]?

Amir. To be sure, we shall let them go before, with my advanced guard.

---

[*] A military rank equivalent to captain. Literally, the person responsible for a group (deriving from *jama*, the Arabic term for an assembly). Amir Khan's trusted *jamadar* was Mirza Haji Beg (see Appendix III).

[†] An early modern term for field guns or mobile artillery, typically small wheeled cannons.

Jamadar. But pray, Sir, may I take the liberty of asking you, what is your errand?

Amir. Oh! It is nothing else, but to seize Sawai Singh, who is said to have taken shelter in that fort, with a few of his followers.

Jamadar. Is it that? Then the task is not so easy as you perhaps suppose it to be; because, I know, this brave Rajput chief possesses there resources enough, to defend himself against our army; and I know the Rajputs of that place will protect the refugees with all their might.

Amir. True, but you must know likewise, that Amir Khan will not undertake any errand, to execute which he has not previously devised the necessary means.

Jamadar. I suppose, you will have recourse to some artifice in this case, as you have done upon many other occasions.

Amir. Aye, that is my way.

Jamadar. But you are mistaken in this matter; because Sawai Singh is so well versed in artifices and intrigues, that it is next to impossible to outdo him in that point.

Amir. But where is the glory of genius to be found, except in outwitting those, who are supposed to be invincible by their skill.

Jamadar. Yes, thus the English are great, because they always outmaneuver their formidable opponents.

Amir. No doubt, you have hit the mark. I assure you that my intellects are so replete with plans and stratagems, both offensive and defensive, that I flatter myself, I can prove to be an overmatch to any power in India.

Jamadar. Yes, you can; you know it was already predicted by a sage *fakir*[*] that you would at one time have the supreme dominion over India; therefore, why don't you seat yourself at once on the throne of Delhi, and restore to the true believers their fallen power and glory in Hindustan? This project, though seemingly rash, is by no means impracticable; because the cabinets of Sindhia, Holkar, Bhonsle,[†] Peshwa,[‡] Nizam[§] and other potentates are at present so corrupted, and their strength is so reduced, that no resistance whatever is to be expected from those quarters.

Amir. Aye, I have this grand object always in my view, and I know likewise how to take the advantage of the present favorable circumstances to put it in execution; but the rising English authority in India will not suffer me or any other adventurer to reach that highest pinnacle of glory; and as to their power, both by land and sea I think it is quite miraculous, and is now-a-days capable of performing wonders in the world.

---

* Muslim religious mendicants drawn from Sufi orders.

† The family name of the ruling dynasty in the Maratha state of Nagpur.

‡ The prime minister of the Maratha Empire.

§ The official title of the ruler of Hyderabad, from the Arabic *nizam* (order).

Jamadar. Surely, your wisdom is unfathomable. I am now fully convinced of the truth of your arguments, but here comes Man Singh's General.

Enter General with cheerful countenance

General. His Highness has directed me to convey to you his most sincere thanks for your ready compliance with his request, and wishes that you will let him know the method of our proceeding in this intricate affair.

Amir. Well, then, tell His Highness, I have a thousand methods before me; let him not be troubled about it, and let him expect the head of Sawai as a present from me within a few days. Do you understand me?

General. Quite clearly. I assure you, Sir, your success in this case will restore everlasting peace to our country; and it is upon that alone that the Raja's prosperity depends.

Amir. Well, then, tell the Raja, I will leave this immediately for Nagaur, and play my part so skillfully, that it shall shine in the theatre of the world as a masterpiece of the kind.

General. I will inform His Highness of that: so I wish you prosperity and success! *(Exit)*

Jamadar. Everything is ready, shall I order the Pathan corps and battalions to march? *(Exeunt)*

Amir. Certainly! Let us move on!

SCENE III.

A TENT, STRONGLY GUARDED BY ARMED PEONS IN A MANGO GARDEN, NEAR THE FORT OF NAGAUR

Enter Sawai Singh.

Sawai. A strange circumstance indeed! But how can this be accounted for, or relied upon? Amir Khan gives out, that he is disgusted with the ingratitude of Man Singh, and now invites me to his camp, in order, as he says, to tell me some secrets verbally! But as my prudence would not allow me to trust him, I have politely declined his invitation. It seems, however, he wishes to have me in his hands, as an instrument to ruin Man Singh. Why, really, this is a lucky incident! God grant, that my suppositions may prove true! But will Amir Khan be sincere, or act traitor in this case? I cannot say one or the other, because, he has already sent me word that he will wait upon me today with a few servants only. Well, if he will be so good as his word, his trust in me is not to be doubted. For then, how can I suspect him of any treacherous designs against me?

Enter Servant.

Servant. Amir Khan is approaching our garden, sir.

Sawai. Does he? What retinue has he along with him?

Servant. No retinue, he only comes in his palanquin with three or four *khidmatgars*[*], and a single horseman who seems to be his favorite *jamadar.*

Sawai. *(aside)* Then he confides in me entirely! *(to the Servant.)* Very well, let him enter unmolested.

Servant. I will convey your orders to our guards. *(Exit.)*

Sawai. What can all this mean? Can so much of apparent confidence be an artifice? By no means; it is more than probable, that he is dissatisfied with the bad conduct of Man Singh, and of course, would[†] have my assistance, in his operations against him; because according to the common course of things, both the friends of our friends, the enemies of our enemies, are our friends, and the friends of our enemies, and the enemies of our friends are our foes. But here he comes unarmed, with a smiling countenance, full of serenity, and seeming innocence.

Enter Amir Khan and his Jamadar,
both saluting Sawai Singh with a good grace,
and sitting down before him on the carpet.

Amir. Well, Sawai Singh, I am very sorry, to see you in this condition!

Sawai. I thank you for your good will towards me; but you need not wonder at this miserable condition of a wretched fugitive, whom fortune persecutes without mercy.

Amir. Pshaw! Do not be hopeless; God will at last display his mercy towards his helpless creatures.

Sawai. No doubt! He did display it already, Sir, by exciting in your heart some pity for my deplorable and forlorn condition.

Amir. But, pray, Sir, I beg your pardon, what made you hesitate at first, then refuse to come? I fear, you doubt my veracity.

Sawai. Oh, no, Sir! The violent agitations, which these reverses have produced in my mind, force me even to doubt of my own existence.

Amir. Aye, do they? Then I was in the wrong to believe, that nothing in the world could deprive Sawai Singh of his innate courage.

Sawai. No, Sir; Courage has not forsaken me, but the comparison of the past with the present circumstances has —

Amir. *(interrupting him)* Changed your sex, I think; *(Laughs.)* But that comparison alone is enough to convince you of the sincerity of my motives; because Man Singh was my pretended friend, and now he is my open enemy, by his ungrateful behavior

---

[*] A servant or attendant of a Muslim nobleman. Originally, one who waited at the nobleman's table.

[†] A printing error in the original edition interposes the word "needs" here.

towards me. And why do you not compare these circumstances one with the other, and conclude thereby, that I am really in want of your friendship and assistance?

Sawai. Aye, you may be, Sir, but —

Amir. There again you stick to your Buts. *(to Jamadar.)* Why, I cannot reason him out of his womanish fears.

Jamadar. Can't you, Sir? then I will do it for you, and will very easily laugh him out of his unaccountable doubts. *(to Sawai.)* It is very true, Sir, that you are at loss to account for this change in our conduct towards Man Singh after what has actually taken place; but this instance is not so uncommon under the moon, because the same person may either be our friend or foe, according to circumstances, you know.

Sawai. Yes; but it is this point of your argument alone, which does not permit me to be so bold as to trust myself implicitly into your hands; because outward appearances are not be considered as a conclusive testimony of inward motives.

Jamadar. Very true; but are deeds too to be viewed in the same light?

Sawai. Oh, no, never; because if this were the case, we should have nothing to depend upon in this world, and consequently no data to proceed upon in the ordinary affairs of this life.

Jamadar. Well, then, you see my master is already come here, without any guards whatever; does he not in this case trust entirely upon your friendship and good will? And now, is not his sincerity towards you clearly demonstrated by these deeds?

Sawai. To be sure, it is; but the disturbed state of my mind requires one thing more, to support my belief.

Jamadar. Still something more? *(Laughs.)* Pray, what is it, Sir?

Sawai. Nothing extraordinary; but I beg your master will be so good as to take an oath, and declare solemnly before any sacred shrine, that he has no bad intentions against me.

Amir. *(laughs)* The most wonderful pusillanimity, that I ever saw in my life. *(to Sawai.)* Since I cannot satisfy you in any other way, I am ready to perform what you require; come, then, shall we go to the neighboring *dargah*?[*]

Sawai. Aye, let us go!

Jamadar. *(laughs)* This is a very remarkable instance of Hindu cowardice: but, let us repair to the holy tomb. *(Exeunt.)*

---

[*] The tomb of a Muslim saint. The reference here was to Tarkin *dargah*, the tomb of Hamiduddin Nagori, a Sufi saint of the Chistiya order. The tomb is located a short distance from Nagaur Fort.

SCENE CHANGES TO A MAGNIFICENT TOMB OF A MAHOMEDAN SAINT

Enter Sawai Singh, Amir Khan, and Jamadar.

Amir. The noble appearance of this sacred building fills the mind at once with awe and reverence; does it not?

Jamadar. It does; but I think these unbelievers, the Hindus, are utter strangers to these enthusiastic emotions; because their knowledge of the Supreme Being and his attributes is very imperfect, when compared to the sublime notions, which we Mussalmans have of the great Allah.

Amir. Well, Sawai Singh, I believe you are displeased with what our Jamadar has just now suggested about the Hindus.

Sawai. Oh, no, not in the least, Sir; I am rather amused with his assertions, because the ideas of Mahommedans concerning our nation, and their bold and erroneous statements are become so proverbially ridiculous, that they never fail to produce laughter among us.

Jamadar. Surely it will continue to produce it, until all infidels are corrected by subversion and conversion. *(Laughs.)*

Sawai. That is to say, they will cease to be Hindus, after they are corrupted irrecoverably. *(Laughs.)*

Amir. Jamadar I assure you, Sawai Singh has combated your reasons very ably; what think you about his head?

Jamadar. Why, Sir, I think it is quite full of wit and wisdom; and I hope you will derive many advantages from it.

Amir. To be sure, I will. I know, it can do miracles: and, therefore, I consider his friendship as the most valuable acquisition in the world.

Jamadar. You are in the right, Sir. *(Aside.)* Surely, two lakhs of rupees and a *jagir* is no small acquisition!

Sawai. *(to Amir Khan)* You do me too much honor by thus overvaluing my merits; and I am determined to show gratitude rather by my deeds than barely expressing it by words.

Amir. Very good! Since that is your determination, I will show you just now by my formal oaths, how sincere I am in my intentions towards you. *(to Jamadar.)* Can you get me the holy Koran?

Jamadar. Yes; here is one, which I have already procured from one of the attendants of this holy place. *(Gives it into his hand.)*

Amir. *(receives the Koran with an affected humility and devotion)* "I do declare solemnly, and swear by all that is sacred, that I have no bad designs whatever against Sawai Singh. I shall be his sincere friend henceforward; let God and his divine agent upon the earth, the great Mohammad, be witnesses of my sincerity." *(keeps the Koran upon his head, and returns it to the Jamadar after kissing it several times.)* Now, Sawai Singh, I have done what you have required of me; are there still some suspicions lurking in the gloomy corners of your heart?

Sawai. Oh! God forbid, that I should be so blind, as not to be able to see the bright sun in the sky. I am perfectly convinced of your sincerity. I will with all my heart wait upon you tomorrow at your camp, and I request, you will excuse my indelicacy in having required an oath from you.

Amir. Pshaw! According to the common course of things, any man in your strange predicament will be under the necessity of requiring it; no matter, if you will be pleased to honor me with your visit at any convenient time, I will receive you with all the military honors due to your high rank; and I assure you again, that if you will depend upon me faithfully, I will prove myself to be the best of friends.

Sawai. I thank you, Sir.

Jamadar. *(to Amir Khan)* Depend upon it, his wise head will be more useful to you than many empty ones like that of mine! Do you understand me, Sir?

Amir. Aye, very clearly; you mean his wise counsels will be of great service to me, is it not?

Jamadar. Aye, that is my meaning: you always hit the mark without missing.

Amir. Well, Jamadar, we have attained the object we had in view; and now, let us return to our tents, and make necessary preparations for the reception of our friend, Sawai Singh. *(Both saluting Sawai Singh.) (Exeunt.)*

Sawai *(to himself)* Amir Khan is undoubtedly mine! Now I will teach Man Singh, how to hate me! I will let him feel the marvelous power of my head; to be sure I will. Aye, the poor fellow may perhaps repent, but what is that to me? I will not pardon him, no, never!

(Exit.)

ACT THE FOURTH

SCENE I.

A VERY LARGE TENT, PITCHED IN THE CAMP OF AMIR KHAN, THE REGULAR INFANTRY THREE DEEP DRAWN UP AROUND IT, WITH SEVERAL FIELD PIECES MOUNTED AND LOADED, THE MATCHES LIGHTED, LINES OF PATHAN CAVALRY ARE SEEN RANGED IN DIFFERENT DIRECTIONS

Enter Sawai Singh and his officers, with several relations and followers, conducted by the Jamadar of Amir Khan.

***Sawai*.** Is not the weather this morning warmer than usual, Jamadar?

***Jamadar*.** Aye, it is very sultry, surely; but when the sun approaches to his meridian glory, you shall find, that the heat of this place will be as intense as that of an oven.

***Sawai*.** I am quite transported with joy, at being received with such particular marks of distinction and honor!

***Jamadar*.** Very true; my master has ordered the whole body of his troops to be under arms, in order to salute you, on your coming to and going from our camp; because, he thinks it necessary, that his great regard for you be known to the public.

***Sawai*.** I am all gratitude for his kindness; but where is your master? I am very eager to embrace him soon.

***Jamadar*.** In obedience to his commands, I came to receive you at some distance from the camp, and thence to conduct you to this pavilion. I think, he is busy in his sleeping tent, in selecting some valuable jewels, and some delicious fruits, such as grapes, oranges, and figs of the best quality, which I know, he intends to welcome you with. *(Aside.)* I mean grape shots, cannon balls, and musket bullets. *(to Sawai.)* But as it is already late, I will go and call him. *(Exit.)*

***Sawai*.** *(to one of his officers)* Let us rejoice, and thank heaven for this happy change of our fortune. We had been nearly reduced to the most miserable condition, by the machination of our enemy; but now, the very person, whom Man Singh employed in ruining me, is become the very instrument in my hands for his destruction; such are the miracles, which heaven works in favor of its favorites. Does it not?

***Officer*.** Yes, Sir, it sometime does; but a sudden change, like this, is a very extraordinary phenomenon, and must have some mystery in it.

***Sawai*.** Some mystery, to be sure, there is; yet what else can it be, but a divine miracle in our favor, as I have just observed?

***Officer*.** Yes; but is it necessary, that such a large body of troops should be arranged in battle array, merely to salute us?

Sawai. Vain suspicions! Did not the Jamadar tell us just now, that his master intends to convince the populace of his great regard for me, by thus treating me with pomp and honor? Well, don't you see, that I am already treated like a prince?

Officer. True; but why should there be so many guns planted in every direction around? I shudder at the very sight of the lighted matches, and of the muzzles of the guns, which are all pointed at us. Are so many deadly implements of war requisite, merely to pay us compliments?

Sawai. No, they are not; but, who know, it may be the intention of Amir Khan to exhibit before me the show of a mock battle, which requires different maneuvers of troops, firing of guns, wheeling about of cavalry and all that.

Officer. Perhaps, it may be; but what signifies this profound silence, which prevails everywhere? And why does no body stir around us? Is not this dismal appearance something like the dead calm, which, they say, precedes a storm at sea?

Sawai. Pshaw! Amir Khan must have these arrangements to show me the regularity, and the strict discipline of his army.

Officer. Be that as it may; why should we be thus deserted by all his people, and why should the Jamadar himself have left us alone in this large tent?

Sawai. Your remarks seem to have some truth in them: they begin to operate on my mind, though I am not certain of anything at present; yet some secret unaccountable agitations of my heart make me uneasy, I feel a kind of chilling sensations throughout my body, my heart palpitates! What can this mean? — Fy! Fy! It is nothing but a chimera; the doleful effects of unfounded fears, excited by your imaginary doubts. *(Laughs.)* It is very true, that bewildered eyes see things in a different light from what they really are. Is it possible that Amir Khan should be so base a perjurer, as to betray me, after taking an oath, before the *dargah* of his saint?

Officer. No, it is impossible; but the strange coincidence of some circumstances has in a manner forced me to doubt the sincerity of this Mussalman.

Sawai. Yes, that is the thing which disturbs the peace of my mind; it is very true. I attempt to banish these gloomy thoughts out of my head, but they in spite of my efforts arise there spontaneously, and prey like vultures on my soul. Oh! what a miserable creature man is! Now I perceive, that this disquietude is the fruit of my unbounded ambition. Cursed be riches and power! They fascinate us by their enchanting charms, then render us a burden to ourselves. What blockheads are we to pursue these phantoms in hopes of happiness? Oh, that I had been content with a moderate fortune!

Officer. You are in the right, Sir; we pursue butterflies, with a view to build our castles in the air by their means.

Sawai. But, alas! What is the use of thus aggravating our sorrows, by ruminating on our past follies! Where is my bodyguard?

Officer. They are scattered about here and there. I think it would be proper to keep them collected in one place; but here comes the brother-in-law of Amir Khan.

Enter Brother-in-law.

Sawai. I am very glad to see you, Sir; but where is Amir Khan? Why does he delay to honor us with his company?

Brother. I don't know, why? I came here of my own accord to be present at this interview; perhaps, he is busy in his tent; but, I think he will be here presently.

Officer. You think, there is no sinister intention? But oh! What is the matter? The tent is in a violent motion! It almost totters: there is no wind at all! Is it the shock of an earthquake? No; the ground is firm enough. But mercy upon us: here it falls down. It is a plot! We are undone! It is a plot. *(The tent falls down on the head of Sawai Singh, his officers, relations, and servants; drums begin to beat, musketry commences a heavy and brisk fire upon the tent; the fieldpieces pour in their fiery hail of grapes from all directions; columns of thick smoke and dust rise and spread on all sides, and cover the whole plain with terrible darkness. Within the tent are heard hideous cries, loud lamentations, screams of agony, and dreadful shrieks of dying sufferers.)*

Oh! We are murdered! Butchered! Massacred! Amir Khan, that scoundrel, that rascal, that monster has deceived us! —Oh God! Mercy! Mercy! —How to extricate ourselves from under this weight? — Alas! We are fired upon! No safety! Help! Help! Who are you? — I am the wretch, Sawai, wounded, exhausted, here I sink! Adieu to the world! —Alas, I am the brother-in-law of Amir Khan! Oh, what is this? What have I done? Why do they kill me? Help me, Oh Mohammad, help me! But no, there is no help! I am murdered! Give me life! Ah, this is death!

(Outside the tent is heard the shouting of Pathan soldiers, intermingled with the confused noise of dying Rajputs &c.)

Cut them to pieces! *Deen*! *Deen*![*] *Maaro*! *Maaro*![†] Put the *kafirs* to death! Here they hide their heads; there they creep and escape from under the tent! Seize those fellows! Shoot them!

Alas! We are surrounded; overpowered: no escaping! Our poor comrades are massacred! They are trodden down! Ah merciless savages! We are deceived! We are undone!

Holla, fire at them! Send them all down to hell! Are they all sabered?[‡] All is over! Success! Victory! Glory! Huzzah!

(The stage appears strewed with dead bodies, the firing ceases, order is restored, profound silence ensues, curtain drops with slow music.)

---

[*] A rallying cry used by Muslim soldiers. Literally, in Arabic, it means religion.

[†] In Urdu, an order to hit or kill.

[‡] To cut down with a saber or scimitar—a long, curved sword typically employed by cavalry.

SCENE II.
A SMALL TENT WELL FURNISHED

Enter Amir Khan and his Jamadar.

Amir. Today our brave troops have behaved remarkably well. I believe they have sacrificed all the victims. Well done! But what is become of Sawai Singh? Did he escape?

Jamadar. No, sir; not a single soul, I am sure, has escaped from the tent; which, according to your device, was so skillfully dropped, that it is impossible for anyone to have come out of it; and had any succeeded in this, he could not have escaped being shot from without.

Amir. That is right; God be praised! My plan is at last crowned with success. But here come the officers of the different corps.

*Enter officers, the foremost of them carrying the head of Sawai Singh in a large salver.**

Officer. We have executed your commands punctually, all Sawai Singh's men, to the number of about six or seven hundred, are killed; here is the trophy of this great exploit. *(They set before him the mangled head of Sawai Singh, which Amir Khan and his Jamadar look at very attentively, with some affected changes in their countenances, exclaiming frequently aloud "O God! O merciful Allah.")*

Amir. This is the fate which awaits evildoers.

Officer. Yes, it is; but we are sorry to inform your Excellency, that the same fate has befallen your innocent brother-in-law; because he was one of the unfortunate victims, who were slain within the tent.

Amir. What? My brother-in-law! That is mournful! — Indeed, the decree of heaven is blind. But how did that happen? *(With tears in his eyes.)* Alas! Poor man, the best of my friends! What could have carried him thither? Where was he found dead?

Officer. We know nothing of the matter; but, somehow, or other, he happened to be within the tent, when the fire commenced. We found his body stretched on the ground close to that of Sawai Singh, both of them shot by many musket bullets.

Amir. Indeed! It is an unhappy blunder! But how can that be helped? It was the doom, to which he was predestined by the Almighty will! Be that as it may, send *this* head immediately to Man Singh, that he may feast his eyes on it; because, I know this skull contained many intrigues, and he dreaded it most in the world. Now you may all go to rest yourselves in your tents. I will reward your exertions.

Officer. We are all very thankful for your kindness. *(Exeunt.)*

---

* A large metal tray or platter, usually made of silver.

Amir. Well, Jamadar, what think you now of the measures, which I have taken to destroy this traitor Sawai Singh and his party?

Jamadar. Why, they are both ingenious and just, Sir. As a friend of Man Singh, you have on one hand done your duty to the satisfaction of that prince; and on the other, as you have cleared the world of this wicked man, who was the scourge of mankind, your general philanthropy is established.

Amir. Aye, you are in the right; that is my laudable object; but here comes my old Khansama*; he always speaks nonsensically, but pretends to have great regard for virtue and religion; let us know what is his opinion about the present affair.

Jamadar. Oh, Sir, he is nothing but an empty-headed simpleton, but —

Enter an old Khansama, with a melancholy air.

Amir. Come, Khansama, what is the matter with you? You seem to be very sorry; what is become of your wonted gaiety?

Khansama. Why, Sir, the sight of this unjust and dreadful massacre has entirely deprived me of it.

Amir. So then, you are sorry because I have destroyed my enemies, are you?

Khansama. No, Sir, I am sorry, because you have destroyed your reputation, and rendered yourself odious among mankind.

Amir. How? In what manner can this my prudent act affect my character?

Khansama. It has metamorphosed you so completely that you are not the same person today, that you were yesterday; because, hitherto you were the ablest commander, and a brave soldier; but now, you are no more than a detestable perjurer, and a cruel murderer.

Amir. You seem to be sure, that I have committed perjury!

Khansama. The whole world is sure of it. Do you suppose then, that you great folks can keep the world ignorant of your deeds? Does not every sepoy† and common porter in the bazar know of your having deceived poor Sawai Singh by your oaths? And then, of having put him to death in spite of it?

Jamadar. Well, what then?

Khansama. What then? Is it not the greatest sin that a man can commit against his Maker?

Jamadar. Oh, by no means. It is as silly as to suppose it a sin, if we ensnare beasts and birds, and then kill them for our use.

Khansama. Then, are our fellow creatures to be considered as beasts and birds?

---

* The principal steward or butler in a household. The term was reserved for Muslims serving in this role.

† The term for a native soldier, from the Persian *sipahi*.

Jamadar. Why, I think they are not in the least better; because they are infidels, do you know?

Khansama. Yes, I do; but this theory, which you have just adduced, is not new; because, in certain parts of the world some ingenious people, who are naturally endowed with superior genius, like that of yours, have already put it in practice long ago: they not only slaughter their own species, as you would have us do, but also they eat them with great pleasure. Now do not you allow them a higher degree of reformation than us true believers?

Amir. Well, Khansama, you have not yet got better of your foolish dogmatism. Would you overturn the whole order of things in the world? I ask you, how is it possible for us to acquire power and wealth, unless recourse is had to some stratagem or other occasionally?

Khansama. If you ask my opinion, it is quite unsafe to deviate from the golden rule of doing to others, as we would they should do to us; and even universal monarchy is not worth a *kaudi**, when we are to obtain it at the expense of our conscience.

Amir. *(laughs)* Be sincere! Will you look at my face, and tell me what you think, at the bottom of your heart about the magnificence of royal state, noble buildings, splendid carriages, rich jewels, fine apparel, exquisite delicacies of the table, and all that? Are not these enchanting temptations capable of stifling your poor conscience within your heart?

Khansama. *(laughs)* True; the temptations are very strong, indeed; but the ideas of the headache, gout, cholic pain, fever, infirmities of old age, and sickness, the screams of agony, pangs of death, the dismalness of the dark grave, and lastly the terrible notion of perpetual tortures in hell, trample all these temptations under foot, and point out to me clearly the necessity of having conscience for my guide in this sublunary state.

Jamadar. *(laughs)* It seems some insipid books of beggarly *fakirs*, which go by the name of Philosophy, have stuffed his empty head with all these foolish romantic notions of groundless fears.

Khansama. Yes, as the Devil has crammed yours with pernicious and blind confidence on the deceitful charms of fortune, and the erroneous opinions about happiness.

Jamadar. *(to Amir Khan)* I think his nonsensical speech has something pernicious in its effects; because, it begins to puzzle my head strangely; but who in the world doubts, that without money and power a man is nothing but a poor two-legged helpless animal? Let this fellow stick to his dull Philosophy, and let us mind our serious business of procuring riches and happiness.

Amir. Yes, it is true; to discourse with wrongheaded people is to disturb the peace of your mind; but this man being my old confidential servant, I cannot help loving him. I

---

* A small, white seashell, which served as a coin of the lowest denomination. In the early nineteenth century, 5,120 *kauris* were equivalent to one *sicca* rupee.

have very often given him the liberty of speaking his mind to me and I must not forget that his opinions were very useful upon several occasions.

Jamadar. Aye, they might have been so upon some trifling occasions; but in the present case, he reasoned very absurdly, and seems to have almost abused that liberty you have given him, by boldly representing our grand political actions in a quite different light from what they really are; he has almost obscured our brilliant exploit by his gloomy reasonings.

Khansama. *(laughs)* Strange depravity! *(to Amir Khan.)* I beg your honor will pardon my boldness: I have done my duty in speaking the truth according to my own way, in which I am determined to continue until my life ends. Now I take leave to go to my own business: God grant you long life and success! *(Exit.)*

Amir. A plague on the devilish arguments of this old fellow! They are not easily controverted; but we need not trouble our heads about them. Let us lose no time to set out for Jodhpur, and demand from Man Singh the promised reward of a *jagir* and money for my services to his state.

(Exeunt.)

ACT THE FIFTH

SCENE I.

A ROOM IN A COUNTRY HOUSE, IN THE NEIGHBOURHOOD OF UDAIPUR

Enter Amir Khan.

Amir. *(to himself)* Man Singh has already rewarded my services according to his promise. The marriages between Man Singh[*] and the sister of Jagat Singh, and another between the daughter of Man Singh and Jagat Singh have at last taken place, through my mediation.[†] This double alliance has brought on a perfect reconciliation between the Rajas of Jaipur and Jodhpur. But I am afraid it will not last long; because the beautiful Krishna Kumari still lives; of course, blind Cupid will, in course of a very short time, rekindle in both their former passion, and thus bring on another bloody war between them. Yes, there is no safety, unless this baneful cause is removed entirely. But it depends upon what will be the result of my mission to Ajit Singh[‡].

Enter Khansama.

Amir. Have you seen the *darbar* of the Maharana?[§]

Khansama. Not only seen it, Sir, but I am well informed of all the characters and dispositions of the people thereof.

Amir. Aye, that is very clever! What sort of men does it consist of?

Khansama. It consists of inconsiderate and barbarous generals, a rash soldiery, rapacious civilians, tyrannical ministers, superstitious Brahmins, crafty priests, deceitful astrologers, intriguing courtiers, prodigal nobles, ignorant relations, designing sycophants, abject slaves of both sexes, and lastly of blockheads and knaves of all descriptions.

Amir. The most ridiculous and heterogenous mass, indeed! But what are the talents of the Maharana?

---

* The original text incorrectly prints this name as Dhonkal Singh. It was Man Singh who married Jagat Singh's sister.

† The "double alliance" had originally been proposed by Ratan Lal, a sober counsellor of Jagat Singh, and not by Amir Khan, who stood to lose from the contest over Krishna Kumari ending.

‡ Ajit Singh was the *thakur* of Asind. He was a son of the Chundawat leader, Arjun Singh, the *rawat* of Kurabad, and brother-in-law to Sawai Singh. He served as Udaipur's *vakil* (representative) to Amir Khan.

§ The customary title of the Maharaja of Udaipur, indicating his preeminence amongst the Rajput clans. Literally, it means the greatest (*Maha*) ruler (*Rana*). The Maharana of Udaipur was Bhim Singh.

Khansama. Why, Sir, he is naturally a man of very good disposition. He knows how to bathe, to eat, to drink, to dress, to enjoy his pleasures, and to perform his daily worship, attend to some ridiculous unmeaning ceremonies, which either the Brahmins or astrologers now and then prescribe to appease, as they say, the wrath of some unpropitious stars and deities, but in fact to gain their own advantages.

Amir. Are there not any virtuous and wise people in the *darbar*?

Khansama. Aye, there are many; but as it is not their proper element, they only float on the surface of it, and never attempt to dive to the bottom, for fear of being devoured by some huge animals which infest it.

Amir. The Hindu Raja is a poor helpless creature, indeed; but what education do they give him in his youth?

Khansama. The Brahmins, who are entrusted with the education of the Hindu princes, generally initiate them into all their superstitious mysteries of priestcraft, then the flatterers on one side, and temptation on the other, corrupt both their head and heart to a degree exceeding belief.

Amir. Well, if this be the case, how do they govern their subjects?

Khansama. Good God! Do you think the princes govern their people? No; on the contrary, they are led on by their nose by courtiers, priests, flatterers, and women.

Amir. *(laughs)* I am quite delighted with the picture, which you have given me of the Maharana's court, and I hope I shall succeed in my design.

Khansama. So I wish you success in all your just undertakings. *(Exit.)*

Enter Jamadar.

Amir. Have you succeeded in your errand?

Jamadar. Completely, Sir; I found Ajit Singh to be a very useful man, because he is the greatest favorite of the Maharana. I think he can act his part to our satisfaction.

Amir. Can he? It is very lucky; but how is it possible for him to persuade his master so far, as to consent to put an end to the life of his lovely daughter Krishna Kumari?

Jamadar. He assured me, that he could do it easily, adding likewise, that if he did not succeed, in persuading the Raja in this case, he could effect it in some other way; and after all, he is so fond of money that I do not think he will hesitate even to sell his master's crowned head to you, if you would offer him a proper prize for it.

Amir. He seems, then, to be a man of business and activity.

Jamadar. To be sure! He is a man of spirit and partakes so much of our brave race that I cannot help doubting the chastity of his mother. Do you understand me, Sir? *(Laughs.)*

Amir. Aye, perfectly well; (*Laughs.*) But there are some among us, who are as timid as Hindus, and some among Hindus, who are as bold as Pathans; for instance, what think you about our old Khansama? Does he not resemble the talkative Brahmin, though he is a genuine Mussalman?

Jamadar. You are in the right, Sir. I think much depends on the bodily and mental powers, which everyone brings along with him into the world, according to his predestination.

Amir. Be that as it may, it is very true, that the establishment of peace and amity between the Rajas of Jaipur and Jodhpur is of great advantage to us; but the necessity we are under, to make it permanent at the expense of a poor princess' life is indeed a very disagreeable alternative: is it not?

Jamadar. Pugh! It is nothing but the common course of things. A noble, high-ranked personage, like you, must always have public good for your principal object, in attaining which, you must not hesitate to sacrifice the life of any individual whatever.

Amir. Aye, that is the strongest motive, which certainly justifies my deed! But when I consider her innocence, beauty, and other accomplishments, I cannot help pitying her.

Jamadar. Very true! But what use is her beauty to you? Can you have her for your mistress? No, never; because these rascals the Hindus, in general, consider us worse than Christians and Parriars*; and I think, we have some reason to kill her; because, she possesses killing beauty. *(Laughs.)*

Amir. *(laughs)* You are the acutest reasoner, that I ever saw in my life. Let us remain here and wait the result of our masterly scheme, which has already begun to work. *(Exeunt.)*

SCENE II.
A SALOON IN THE PALACE OF UDAIPUR

Enter the Maharana and Ajit Singh.

Maharana. Ajit Singh, why, you look so pale and pensive today —

Ajit. Pensive? To be sure! An anticipation of being buried alive in an expected earthquake must make one so.

Maharana. An earthquake? How, what do you mean?

Ajit. Why, Sir, I mean, that our kingdom shall within a few days hence be the principal seat of a destructive war, between the great potentates of Rajputana; and that we are certainly going to fall a sacrifice to the burning rage of contending parties.

Maharana. Pshaw! Foolish fears! Pray, what should be the cause of this your imaginary war?

* In nineteenth-century South India, this term referred to outcaste groups, now called Dalits, who were shunned and maltreated by caste groups.

Ajit. Cause, Sir? Your daughter; the amiable princess Krishna Kumari is the cause of it.

Maharana. My daughter the cause of war? How?

Ajit. Because, her noble birth in your most illustrious family, her incomparable beauty, and other valuable endowments have so completely fascinated the minds of all the Rajas, that every one of them is anxious to possess her hand; and in consequence, an obstinate war between these suitors is inevitable; don't you see?

Maharana. Yes, it seems probable; but why should we involve ourselves in this war? Let us remain neutral, and we shall have nothing to fear from it.

Ajit. Oh! Sir, when war rages with all its fury at the very vestibule of our palace, the neutrality on our part is impossible.

Maharana. Is it? Then let us join one of the Rajas, and try our chance in that way.

Ajit. You are in the wrong, Sir; because the prince whom you would choose for your ally, will first demand your daughter in marriage.

Maharana. Very well, let him marry her; what then?

Ajit. There you are mistaken again, because all the other disappointed suitors will form a strong confederacy against both of you; and then, having overpowered you by their united forces, will unmercifully ransack your capital, pillage your palace and make you and all your family prisoners of war; and if so, who knows, what horrible fate awaits the new married couple, in the heat of the action! Perhaps, rape will be committed and our helpless Krishna Kumari, forced by some merciless ravisher, may have recourse to suicide as the only means to save the honor of her family. As to our country, it may probably be divided among the confederate princes.

Maharana. God have mercy upon us! The picture you have just drawn seems to me more horrible than an earthquake, deluge, and even death itself; but I trust God will help suffering virtue.

Ajit. *(laughs)* These are foolish hopes! Leave them to the idle Brahmins, and let us seriously consider about some proper means to avoid the impending danger.

Maharana. Alas! What is to be done? My mind is quite perplexed! I think it advisable to declare to all the Rajas that my daughter shall marry none, but shall remain a virgin devotee all her lifetime.

Ajit. Aye, this plan will parry off the war; but as it is contrary to the law,* it will not fail to expose you to the ridicule of the people, and to bring a perpetual odium upon your noble family.

Maharana. That is right enough. The most vexatious, insurmountable difficulty indeed! I can neither marry her to any prince, nor keep her without marriage! Can you propose any method of extricating myself from this dilemma?

---

* In the sense of norm or custom.

Ajit. Yes, I think I can; but —

Maharana. Why are you embarrassed, my friend? Tell me your mind freely. You know I have no other confidant but you to depend upon in this delicate affair.

Ajit. Yes, I know; and that alone is the cause of my hesitation and embarrassment.

Maharana. Strange paradox! How is that to be accounted for?

Ajit. Why, because the measure I would propose to you is seemingly so horrible, that I cannot help trembling at the very thought of it. I attempt to speak, but the words die on my lips; and yet I think the measure is indispensably necessary, and the only one we can adopt in this critical juncture.

Maharana. Pray, don't keep me in suspense: tell me anything you think proper; I am already prepared for the worst.

Ajit. I humbly request, Your Highness will pardon my boldness — Do you remember the cruel custom, which certain tribes of Khatris* observe, when the birth of a female child takes place in their families?

Maharana. Aye, these wretches are said to put their female children to death, for want of proper means, as they say, to settle them honorably in the world, when they are grown up.

Ajit. Yes, that is it. This hint is, I think quite enough. I need say no more.

Maharana. God be merciful! Now, I understand what you mean: you would have me follow this diabolical custom! Would you? Oh, no; never! Never! My lovely Krishna Kumari is the dearest of all that I possess in the world. I will with all my heart, sacrifice my own life, to save hers! O God! Even to think of this atrocious brutality, is worse than death! Oh! What made your heart all at once so dead to every feeling? Ah! My throat is choked! No! I can utter no more.

Ajit. I know, and I have already told you, that the act is very cruel; but the public good, and the honor of your family, require that we should have recourse to some bold measure, even against the feelings of nature.

Maharana. Enough, enough! Hold your tongue! This is brutal ferocity, surely; yea, the brutes even will shame us. Ah! Never mind, let my kingdom and everything else go to ruin and destruction; but let my Krishna Kumari live!

Ajit. I own, Sir, these emotions are natural and praiseworthy in a good prince, like you; but the world, you know, is always busy in disappointing the just and persecuting the innocent.

---

* A caste group in North India, which spans Hindus and Sikhs. The reference here appears to be to the Bedis, a sub-caste of Khatris from Punjab, whom the British publicly castigated for practicing female infanticide (or *kudi-maar*). The terrible reality is that a number of North Indian communities, including the Rajputs, practiced this "diabolical custom" (see A. J. O'Brien, 'Female Infanticide in the Punjab', *Folklore*, Vol. 19, No. 3, 1908, 261–75).

Maharana. Yes: but I hope, Divine Mercy will at last be manifested in the preservation of virtue.

Ajit. Oh chimerical hopes, founded on the old-school maxims! I know the divine hands are as busy in the ruin of innocence, as in that of piety.

Maharana. Well, what then? How can we help it?

Ajit. Why, Sir, when heaven afflicts us with its injustice, you must resort to the help of the Devil to counteract it! Do you know what I mean?

Maharana. Aye, very clearly; but no, I would rather endure the afflicting hand of God, than be cured by the hand of the Devil. *(Exit.)*

Ajit Singh, alone.

Ajit. *(to himself)* A plague upon these obstacles! The Raja is so obstinate and inflexible, that I cannot persuade him to coincide with my views. Is there not any other way to put an end to the life of the princess? No, I do not think it practicable, unless some one of her immediate female servants or relations can be bribed to assist me; but whom could I employ? The least imprudence in this matter will cost me my life! Is not Chand Bai*, the aunt of Krishna Kumari, the proper person?† Yes, it is she only, who possesses manly courage and expertness, an energetic mind, not common to her sex; but here she comes.

Enter Chand Bai.

Ajit. You are welcome Chand Bai; how do you do? It is long time since I have had the honor of seeing you.

Chand. I am very well, I thank you, Sir; but what was the purport of your long conference with His Highness my brother?

Ajit. Oh, Madam, the secret upon which we conversed together is of very great importance; but the Rana your brother is inconceivably stubborn, and as immoveable as a rock, and cannot be roused to any action whatever.

Chand. Aye, that is his way; but, will you be so kind as to let me into the secret?

Ajit. Yes, I will do it on condition, that you will promise me solemnly, not to divulge it, and to assist me in this affair, as far as it lies in your power.

Chand. Oh, upon my life, I will not abuse your confidence; but only tell me what the matter is, that I may see whether I can in any way be useful to you.

---

* A respectful term for lady. Her proper name was Chandra Kumari Bai.

† Chandra Kumari Bai had been engaged to Pratap Singh, the former Maharaja of Jaipur. He died in 1803 before the marriage could be completed, whereupon Chandra Kumari Bai adopted the life of a widow and declared Jagat Singh, his son and successor, her adoptive son. Chandra Kumari Bai and Ajit Singh had led the faction in Udaipur that had encouraged the Maharana to wed Krishna Kumari to Jagat Singh (Shyamlal Das, *Vir-Vinod, Mevad Ka Itihas, Vol. 2,* New Delhi: Motilal Banarsidass, 1986, 1736). Whether Chandra Kumari Bai was involved in administering poison to Krishna Kumari is unclear. James Tod and Amir Khan do not follow John Malcolm in highlighting her role (see the Appendices).

Ajit. As to the matter, it appertains solely to the public good of the country: your familiarity with and your free access to the person of Krishna Kumari never leaves me any doubt of your success, if you will but lend your powerful aid.

Chand. You still leave me in doubt! Do you wish then to attain your object through the great, but baneful influence of this haughty princess with her father the Raja?

Ajit. No; I desire to attain my object by the total extinction of both her influence and her life at once.

Chand. Do you? That is very just. It is very true, she is a beautiful girl, but her pride is insufferable. Be that however as it may, tell me in what manner her existence proves to be repugnant to the public welfare.

Ajit. Why, Madam, the fame of her beauty, having rendered her the idol of all the princes, has multiplied the number of suitors amazingly; and the consequence is that an everlasting war is very likely to ensue among them, and our poor country is going to be crushed under its deadly weight. Do you understand me now?

Chand. Aye, quite plainly; but did you explain to my brother clearly, that the safety of his country and of himself depends entirely upon his getting rid of his daughter?

Ajit. Yes; I have exhausted all my rhetoric, and have almost silenced him by my arguments, and by pointing out to him, the well-known instance of the Khatris putting their children to death, for the sake of their honor.

Chand. Well, and what was the result?

Ajit. Why, it was quite the reverse of what I had expected; because, he seems to be resolved to preserve his daughter, at the expense of his honor, his dignity, his kingdom, and even of his own life.

Chand. Is he? A poor wrong-headed prince indeed! But, did he give you any reasons for his resolution?

Ajit. No; none whatever. His head seems to be puzzled by some old foolish maxims of morality and religion, and a jargon of words* which they contain; because, he talks of the Divine Mercy, the rewards and punishments in the next world, the advantages of virtue and a good conscience, and many such things besides.

Chand. Pugh! Nonsense! He must have imbibed these romantic notions from some idle Brahmins, I assure you; but since he thinks so highly of the happiness of the next world, why does he hesitate to send his daughter thither a little sooner?

Ajit. *(laughs)* Your reasons are very strong; but your brother is so weak, that nothing can rouse him from his mental lethargy—and none can persuade him to act like a prince: therefore let us give him up for lost, and for his sake and for his country's, let us rather bestir ourselves in this affair, and effect by our united exertions that which pure philanthropy requires of us. Do you know?

---

* A nineteenth-century English phrase, "a jargon of words" means balderdash or nonsense.

Chand. Yes, I do; and I know likewise how to settle this business in the genteelest manner possible; but the reward I expect for my trouble must be proportionate to the risk I run in this case.

Ajit. Aye, to be sure; Amir Khan will take care of that. But for the present accept this from me, as a token of my esteem. *(Gives her a purse full of gold mohurs.)*

Chand. I thank you for your liberality. (*Exit.)*

Ajit. *(to himself)* The appearances are promising and indicate speedy success. I must lose no time to inform Amir Khan of what has passed: and this opportunity must not be suffered to slip. A proper arrangement must be made about the reward, which he has offered me; for these men of business will soon forget their promises, when they have attained their purpose. No! I will not be deceived though. As to Chand Bai, I have in the meantime satisfied her with some trifles; and in regard to my other promises, she need not be oversanguine. *(Exit.)*

SCENE III.
AN ELEGANT APARTMENT OF KRISHNA KUMARI

Enter Krishna Kumari and her maid.

Krishna. It is true, my father intends to marry me soon to some virtuous prince of his own choosing; but then I must have a new set of superior jewels, adorned with gems, which will suit the occasion, and set off my person to advantage. Don't you think so?

Maid. Yes; those glittering pebbles are necessary to those only who would dazzle the eyes of their lovers by the luster of these stones; because they know their persons alone are not capable of doing it. But as for *you,* whose charms are so captivating, I do not think you need any such auxiliaries to enchant the world.

Krishna. I thank you for your compliment; but I doubt whether my intended husband will be of your opinion?

Maid. You may try if you like, and see whether there is any man in this world, who can be a proof against that pair of sparkling eyes. Is not that bewitching smile alone capable of melting any adamantine heart, though it be proof against every soft passion?

Krishna. You may flatter me in any way you like, but the mirror tells me, that my face has nothing extraordinary in it.

Maid. Your modesty and humility are the finishing touches of heaven, which give your person an air of negligent beauty, equal to that of Venus, I assure you; but here comes your aunt, she wishes perhaps to speak with you in private. I must retire now. *(Exit.)*

Enter Chand Bai, with a grave melancholy countenance.

Krishna. How do you do, my dear aunt? What makes your bright visage so pale today?

Chand. Aye, my love, my health is as good as I can wish it to be; but I am so dismayed by some unpropitious circumstances, that I cannot by any efforts whatever prevent my face from betraying the disordered state of my mind.

Krishna. You frighten me, indeed! Pray, will you be so kind as to let me know what those circumstances are?

Chand. Yes, I will; but the very blood of my heart freezes within me, when I attempt acquaint you with the cause of my sorrow; for the shock, which it must give to your mind, will be too violent to be borne by your tender frame.

Krishna. Well, if it be so, I think it necessary that I should insist on knowing it.

Chand. Then, I must tell you plainly, that you alone are the sole cause of our misfortune; for your extraordinary beauty, your good disposition, excellent sense and many other superior qualities, instead of being a blessing to our family, are unluckily become the scourge of whole Rajputana, so that the ruin of our country and family is inevitable. Do you understand?

Krishna. Not clearly. God have mercy! I, the cause of ruin? How is that?

Chand. Be composed; I will explain the matter fully. They say, that the fame of your beauty and other accomplishments, having multiplied the number of your suitors, who are potentates of Rajputana, a very destructive war is soon to break out among them, and our country and capital are very likely to fall a sacrifice to the rage of the parties; and in consequence, the honor of our family is at stake; because the furious invaders will not fail to commit all sorts of excesses: and then, as to the safety of our persons, what think you about it? No! for shame I cannot proceed farther — my voice fails me.

Krishna. Now I understand your meaning. Alas! I am an unfortunate wretch! Would to God, I had not been born at all in this family!

Chand. Oh, my dear, it would have been better indeed! But it is too late now to wish so; all the members of our family are thrown into such a consternation, that they are at a loss how to extricate themselves from the danger which threatens them. As to your parents, their grief knows no bounds, and they intend — no, my tongue denies me utterance.

Krishna. Why do you hesitate, my dear aunt? Go on, let me know the worst. What is their intention, pray?

Chand. Oh, my dear, I tremble at the very thought, but I cannot help mentioning. They seem to be determined to put an end to their own existence; because they know that death alone can rescue them from the woeful misery of seeing, with their own eyes, the pillage of their capital, and the dishonorable treatment of their family.

Krishna. God have mercy upon them! These are most horrible news indeed! But why did they not all this time inform me of these dreadful circumstances? Why are they so circumspect in their conversation with me?

Chand. They have their reasons to be so, because they dare not vex you, whom they love more than their life.

Krishna. Very true; that appears to be the case; but is there not any way to prevent this misfortune? May we not at least hope the intercession of Heaven in behalf of such virtuous parents? *(Weeps.)*

Chand. Ah! Poor, innocent, lovely creature! Now-a-days, virtue being the victim of vice, and innocence a prey to intrigue, alas we cannot expect any such miracle in our favor. *(Pretends to weep.)*

Krishna. Is God then so cruel, as to suffer us poor helpless creatures to perish by the injustice of our merciless enemies?

Chand. Why, is not the blindness of the divine decree become quite proverbial among the learned? And does not the wrath of Heaven descend on both the criminal and innocent promiscuously? Are not the most detestable barbarians and tyrants always victorious and prosperous in the world, while the poor are subjected to their tyrannical sway? Are not whole nations, which consist of good and wicked, either swept away by war and pestilence, or swallowed up by earthquakes or volcanoes? Therefore, we must not cherish the foolish hopes of any help from above.

Krishna. The most shocking truths indeed! But what think you about the blessings, which are promised to the votaries of virtue in the next world?

Chand. Aye, our books and Brahmins always assure us, that perfect happiness is not to be found in this, but only in the world to come.

Krishna. Do they? Then I think it will be both prudent and necessary to bid farewell to this miserable world, and flee to the happy regions of paradise.

Chand. A very bold step indeed! But it is not an uncommon one, in India; because some virtuous individuals of our sex burn themselves with their dead husbands, for fear of dishonor incident to widowhood. Among us, you know, these are called *satis.**

Krishna. Yes, now I think on it: your argument is a very decisive one. This noble instance of self-devotion and voluntary death of *satis* has strengthened my resolution of finishing my wretched career.

Chand. Oh, mercy on me! Are you then resolved to put an end to your life?

Krishna. I am; because nothing else can save the life of my parents, the state of Udaipur, and the honor of my noble family.

Chand. Ah! What do I hear? Every one of your words pierces my heart, like a fiery arrow. I will most willingly sacrifice my own life to save yours; but alas *(pretends to weep)* it will not avail anything.

Krishna. Now, my dear aunt, you shall not die, it is I that deserve it; because I am charged with the capital crime of having beauty. *(Weeps.)*

---

* The practice of a widow being cremated alongside the corpse of her husband. Though enacted in various Hindu principalities in medieval India, British travelogues led to this rite being especially associated with Rajputs.

Chand. No, my dear, can I screen this valuable gem, this angel, from the eyes of people by flight? No vain attempt can conceal her shining beauty!

Krishna. My beauty, call it rather my misfortune: it is my malady. And I am resolved to be cured of it by a dose or two of poison. Yes, that is the surest specific. Will you be so kind as to procure me a potion of it?

Chand. I, to procure you poison? Mercy on me! No, I dare not even think of it. *(Trembles.)*

Krishna. Pshaw, my dear aunt, do not indulge this weakness; throw it aside, and be useful to me this last time. I am resolved to surpass *sati* by my courage; come, make haste, go and fetch me a chalice of powerful poison. Won't you?

Chand. No, my dear, I will not; I would rather die than to render you this dismal service.

Krishna. Well, then, if you deprive me of these gentle means, the poniard* may as well decide my fate; but no, I cannot handle it well; the tank or well, anything will serve my purpose, you know?

Chand. Ah! Is it come to that extremity? Well, then, I will go, and bring the chalice: let us both taste it at once, and leave this world together. *(Aside)* This scene affects me in spite of myself. My heart begins to palpitate violently! But no, since I have begun, I must finish it. *(Goes and returns with a chalice, which she fills and presents to Krishna Kumari.)*

Krishna. *(to the cup)* Well, my friend, I choose you as the safest vehicle, to carry me to the next world! O woeful world! Adieu to you and your miseries, forever! *(Drinks.)* Aye, it is as bitter as my life! Well, my dear aunt, fill me another.

Chand. *(fills another cup, with tears in her eyes)* Oh my dear, I will not survive you *(attempts to carry it to her mouth, under pretense of drinking it herself, but Krishna Kumari snatches it from her)*

Krishna. No, my dear aunt, you shall live, and let my parents know, that I die for them and their country. Do you know? O God! have mercy upon my soul (*Drinks.*) Ah! It operates already. Strange sensations! I know death approaches; but enough. Give me more —

(Chand Bai gives her a third cup, which Krishna Kumari applies to her mouth, exclaiming aloud, with a faltering voice.) Oh God! This is the marriage to which I was foredoomed. *(Drinks, falls convulsed on her pillow, and dies. Chand Bai rushes out of the apartment, and gives the alarm of the sudden death of the princess.)*

Enter Queen, with some of her female attendants.

Queen. Oh! my Krishna Kumari, my dear, my love, my angel, where are you gone? Why have you left me behind? Will not you speak with me? Oh! What has become of

* A slender, tapered dagger.

your sweet words? Where are your smiles? Alas! Everything is hushed in deadly silence! All is over! My hopes are frustrated! I am undone! I am ruined! No, I can't endure! Gloomy darkness surrounds me everywhere! I can see nothing — *(She falls down in a deep swoon, and is carried away by her servants.)*[*]

SCENE CHANGES TO A GREAT PLACE OF AUDIENCE, CROWDED BY COURTIERS, SERVANTS, &.c.

Enter the Maharana, supported by Ajit Singh and servants, sobbing; his face bedewed with tears, which flow in torrents from his eyes.

Maharana. *(leaning on his pillow)* O! Ajit Singh! Why did God hurl such dreadful thunder upon my head? Alas! What could have been her motive in killing herself by poison?

Ajit. God knows, what it was; but it is more than probable that, being well informed of the dangers with which this kingdom is threatened on her account, she might have chosen this way of putting an end to her life, and thereby to all troubles, at once.

Enter Sangram Singh, the Chief of Sardargarh,[†] *almost breathless.*

Sangram. *(to the Maharana)* Is the princess dead or alive?

Ajit. Do not disturb the grief of a father for a lost child.

Sangram. *(unbuckling his sword, which with his shield he lays at the feet of the Maharana)* My ancestors have served yours more than thirty generations, and to you I cannot utter what I feel; but these arms shall never more be used in your service. *(to Ajit Singh.)* As for you, villain, who hast brought this ignominy upon the Rajput name, may the curse of a father light upon you! May you die childless![‡]

(Exeunt.)

THE END

---

[*] This was Chawadi Bai. She fasted unto death a few days hence.

[†] Subba Rao followed John Malcolm in mistakenly describing Sangram Singh as the chief of Kurabar (now known as Kurabad), which was in fact the stronghold of the Chundawat clan. Sangram Singh was a prominent figure in the rival Shaktawat clan, whose bastion at the time was Sardargarh.

[‡] Incredibly, Ajit Singh lost his wife and two sons shortly after this event. The shock led him to take up, temporarily, the life of a penitent. He continued however to play a central role in the *darbar*. In 1818 he signed, on Bhim Singh's behalf, the treaty that brought Udaipur under British protection.

APPENDICES

In the following extracts, original footnotes are marked by symbols and editorial comments are marked by numerals.

An Extract from *A Memoir of Central India*[1]

[. . .] The history of Amir Khan is comprehended in that of Jaswant Rao till their separation [. . .] He at that period entered the service of Jagat Singh, Raja of Jaipur, who engaged his aid in an approaching contest with the Raja of Jodhpur, for the disputed hand of the daughter of the Udaipur Rana.[*] The latter family is the highest in rank among the Rajputs, and an alliance with it has always been esteemed the greatest honour to which a prince of that tribe can aspire. The princess Krishna Kumari added to her high birth the reputation of extraordinary beauty. She had been betrothed to the deceased Bhim Singh, Raja of Jodhpur. On his death Man Singh,[†] a distant relation, succeeded to the throne, but two years afterwards Sawai Singh (who had been minister to Bhim Singh) brought forward a real or supposed son of that prince, in support of whose claims he formed a strong party, and as one means of accomplishing his ends, he used every effort to render the princes of Jodhpur and Jaipur implacable enemies. With the knowledge that Man Singh cherished hopes of obtaining the hand of the Udaipur princess, Sawai Singh instigated Jagat Singh,[‡] the Raja of Jaipur, to demand her in marriage, and this prince, inflamed by the accounts of her beauty, fell immediately into the snare. A negotiation was opened with the Rana of Udaipur for the hand of his daughter, and the marriage seemed at one period certain, but the art of Sawai Singh was farther employed to prevent such a result, and the Raja of Jodhpur was excited not only to insist upon his prior claim to the hand of the disputed princess, but to adopt violent measures to arrest the progress of his rival's suit.

---

1 John Malcolm, *A Memoir of Central India, Vol. I*, London: Kingsbury, Parbury & Allen, 1824, 329–42.

* The celebrated but now fallen family of the Rajas or princes of Udaipur are considered by many (I believe erroneously) to be descended from Porus, who opposed the progress of Alexander the Great. There can, however, be no doubt that they are among the most ancient and renowned of the princes of India, and that they formerly possessed the whole of that tract now termed Rajputana, or the country of the Rajputs, which is situated between the western part of the province of Agra and the northeast of Gujarat. It has Malwa as its boundary to the east, and the Sandy Desert to the west. Its extreme length is computed at 330 miles, and its breadth in the broadest part 200. The chief states are the Rajas of Jaipur, Jodhpur, and Udaipur. The territories of the former are the most fertile. Those of Jodhpur, or Marwar, as it is more commonly called, are still very extensive, while Udaipur, or Mewar, is now a limited and desolate principality, but it is fast reviving under the liberal protection it has received from the British government. The whole of Rajputana is a succession of hills and narrow valleys.

† It was settled at Man Singh's elevation, that if any of the Ranis had a son, he should be Raja. This posthumous pretender to the throne was not brought forward for two years, and the circumstance of the reputed mother (Sawai Singh's sister) denying the fact that its being hers, and his being brought forward by Sawai Singh, a discontented minister, has led to a belief, that the child Dhonkal Singh was spurious. The point, however, appears never to have been clearly established.

‡ Jagat Singh was a weak, dissolute prince, who devoted himself to sensual pleasures. The history of his low amours, and of those who were elevated by him as favourites, would be received as an incredible tale. Ruskapur, a Mohammadan dancing-girl, was raised to the first rank in the principality. He followed himself in her train of attendants, and gave her great estates. The high Rajput females of his family were ordered to salute and visit her as their superior, but they rejected the command, offering to swallow poison or stab themselves if he desired it, but they never would, they said, condescend to the degradation of placing themselves on a level with a female of her character.

It is neither necessary to detail the intrigues that took place, nor to enter into the particulars of the war that ensued: every feeling that could excite Rajput princes to desperate hostility was inflamed, and assistance was solicited from all quarters. The British government was in vain entreated to interfere.* Sindhia gave his countenance to enable two of his most unprincipled partisans, Bapuji Sindhia and Sirji Rao Ghatke, to support their predatory bands upon the quarrels of these Rajput chiefs, while Holkar made them, as has been before stated, the still more baneful present of Amir Khan and his Pathans. The consequence was, the almost complete destruction of both principalities. That of Jaipur expended, at the lowest computation, one crore and twenty lakhs of rupees in prosecution of this unhappy war, which, although successful at the commencement, terminated in disgrace and defeat.

Sawai Singh, when he saw Man Singh completely involved, renewed his demand in favour of Dhonkal Singh, the posthumous prince, whose pretensions he supported. On the Raja's having recourse to evasion, he not only left him, but prevailed upon almost every other chief to desert, and Man Singh, who had taken the field, was, in consequence obliged to fly, attended by only a few adherents, leaving his camp to be plundered by Jagat Singh and his auxiliaries. The misfortunes of Man Singh did not terminate with this reverse: he was pursued to Jodhpur, and his whole country was overrun by his enemies. Dhonkal Singh was proclaimed Raja, and the allegiance of almost every Rathore chief transferred to the young prince. The contest appeared decided, yet still the courage of Man Singh, and of the few troops who remained faithful to him, was unsubdued. He had early endeavored to divide his enemies, and the difficulties attendant on a lengthened siege now promoted his efforts. Amir Khan listened to his overtures, and, on the usual pretext of want of pay, separated from the besieging army, and began to plunder and levy contributions indiscriminately over the districts of Jodhpur and Jaipur. The interest of almost every chief of the latter state was affected by his excesses in laying waste his lands, and their clamors obliged Jagat Singh to detach a force to punish the Pathan leader, who at first retreated towards Tonk, but having been reinforced by some battalions and guns, he attacked and defeated the Jaipur troops. After this success, which was very complete, Amir Khan was expected at Jaipur, the inhabitants of which were thrown into great consternation, but on this, as on many other occasions, he showed that he was only a leader of freebooters. Shunning, from apprehension of danger, the great prize of victory, he contented himself with plundering in the vicinity of the capital, which was out of danger the moment that its inhabitants recovered from their panic.

The intelligence of the discomfiture of the Jaipur troops spread such dismay and confusion in the besieging army, that Jagat Singh determined to return to his capital, and offered a large sum to the auxiliaries sent by Sindhia to convey him there in safety. The cannon and spoils taken in his first action were sent in front, and some Rathore chiefs, who had remained faithful to Man Singh, but, from becoming objects of his

* When I was at Delhi with Lord Lake in 1805, every argument was tried, and every offer made by the Jaipur *vakils* to engage me to become the advocate of their master's cause, and to give him the support of an English force. Aid from the British government was subsequently solicited by the Raja of Jodhpur, who desired to purchase it by cessions of territory.

suspicion, had been obliged to leave Jodhpur, now determined to give their prince a convincing proof of their fidelity, and having concerted an attack upon the troops escorting the trophies of their country's disgrace, they completely defeated them, retook forty pieces of ordnance, with much other booty, and, having effected a junction with Amir Khan, marched with that chief in triumph to Jodhpur.

The fortunes of Man Singh were restored by these events, but, while his enemy Sawai Singh lived, he entertained the most serious apprehensions. That chief had taken refuge in Nagaur. The Raja entreated Amir Khan to march against him, and made him an advance of two lakhs of rupees, promising future wealth and favour as the reward of success in this important enterprise. The Pathan leader undertook the service, but seems from the first to have trusted more to art than force, for its accomplishment. He moved to within a few miles of Nagaur, and under a pretext of discontent, caused by some discoveries he had made of the ingratitude of Man Singh, he made overtures to establish a connection with Sawai Singh. The latter suspected treachery, but the officer employed by Amir Khan, pledged himself for the fidelity of his commandant, and obtained a promise that he would visit his leader. The Rajput chief faltered when the time for fulfilling his promise arrived, but Amir Khan went to meet him, and succeeded, by protestations and oaths, in lulling him into complete security. The consequence was, he went to the camp of his supposed friend, and was murdered,* with the great majority of those by whom he was accompanied. Though Sawai Singh, as the author of a war which brought ruin on his country, may be considered to have merited his fate, that fact in no degree extenuates the deep guilt of Amir Khan, who evinced on this occasion that he was alike destitute of humanity and principle.

[. . .] Amir Khan [later] became the chief actor in a tragedy, in which a good end was obtained by a deed which revolts every feeling of humanity. A reconciliation between the Rajas of Jaipur and Jodhpur was an object of just and wise policy, and it suited the

---

* The following is an account of this transaction, as stated by a respectable eyewitness:

"Mahomed Shah Khan succeeded by his protestations in persuading Sawai Singh to promise a visit to Amir Khan, but when the hour came, the Rajput chief, who probably had received some intelligence of the designs against his life, hesitated. Amir Khan, when he learned his irresolution, mounted, and proceeded with a few followers to the shrine of a Mahomedan saint, close to the walls of Nagaur. He was here joined by Sawai Singh, whom he reproached for his fears, and asked him if he thought it possible that a man who cherished evil designs, could shew such confidence as he had that day done, by placing himself in the power of the person he meant to betray? Sawai Singh confessed his error. Presents, dresses and even turbans (a pledge of brotherhood) were exchanged, and Amir Khan swore, at the tomb of the saint, to be faithful to his new ally, who was persuaded to go next day to his camp, where splendid preparations were made for his reception, and a number of chiefs appointed to meet him. The troops were under arms, some on pretext of doing honour to the visitor, others apparently at exercise. The guns were loaded with grape, and pointed at the quarters prepared for the Raja, who with his principal adherents, to the number of two hundred, were seated in a large tent, when it was let fall upon them at a concerted signal, and while the officers of Amir Khan saved themselves, all the Rajputs were inhumanly massacred by showers of grape and musketry from every direction. Of seven hundred horse that accompanied Sawai Singh, and continued mounted near the tent, only two hundred escaped; the rest were slain, and a number of Amir Khan's people, among whom was one of his own relations, fell under the promiscuous fire of the cannon. Sawai Singh had been killed by grape, but his head was cut off and sent to Man Singh, who rewarded Amir Khan with a *jagir* and a large sum of money."

views of the Pathan chief to promote its accomplishment. It was proposed, that this should be effected by a double marriage. Jagat Singh was to espouse the daughter of Man Singh, and the latter the sister of his rival and enemy. To propitiate these nuptials, it was conceived that the honour of all parties required the death of Krishna Kumari, the princess of Udaipur. The question of this sacrifice was agitated when Amir Khan was at Udaipur, and that chief urged it strongly on the counsellors* of the Prince, representing the difficulty of establishing peace while the cause of the war existed, and then pointing out the impossibility, without offending the two most powerful Rajput rulers in India, of giving his daughter to any other chief. To these he added arguments well suited to the high, though mistaken, pride of a Rajput, regarding the disgrace of having in his family an unmarried daughter.

It is stated, and for the honour of human nature let us believe it, that neither arguments nor threats could induce the father to become the executioner of his child, or even to urge her to suicide. But his sister Chand Bai[2] was gained to the cruel cause of policy and she presented the chalice to Krishna Kumari, entreating her to save her father, family, and tribe, from the struggles and miseries to which her high birth and evil destiny exposed them. The appeal was not in vain: she drank three poisoned cups, and before she took the last, which proved instantly fatal, she exclaimed, "This is the marriage to which I was foredoomed."

All were acquainted with what was passing in the palace, and the extraordinary beauty and youth of the victim excited a feeling, which was general in a degree that is rare among the inhabitants of India. This account is written from the report of several persons who were on the spot, and they agree in stating that the particulars of Krishna Kumari's death were no sooner spread through the town of Udaipur than loud lamentations burst from every quarter, and expressions of pity at her fate were mingled with execrations on the weakness and cowardice of those who could purchase safety on such terms. In a short period after this tragical event, the public feeling was again excited by the death of the mother of the princess, who never recovered [from] the shock she received at the first intelligence of the fate of her beautiful† and cherished daughter.

If it is to the disgrace of the nobility of Udaipur that one of them (Ajit Singh, a man of high rank, who possessed unbounded influence over the mind of his prince) proved base enough to act throughout as the instrument of Amir Khan, the character of this proud race was redeemed by the conduct of Sangram Singh, chief of Sardargarh,[3] who,

---

2 The correct name is Chandra Kumari Bai. Her role is not cited in any subsequent account of the event.

3 The original text mistakenly cites this as Karradur, a poor transliteration of Kurabar, which is now known as Kurabad.

* He is stated never to have proposed it direct to the Rana. The *thakur*, Ajit Singh, of [Asind], was the Rajput lord, who is reproached with being his instrument upon this memorable occasion.

† I visited the court of Udaipur in March 1821, eleven years after the occurrence of the events I have stated, and possessed complete means of verifying every fact. I could have no doubt of the beauty of Krishna Kumari, after seeing her brother Jawan Singh, the present heir to the *musnud*, whom she is said to have exactly resembled. His complexion is very fair, and his features are fine, and though they have the softness which characterizes Hindu physiognomy, they are full of animation and intelligence.

the moment he heard of the proceedings in the palace, hastened from his residence to Udaipur, and dismounting from a breathless horse, went unceremoniously into the presence of his prince, whom he found seated with several of his ministers in apparent affliction. "Is the princess dead or alive?" was his impatient interrogation, to which, after a short pause, Ajit Singh replied by intreating him "not to disturb the grief of a father for a "lost child." The old chief immediately unbuckled his sword, which, with his shield, he laid at the feet of the Maharana,* saying, in a calm but resolute tone, "My ancestors have served yours for more than thirty generations, and to you I cannot utter what I feel, but these arms shall never more be used in your service. As to you, villain!" he exclaimed, turning to Ajit Singh, "who have brought this ignominy upon the Rajput name, may the curse of a father light upon you! May you die childless!" He retired from the assembly, leaving, according to the account of those that were present, an impression of awe and horror in the minds of all who heard him. Sangram Singh lived for eight years after this occurrence, but, though he continued in his allegiance, he never could be prevailed upon to resume his arms. The last child of Ajit Singh died a short time ago, and the event was deemed by the superstitious Rajputs a fulfilment of the curse that had been pronounced upon him. He maintained his influence over the mind of his weak prince till very lately, when he was disgraced,† to the joy of the inhabitants of Udaipur, who continued to consider him as the chief cause of the self-murder of their regretted princess.

* Maharana means Great Prince, the title by which the rulers of Udaipur are always distinguished.

† The intelligence of his disgrace, and the sentiments of joy it had caused, were communicated to me by Captain [James] Todd, Political Agent at Udaipur, in June 1821.

An Extract from *The Annals and Antiquities of Rajasthan*[1]

[. . .] It would be imagined that the miseries of Rana Bhim were not susceptible of aggravation, and that fortune had done her worst to humble him, but his pride as a sovereign and his feelings as a parent were destined to be yet more deeply wounded. The Jaipur cortege had encamped near the capital, to the number of three thousand men, while the Rana's acknowledgements of acceptance were dispatched, and had reached Shahpura. But Raja Man of Marwar also advanced pretensions, founded on the princess having been actually betrothed to his predecessor, and urging that the throne of Marwar, and not the individual occupant, was the object, he vowed resentment and opposition if his claims were disregarded. These were suggested, it is said, by his nobles to cloak their own views, and promoted by the Chundawats (then in favor with the Rana), whose organ, Ajit, was bribed to further them, contrary to the decided wishes of their prince.

Krishna Kumari (the Virgin Krishna) was the name of the lovely object, the rivalry for whose hand assembled under the banners of her suitors (Jagat Singh of Jaipur, and Raja Man of Marwar), not only their native chivalry, but all the predatory powers of India, and who like Helen of old, [was] involved in [the] destruction [of] her own and the rival houses. Sindhia having been denied a pecuniary demand by Jaipur, not only opposed the nuptial, but aided the claims of Raja Man, by demanding of the Rana the dismissal of the Jaipur embassy, which being refused, he advanced his brigades and batteries, and after a fruitless resistance, in which the Jaipur troops joined, forced the pass, threw a corps of eight thousand men into the valley, and following in person, encamped within cannon-range of the city. The Rana had now no alternative but to dismiss the nuptial cortege, and agree to whatever was demanded. Sindhia remained a month in the valley, during which an interview took place between him and the Rana at the shrine of Eklinga.[*]

The heralds of Hymen being thus rudely repulsed and its symbols intercepted, the Jaipur prince prepared to avenge his insulted pride and disappointed hopes, and

---

1 James Tod, *Annals and Antiquities of Rajasthan, Vol. I & Vol. II*, Calcutta: The Society for the Resuscitation of Indian Literature, 1902, 198–203.

* To increase his importance, Sindhia invited the British envoy and suite to be present on the occasion, when the princely demeanor of the Rana and his sons was advantageously contrasted with that of the Maratha and his suite. It was in this visit that the regal abode of this ancient race, its isles and palaces, acted with irresistible force on the cupidity of this *scion of the plough*, who aspired to, yet dared not sit himself in, "the halls of Caesars." It was even surmised that his hostility to Jaipur was not so much from the refused war-contribution, as from a mortifying negative to an audacious desire to obtain the hand of this princess himself. The impression made on the author upon this occasion by the miseries and noble appearance of "this descendant of a hundred kings," was never allowed to weaken, but kindled an enthusiastic desire for the restoration of his fallen condition, which stimulated his perseverance to obtain that knowledge by which alone he might be enabled to benefit him. Then a young Sub [Subaltern], his hopes of success were more sanguine than wise, but he trusted to the rapid march of events, and the discordant elements by which he was surrounded, to effect the redemption of the prince from thraldom. It was long a dream—but after ten years of anxious hope, at length realized—and he had the gratification of being instrumental in snatching the family from destruction, and subsequently of raising the country to comparative prosperity.

accordingly arrayed a force such as had not assembled since the empire was in its glory. Raja Man eagerly took up the gauntlet of his rival, and headed "the swords of Maru."[2] But dissension prevailed in Marwar, where rival claimants for the throne had divided the loyalty of the clans, introducing there also the influence of the Marathas. Raja Man, who had acquired the scepter by party aid, was obliged to maintain himself by it, and to pursue the demoralizing policy of the period by ranging his vassals against each other. These nuptials gave the malcontents an opportunity to display their long-curbed resentments, and following the example of Mewar, they set up a pretender, whose interests were eagerly espoused, and whose standard was erected in the array of Jaipur.

The [Jaipur] prince at the head of 120,000 men advancing against his rival, who with less than half the number met him at Parbatsar, on their mutual frontier. The action was short, for while a heavy cannonade opened on either side, the majority of the Marwar nobles went over to the pretender. Raja Man turned his poniard against himself, but some chiefs yet faithful to him wrested the weapon from his hand, and conveyed him from the field. He was pursued to his capital, which was invested, besieged, and gallantly defended during six months. The town was at length taken and plundered, but the castle of Joda[3] "laughed a siege to scorn," in time with the aid of finesse, the mighty host of Jaipur, which had consumed the forage of these arid plains for twenty miles around, began to crumble away, intrigue spread through every rank, and the siege ended in pusillanimity and flight. The Xerxes of Rajwada,[4] the effeminate Kachwaha,[5] alarmed at length for his personal safety, sent on the spoils of Parbatsar and Jodhpur to his capital, but the brave nobles of Marwar, drawing the lines between loyalty and patriotism, and determined that no trophy of Rathore degradation should be conveyed by the Kachwahas from Marwar, attacked the cortege and redeemed the symbols of their disgrace. The colossal array of the invader was soon dismembered, and the "lion of the world" (Jagat Singh) humbled and crestfallen, skulked from the desert retreat of his rival, indebted to a partisan corps for safety and convoy to his capital, around whose walls the wretched remnants of this ill-starred confederacy long lagged in expectation of their pay, while the bones of their horses and the ashes of their riders whitened the plain, and rendered it a Golgotha.[*6]

By the aid of one of the most notorious villains India ever produced, the Nawab Amir Khan, the pretender's party was treacherously annihilated. This man with his brigade of artillery and horse was amongst the most efficient of the foes of Raja Man, but the *auri*

---

2 A Rajasthani term, deriving from Sanskrit, meaning "the desert."

3 Referring to the famed Mehrangarh Fort, which was built in the fifteenth century by Rao Jodha, the founder of Jodhpur.

4 The vernacular name for Rajasthan, meaning the abode or land of kings.

5 The Rajput clan that founded Jaipur, who were scorned for submitting to the Mughals. They served in Mughal armies and married their daughters to Mughal rulers.

6 A Biblical phrase, referring to the place where Jesus was crucified, a skull-shaped hill called Golgotha (from the Aramaic word for skull). Tod thus means a place of suffering and death.

* I witnessed the commencement and the end of this drama, and have conversed with actors in all the intermediate scenes. In June 1806 the passes of Udaipur were forced, and in January 1808, when I passed through Jaipur in a solitary ramble, the fragments of this contest were scattered over its sandy plains.

sacra fames[7] not only made him desert the side on which he came for that of the Raja, but for a specific sum offer to rid him of the pretender and all his associates. Like Judas, he kissed whom he betrayed, took service with the pretender, and at the shrine of a saint of his own faith exchanged turbans with their leaders, and while the too credulous Rajput chieftains celebrated this acquisition to their party in the very sanctuary of hospitality, crowned by the dance and the song, the tents were cut down, and the victims thus enveloped, slaughtered in the midst of festivity by showers of grape.

Thus finished the underplot, but another and more noble victim was demanded before discomfited ambition could repose, or the curtain drop on this eventful drama. Neither party would relinquish his claim to the fair object of the war, and the torch of discord could be extinguished only in her blood. To the same ferocious Khan is attributed the unhallowed suggestion, as well as its compulsory execution. The scene was now changed from the desert castle of Joda to the smiling valley of Udaipur, soon to be filled with funeral lamentation.

Krishna Kumari Bai, the "Virgin Princess Krishna," was in her sixteenth year, her mother was of the Chavda race, the ancient kings of Anahilavada.[8] Sprung from the noblest blood of Hind, she added beauty of face and person to an engaging demeanor, and was justly proclaimed the "flower of Rajasthan." When the Roman father pierced the bosom of the dishonored Virginia, appeased virtue applauded the deed. When Iphigenia was led to the sacrificial altar, the salvation of her country yielded a noble consolation. The votive victim of Jeptha's success had the triumph of a father's fame to sustain her resignation, and in the meekness of her sufferings we have the best parallel to the sacrifice of the lovely Krishna, though years have passed since the barbarous immolation, it is never related but with a faltering tongue and moistened eyes, "albeit unused to the melting mood."[9]

The rapacious and bloodthirsty Pathan, covered with infamy, repaired to Udaipur, where he was joined by the pliant and subtle Ajit. Meek in his demeanor, unostentatious in his habits, despising honors, yet covetous of power, religion, which he followed with the zeal of an ascetic, if it did not serve as a cloak, was at least no hindrance to an immeasurable ambition, in the attainment of which he would have sacrificed all but himself. When the Pathan revealed his design, that either the princess should wed Raja Man, or by her death seal the peace of Rajwada, whatever arguments were used to point the alternative, the Rana was made to see no choice between consigning his beloved child to the Rathore prince, or witnessing the effects of a more extended dishonor from the vengeance of the Pathan, and the storm of his palace by his licentious adherents: the fiat passed that Krishna Kumari should die.

---

7 A line from Vergil's *Aeneid*, typically translated as the "sacred hunger for pernicious gold" (Vergil, *Aeneid*, trans. John Dryden, New York: P.F. Collier and Son, 1909, 3.57).

8 Anahilvada, now known as Patan in Gujarat, was founded in 746 CE by Vanraj Chavda. The Chavda dynasty ruled the region until 942 CE.

9 A line from Othello's farewell speech (William Shakespeare, "Othello, The Moor of Venice" in *The Complete Works of William Shakespeare*, Philadelphia: Gebbie & Co., 1891, 404).

But the deed was left for women to accomplish—the hand of man refused it. The *Rawula*[10] of an eastern prince is a world within itself: it is the labyrinth containing the strings that move the puppets which alarm mankind. Here intrigue sits enthroned, and hence its influence radiates to the world, always at a loss to trace effects to their causes. Maharaja Daulat Singh,[*] descended four generations ago from one common ancestors with the Rana, was first sounded "to save the honor of Udaipur," but, horrorstruck, he exclaimed, "accursed the tongue that commands it! Dust on my allegiance, if thus to be preserved!" The Maharaja Jawan Das, a natural brother, was then called upon, the dire necessity was explained, and it was urged that no common hand could be armed for the purpose. He accepted the poniard, but when in youthful loveliness Krishna appeared before him, the dagger fell from his hand, and he returned more wretched than the victim. The fatal purpose thus revealed, the shrieks of the frantic mother reverberated through the palace, as she implored mercy, or execrated the murderers of her child, who alone was resigned to her fate. But death was arrested, not averted. To use the phrase of the narrator, "she was excused the steel—the cup was prepared"—and prepared by female hands! As the messenger presented it in the name of her father, she bowed and drank it, sending up a prayer for his life and prosperity. The raving mother poured imprecations on his head, while the lovely victim, who shed not a tear, thus endeavored to console her: "Why afflict yourself, my mother, at this shortening of the sorrows of life? I fear not to die! Am I not your daughter? Why should I fear death? We are marked out for sacrifice from our birth.[†] We scarcely enter the world but to be sent out again. Let me thank my father that I have lived so long!"[‡] Thus she conversed till the nauseating draught refused to assimilate with her blood. Again the bitter potion was prepared. She drained it off, and again it was rejected, but, as if to try the extreme of human fortitude, a third was administered, and, for the third time, Nature refused to aid the horrid purpose. It seemed as if the fabled charm, which guarded the life of the founder of her race,[11] was inherited by the Virgin Krishna. But the bloodhounds, the Pathan and Ajit, were impatient till their victim was at rest, and cruelty, as if gathering strength from defeat, made another and a fatal attempt. A powerful opiate was presented—the *kasoomba* draught.[§] She received it with a smile, wished the scene over and drank it.

---

10 A Rajasthani term referring to the *zenana* or the secluded quarters for women.

11 Referring to Bappa Rawal, the famed eighth-century chieftain described in bardic chronicles as having founded Mewar in 734 CE.

* I knew him well—a plain honest man.

† Alluding to the custom of infanticide—here, very rare, indeed almost unknown.

‡ With my mind engrossed with the scenes in which I had passed the better part of my life, I went two months after my return from Rajputana, in 1823, to York Cathedral to attend the memorable festival of that year. The sublime recitations of Handel in "Jeptha's Vow," the sonorous woe of Sapio's "Deeper and Deeper Still," powerfully recalled the sad exit of the Rajputni, and the representation shortly after of Racine's tragedy of "Iphigenie," with Talma as Achille, Duchesnois as Clytemnestra, and a very interesting personation of the victim daughter of Agamemnon, again served to waken the remembrance of this sacrifice.

§ The *kasoomba* draught is made of flowers and herbs of a cooling quality, into this an opiate was introduced.

The desires of barbarity were accomplished. "She slept!",[12] a sleep from which she never awoke.

The wretched mother did not long survive her child. Nature was exhausted in the ravings of despair: she refused food, and her remains in a few days followed those of her daughter to the funeral pyre.

Even the ferocious Khan, when the instrument of his infamy, Ajit, reported the issue, received him with contempt, and spurned him from his presence, tauntingly asking "if this were the boasted Rajput valor?" But the wily traitor had to encounter language far more bitter from his political adversary, whom he detested. Sangram Shaktawat reached the capital only four days after the catastrophe—a man in every respect the reverse of Ajit, audaciously brave, he neither feared the frown of his sovereign nor the sword of his enemy. Without introduction he rushed into the presence, where he found seated the traitor Ajit. "Oh dastard! who hast thrown dust on the Sisodia race, whose blood which has flowed in purity through a hundred ages has now been defiled! This sin will check its course for ever, a blot so foul in our annals that no Sisodia[*] will ever again hold up his head! A sin to which no punishment were equal. But the end of our race is approaching. The line of Bappa Rawal is at an end! Heaven has ordained this, a signal of our destruction." The Rana hid his face with his hands, when turning to Ajit, he [Sangram] exclaimed, "thou stain on the Sisodia race, thou impure of Rajput blood, dust be on thy head as thou hast covered us all with shame. May you die childless, and your name die with you![†] Why this indecent haste? Had the Pathan stormed the city? Had he attempted to violate the sanctity of the *Rawula*? And though he had, could you not die as Rajputs, like your ancestors? Was it thus they gained a name? Was it thus our race became renowned—thus they opposed the might of kings? Have you forgotten the *shakas*[13] of Chittor? But whom do I address—not Rajputs? Had the honour of your females been endangered, had you sacrificed them all and rushed sword in hand on the enemy, your name would have lived, and the Almighty would have secured the seed of Bappa Rawal! But to owe preservation to this unhallowed deed! You did not even await the threatened danger. Fear seems to have deprived you of every faculty, or you might have spared the blood of Srijee,[‡] and if you did not scorn to owe your safety to deception, might have substituted some less noble victim! But the end of our race approaches!"

The traitor to manhood, his sovereign, and humanity, dared not reply. The brave Sangram is now dead, but the prophetic anathema has been fulfilled. Of ninety-five children, sons and daughters, but one son (the brother of Krishna)[§] is left to the Rana, and though his two remaining daughters have been recently married to the princes of

---

12 The title of the Maharana's clan.

13 A storied ritual in which, when faced with the prospect of rape and plunder by invading Muslim armies, Rajput soldiers would lead a suicide charge, while the women of the household would commit *jauhar* (self-immolation).

* The simple but powerful expression of the narrator.

† That is, without adoption even to perpetuate it.

‡ A respectful epithet, meaning "sire" or "great being."

§ By the same mother.

Jaisalmer and Bikaner, the Salic law,[14] which is in full force in these states, precludes all honor through female descent. His hopes rest solely on the prince, Jawan Singh[*] and though in the flower of youth and health, the marriage bed (albeit boasting no less than four young princesses) has been blessed with no progeny.[†] The elder brother of Jawan died two years ago, had he lived he would have been Amar III.[15]

With regard to Ajit, the course has been fully accomplished. Scarcely a month after, his wife and two sons were numbered with the dead, and the hoary traitor has since been wandering from shrine to shrine, performing penance and alms in expatiation of his sins, yet unable to fling from his ambition, and with his beads in one hand, Rama! Rama! ever on his tongue, and subdued passion in his looks, his heart is deceitful as ever. Enough of him: let us exclaim with Sangram, "Dust on his head,"[‡] which all the waters of the Ganges could not purify from the blood of the Virgin Krishna, but "rather would the multitudinous sea incarnadine."[16]

His coadjutor, Amir Khan, is now linked by treaties "in amity and unity of interests" with the sovereigns of India, and though he has carried mourning into every house of Rajasthan, yet charity might hope forgiveness would be extended to him, could he cleanse himself from this deed of horror—"throwing this pearl away, richer than all his tribe!"[17] His career of rapine has terminated with the caresses of the blind goddess, and placed him on a pinnacle to which his sword would never have traced the path. Enjoying the most distinguished post amongst the foreign chieftains of Holkar's state, having the regulars and park[18] under his control, with large estates for their support, he added the

---

14 The *Lex Salica* or Salic Law of the Franks, wherein succession was only permitted through males.

15 Maharanas that shared the name were Amar Singh I (1559–1620) and Amar Singh II (1672–1710).

16 A passage from *Macbeth* (William Shakespeare, *Macbeth*, in W. G. Clark and W. Aldis Wright, eds., *The Globe Shakespeare*, New York: Nelson Doubleday, 1900, 61). The original reads:

> Will all great Neptune's ocean wash this blood,
> Clean from my hand? No, this my hand will rather
> The multitudinous seas incarnadine,
> Making the green one red.

17 Shakespeare, *Othello, the Moor of Venice*, 404.

18 An archaic reference to artillery, which was encamped or parked in a section.

* He was nearly carried off by that awful scourge, the cholera, and, singular to remark, was the first person attacked at Udaipur. I remained by his bedside during the progress of this terrible visitation, and never shall I forget his grateful exclamation of surprise, when after a salutary sleep he opened his eyes to health. Sheerji Mehta, his chief adviser and manager of his estates, merry as ever, though the heir of Mewar was given over, was seized with the complaint as his master recovered—was dead and his ashes blanching on the sands of the streamlet of [Ahar] within twelve hours. Jovial and good humored he was, "we could have better spared a better man." He was an adept in intrigue of [Ambaji Ingle's] school, and till death shall extinguish the whole of this, and better morals are born, the country will but slowly improve.

† Since this work has gone to press, the author has been rejoiced to find that an heir has been born from the last marriage by a princess of Rewa of the Bhagela tribe.

‡ This was written at Udaipur, in 1820. This old intriguer then attempted to renew the past, as the organ of the Chundawats, but his scheme ended in exile to the sacred city of Benares, and there he may now be seen with his rosary on the consecrated *ghat* of the Ganges.

epithet of traitor to his other titles, when the British government, adopting the leading maxim of Asiatic policy, *divide et impera*,[19] guaranteed to him the sovereignty of these districts on his abandoning the Marathas, disbanding his legions, and surrendering the park. But though he personally fulfilled not, nor could fulfil, one single stipulation, this man, whose services were not worth the pay of a single sepoy—who fled from his camp[*] unattended, and sought personal protection in that of the British commander—claimed and obtained the full price of our pledge, the sovereignty of about one-third of his master's dominions, and the districts of Sironj, Tonk, Rampura, and Nimbahera, from the domain of the Nawab Amir Khan, etc., etc., etc.! This was in the fitful fever of success, when our arms were everywhere triumphant. But were the viceroy of Hind to summon the forty tributaries[†] now covered by the aegis of British protection to a meeting, the murderer of Krishna would still occupy a place (though low) in this illustrious divan. Let us hope that his character being known, he would feel himself ill at ease, and let us dismiss him likewise in the words of Sangram, "Dust on his head."

---

19 A Latin phrase that means "to divide and rule".

* Brigadier-General Alexander Knox had the honor of dissolving these bands in the only way worthy of us. He marched his troops to take their guns and disperse their legions, and when in order of battle, the gallant General taking out his watch, gave them half-an-hour to reflect, their commander Jamshid, second only in villainy to his master, deeming "discretion the better part of valor," surrendered.

† There are full this number of princes holding under the British.

An Extract from Amir Khan's *Memoirs*[1]

[. . .] Raja Man Singh sending for the Ameer said that although his obligations to him were such that as long he lived he should never forget or be able to requite them, yet as Sawai Singh was still holding out at Nagaur, and Dhonkal Singh was there set up as the pretended rightful heir of the Raj, to the prejudice of his own authority, he could not be quite satisfied, until these chiefs were subdued. The Ameer said, "God is the disposer of events, and all powerful. Having already done so much for you, what is there in this service that it should not also be accomplished?" The Raja was much assured by the Ameer's readiness to undertake the business and, thereupon, executed a written engagement, stipulating to pay four lakhs and fifty thousand rupees per mensem[2] for the expenses of the army, to assign *parganas*[3] yielding four lakhs per annum as a personal *jagir*[4] to the Ameer's son Wazir-ud-Daula, and further, to take a brigade into permanent service at an annual charge of thirteen lakhs of rupees, and to distribute *jagirs* of a lakh and a half to the Ameer's *sardars*[5] and officers, such as his father-in-law, Mohammed Ayaz Khan, and Ghulami Khan, also to Rai Himmat Rai, and Mirza Haji Beg.

The Ameer having concluded this negotiation, started with only five hundred horse, and made a march in the direction of Nagaur. The main army being somewhat out of humour, and distressed for money to clear themselves from Jodhpur, came up the following day. The whole were collected, however, by the time the camp arrived at Kharnal, which is one stage[6] only from Nagaur. The Hyderabad Afghans, who had left Jaswant Rao Holkar's service, and subsequently entered that of Jaipur, came here and joined the Ameer's standard, making altogether a force of twenty thousand men or more. The Ameer had left the brigades of Lal Singh and Mehtab Khan, under the Nawab Mohammed Shah Khan, at Merta, where they had been employed, since the battle with Bakshi Shiv Lal, in reducing the country to obedience, and punishing the *zamindars*[7] and *thakurs*[8] who adhered to Sawai Singh and Dhonkal Singh in rebellion against the authority of Raja Man Singh. He had further given the command of his personal guards to Colonel Mohan Singh, who had recently returned from his home and joined the Ameer. These troops, with the horse immediately attached to the Ameer, had sent along with Mohammed Ghafoor Khan, a relation of the Ameer's father-in-law, Mohammed Ayaz Khan, to make the collections in Kuru, a dependency of Jodhpur.

---

1 Basavan Lal, *Memoirs of the Puthan Soldier of Fortune: The Nuwab Ameer-Ood-Doulah Mohummud Ameer Khan, Chief of Seronj, Tonk, Rampoora, Neemahera, and Other Places in Hindoostan*, trans. Henry T. Prinsep, Calcutta: G. H. Huttman, 1832, pp. 346–60, 398–400. Lal was Amir Khan's *naib munshi* (deputy secretary).

2 Month.

3 A subdivision of a revenue district, sometimes compared with a barony.

4 A grant of the revenue from a specified territory.

5 An honorific for landed nobles and minor chieftains. Here the term is used presumptuously.

6 A variable measure of riding distance, equivalent to about six *kos* or twelve miles.

7 A landlord or revenue farmer.

8 An honorific for chieftains in Rajputana.

By way of stratagem, and to lay a net for the wily chief he had to deal with, the Ameer sent Mirza Haji Beg, an independent *sowar*[9] of much intelligence, to negotiate with Sawai Singh of Pokhran. Through him it was insinuated to the Rathore, that notwithstanding all Raja Man Singh's apparent favors and good offices, especially in the matter of the *dharna*,[10] when he saved the Ameer's life from the violence of the Afridi mutineers, still there was dissatisfaction felt by the Ameer at his short cash payments, and if Sawai Singh desired it, Dhonkal Singh might be put on the *musnud*[11] of Jodhpur in the room of Man Singh, for a due consideration.

To Bapu Sindhia, who was also at Nagaur, the Ameer sent *jamadar*[12] Namdar Khan to propose a meeting for the consideration of matters of mutual advantage. The chief was at that time on bad terms with Sawai Singh, in consequence of the irregularity of the latter's provision of funds for the payment of the Sindhia contingent, and for his general bad faith and selfishness, for he had invited many of Lakhwa Dada's officers under promises which he never performed, so much so as to have entirely lost character with all the supporters of his cause. Bapu Sindhia indicated through the Ameer's agent, that he would meet him at Khuwan, midway between Nagaur and Kharnal, to which the Ameer agreed. He accordingly went to Khuwan with an escort of a thousand horse, and there represented to Bapu Sindhia that Sawai Singh had deceived Raja Jagat Singh to ruin, and was doing the same by him, that if he was wise he would get out of the connection as quickly as possible, make his peace with Raja Man Singh and leave the Jodhpur country, and the Ameer concluding by tendering some aid in money, if it should be indispensable, to enable his troops to move.

Bapu Sindhia replied to this overture that the *subadari*[13] of Jodhpur was his, and if the Ameer would undertake to pay him half of what he might realize from it, besides discharging the present arrears of his troops, he was ready to march immediately. The Ameer, on hearing this proposition, thought to himself, that the man's feet were somewhat longer than his blanket, and, while he was so unreasonable, there could be no coming to terms with him. With considerable art, therefore, in order to circumvent him, he began an intrigue with Munir Khan, Khuda Baksh Khan, Dara Khan, Deendar Khan, Faizullah Khan of Pachpahar, and others, who, to the number of about one thousand *sowars*, were in service with Bapu Sindhia at Nagaur, but dissatisfied at the same time from delay in the payment of their arrears. These men happened now to be on escort duty with Bapu Sindhia, and the Ameer instigated them to raise a tumult and mutiny. They did so, in consequence, and got Bapu Sindhia into their power, subjecting him to considerable severities, and not letting the members of his family or his private servants approach him. The Ameer, fighting still the battle of circumvention, came up now with his troops, and professing to be very angry with the Afghans, said, "You have availed yourselves of the opportunity of Bapu Sindhia's coming to meet me to seize him. This I must resent as an indignity to myself." The Afghans said, "We have a right to get our arrears as we can, we will not liberate him till they are paid." The Ameer then

---

9 A mounted soldier.

10 A form of protest where the creditor refuses to quit the doorstep until the debtor complies.

11 A throne (literally, the cushion on which the ruler would be seated).

12 A commissioned officer equivalent to a lieutenant, who typically served as a deputy commander.

13 A Mughal-era term referring to the governorship (*subadar*) of a province (*suba*).

went with two or three attendants to Bapu Sindhia, and said, "There is no getting the Afghans to consent to your release without a present payment, which neither you nor I are well able to provide. On the other hand," continued the Ameer, "my credit is concerned at your capture under these circumstances, something, therefore, must be done, what do you advise?" Bapu Sindhia, who had been very severely treated by the Afghans, said "At all events, get me out of the hands of these villains." The Ameer asked what was due to the Afghans, and how much was to be received from Sawai Singh. He said, "I owe them about three lakhs, and have the same amount to receive from that chief." The Ameer then said, "If you will engage to leave the Jodhpur territory, I will take the debt on myself." Bapu Sindhia agreed to the condition, but said "Jean Baptiste is here at Nagaur along with me, how will he be able to get away without receiving his arrears?" The Ameer asked how much might be due to him, and the Bapu said, a lakh of rupees. The Ameer said, "I can give him an assignment for that sum on the revenues of Asop, a dependency of Jodhpur, he may get it from thence. If he does not like what I propose thus in good will for you, let him levy his arrears as he can."

Bapu Sindhia being completely over-reached, went away, professing great obligations to the Ameer, in order to persuade Jean Baptiste to agree to the terms. He was at the time encamped at Sandwa, five *kos*[14] from Nagaur, and sending thither for Sawai Singh, they told him of the terms agreed upon. Jean Baptiste said, at the consultation held, that, if the Ameer would come in person, and add an undertaking to be answerable for the lakh of rupees, if it were not realized from Asop, he should agree at once. The Ameer hearing of this, and thinking his object gained, went with a few troops to give to Jean Baptiste the assurance he desired, and though he was warned to be careful of treachery, he paid no attention, but went boldly to Bapu Sindhia's encampment, and satisfied both Jean Baptiste, and the Afghans, to whom he gave the guarantee he had promised of their arrears, and then returned to his own ground at Kharnal. Bapu Sindhia and Jean Baptiste immediately broke up their camp, and moved towards Asop, where they levied eighty thousand rupees of the lakh, and forty thousand rupees more from the villages and towns round about, and then went to Ajmer. Sirji Rao Ghatke had also separated his troops, and Hira Singh's brigade, from the Ameer at Jodhpur, and he too marching on Ajmer, met there Bapu Sindhia, so the field was now open to the Ameer without a rival.

Bapu Sindhia's Afghans had come over to the Ameer, from whom their arrears were to be realized. With their troops and his own, he marched from Kharnal to Sandwa, which is five *kos* from Nagaur, and there encamped, waiting for Mukhtar-ud-Daula's[15] force, consisting of the brigades of Lal Singh and Mehtab Khan, and for the other troops, which were on detached service in different parts of the Jodhpur territory, under Colonel Mohan Singh, and Mohammed Ghafoor Khan. In this interval, the intrigue of Mirza Haji Beg, the Ameer's agent with Sawai Singh, began to work: that chief agreed to pay forty lakhs of rupees, and the agent brought a proposition to this effect in writing from Sawai Singh. The Ameer being determined to bring this wily chief into his net one way or other, replied,

14 A variable measure of distance based on prevailing custom such as audible range. Typically, one *kos* was between one and a half and two and a half miles.

15 A title meaning representative (*mukhtar*) of the state (*ud-Daula*). The holder of the office was Mohammed Shah Khan, one of Amir Khan's principal brigadiers.

"The amount will do, but how is it to be paid? What are the instalments and periods of payment?" Sawai Singh upon this agreed to pay thirteen lakhs, in as many days from the date of his first interview with the Ameer, and the remaining twenty-seven lakhs on the day of Dhonkal Singh's instalment, and Raja Man Singh's expulsion, and he added that if Mukhtar-ud-Daula, Mohammed Shah Khan, would be the guarantee of the engagement, he was ready immediately to give the Ameer the interview. The Ameer consented to all this, and sent Mukhtar-ud-Daula to Sawai Singh, who required this officer to give him a guarantee on oath, whereupon he came away to ask the Ameer, what he was to do. "Determine", said the Ameer, "for yourself what is best for my service, and for the cause of the army of the faith." Although the known perfidy of Sawai Singh, and the many attempts he had made to undermine and ruin the Ameer, were quite sufficient to justify the getting rid of him by treachery, and indeed to make any means employed against him, meritorious, still, in order to satisfy certain doubts and scruples which the Nawab Mukhtar-ud-Daula had conceived on the score of morality, all the officers united in declaring, that to shed the blood of an enemy to the faith, by treachery, when necessary for the good of the general cause of the faith, and its army, or for the service of one's chief, was lawful. Thus the Nawab was brought to agree.

The place fixed for the meeting to complete the compact with Sawai Singh was Markeen Saheb's house, midway between Nagaur and Sandwa. Sawai Singh, the accursed, came thither with one or two thousand horse, in perfect confidence and security, and Mukhtar-ud-Daula met him and made the oaths required. But as Sawai Singh was not satisfied unless the Ameer also set his hand to the compact, and as he urged Mukhtar-ud-Daula to send for him for the purpose, the Ameer too went, and gave him his hand to an engagement to this effect: that if Sawai Singh should keep his promise, and be punctual in the payment of the money stipulated, the compact should stand as arranged, but upon any the least failure on his part, it was to be null and void. The Ameer said further, "Truth is a looking-glass to shew the face, and according to the Hindi proverb, *har jaise ko taisi*,[16] if there lives in your heart any remnant of the old enmity, you must be prepared to stand the consequences." The accursed Sawai Singh was satisfied with these ambiguous assurances, and to outward appearance, forming a wolf's friendship, came and pitched his tents near the Ameer's encampment, along with his troops and attendants. But the dust of hate and rancor was not washed from his mind, and he was watching an opportunity to circumvent the Ameer. Anoop Ram Chobe, Raja Man Singh's *vakil*[17] in attendance on the Ameer, wrote to the Raja, informing him of the intrigue which was carried on, and of the result apparent in Sawai Singh's having joined the camp, and he added, that it would now seem that the Ameer had engaged himself to seat Dhonkal Singh on the *musnud* of Jodhpur. The Raja saw through the plot, and feared not for the Ameer's fidelity, still, to keep up appearances, he wrote in reply, "Let him do his worst".

In the meantime, Sawai Singh, whose heart was not clean from the rust of hate and enmity, and who, notwithstanding the oaths interchanged, was still planting the seeds

[16] A colloquial phrase meaning measure for measure. Used here in the sense of "the same goes for you."

[17] A legal representative employed to negotiate or communicate on behalf of a principal.

of treachery and guile, hired four assassins for one hundred gold *mohurs*,[18] and the promise of a village to each in *jagir*, to lay in wait for the Ameer and slay him, and the four men, for the execution of their wicked purpose, came to the camp, and professing to be seeking service, and to be of the Mahommedan faith, put up at a tent pitched by the Ameer's father-in-law, Mohammed Ayaz Khan, for the entertainment of the strangers, in front of his own. As the scent of the flower of wickedness will betray itself, though it be covered with a hundred folds of linen, it so happened that one of the faithful servants of Raja Man Singh, who was about Sawai Singh as a spy, got to a knowledge of this plot, and let the Raja know of it, and he wrote to the Ameer a detailed account, with the names, and a description of the persons of the assassins, even to the fact of their coming into camp in the manner related.

The Ameer being thus put on his guard, went in the night, followed by two or three *khidmatgars*,[19] with a dagger in his hand, to the tent of his father-in-law where the assassins were lying, and that he might not be recognized, he wrapped up his face in a handkerchief, and so creeping into the tent waked the miscreants, and sitting down as a stranger, asked them what their plans were. They replied, "We are looking out for service, and have no other plans in view." The Ameer said, "What you are looking out for is not service. You are come to assassinate the Ameer." They put on the appearance of alarm, and said, "What is this you say? Are you bent on ruining us and spoiling our hopes and prospects, and getting us turned out of camp?" The Ameer replied, "Why do you conceal your purpose from me? Sawai Singh has sent me to execute the same, and has told me of your coming, and of your having received a hundred gold mohurs and a promise of a village in *jagir*. I know all your real names—you are so and so, natives of such and such villages, I too have my hundred gold *mohurs*, and Sawai Singh has told me to concert matters with you, which is the reason of my coming to you at this time in secret." They were silent at hearing this, and the Ameer saw that they had still some doubts, and required some pledge or further proof on his part, so he said in a low tone of voice, "Come to a distance from this place, and tell me all your plans, and I will communicate mine." They accordingly got up to go with the Ameer, and came out of the tent. The Ameer's servants, who were waiting outside with *mashals*[20] joined the party upon a motion from him, whereupon they asked, who these were? upon which, the Ameer said, "These are all fellow conspirators." When the Ameer had led them to a retired place outside the camp, he made them sit down, and asked what plan they had settled for the assassination. Each of them told a separate story—one was to slit the tent *kunats*[21], and so get at the Ameer when asleep—another to endeavour to get enrolled amongst the personal servants and guards—another was for attacking him openly as he went through the camp. Having now heard enough to satisfy himself of their purpose, the Ameer ordered the lamps to be brought forward, and then taking off the handkerchief which concealed his face, and showing himself, he said, "See, I am the person you have come to assassinate: Tell me now how you will effect your purpose?" Of a truth, the Divine protection watches over

[18] A gold coin representing approximately fifteen rupees.

[19] A personal servant, serving variously as a valet, bodyguard, and attendant.

[20] Torches.

[21] The cloth walls of a tent.

the great in this world, and their presence inspires awe: the four assassins fell on their knees trembling, and asked pardon and forgiveness. The Ameer released one of the four, in order that he might go and report what had happened to Sawai Singh.[22] The other three he took to his own father-in-law, and committing them to his custody, told him to be more careful in the future whom he admitted to his hospitality, and received into his tents. Mohammed Ayaz Khan made many excuses, and professed his entire ignorance, as to who or what the men were, and the Ameer then retired to his own tents.

The Ameer now reflected, that having this proof that Sawai Singh was plotting for his assassination, notwithstanding the oaths interchanged between them, besides which, the first stipulated period had passed, and no money was forthcoming, he might fairly consider, that he was absolved entirely from his engagement, and free to pursue his own designs against the accursed one. Accordingly, going one day with a few attendants to his tents, the Ameer said, "The thirteen days are out, and you have not paid the thirteen lakhs, indeed twice the time has elapsed that was agreed upon, and you have paid nothing, my compact therefore is null and void, and in return for your conduct in this matter, I have come to tell you, that I am prepared to send you safe to Nagaur, or where else you will." Sawai Singh resorted to flattering speeches to soothe and appease the Ameer, but he made at the same time signs, and to his people whispered, that now was the time to get the better of the Ameer by treachery. The Ameer, however, was too deeply versed in the game of cunning to be so over-reached, and saw what was designed. Mounting, therefore, without giving them time to effect their purpose, he went immediately to his own tents, and thence in order to finish the game with this false one, he sent immediately Nawab Mukhtar-ud-Daula Mohammed Shah Khan, and Rai Himmat Rai, to wait upon Sawai Singh as [a] compliment, and to bring him to take leave of the Ameer.

VERSE

Sawai Singh has come to the tents of the Ameer,
He comes to the toils like a noose-stricken deer;
The troops are drawn out, not in open parade,
But concealed by *kunats*, and in close ambuscade;
Without—every tent rope is fast to its pin,
But all are in hand manned by *khalasis*[23] within;
The guards are all ready, with weapons all bright,
Not presented for honor, but loaded for fight;
The cannon are pointed, with matches in hand,
The cannoneers wait for the note of command.
The fife's[24] thrilling tone is the signal assigned,

---

22 The entire episode appears to be fabricated with a view to excusing Amir Khan's subsequent conduct. There is no evidence of it in other accounts. Besides, had Sawai Singh been made aware of the failure of the alleged plot, he would have had little reason to subsequently visit Amir Khan's camp with only a modest bodyguard.

23 A soldier or serviceman responsible for pitching and managing tents.

24 A high-pitched flute, commonly used by eighteenth-century military bands for marching and signaling purposes.

And to all the Ameer has their parts well defined;
When the fife shall strike up, every tent-rope must go,
And the tent be let fall on the heads of the foe;
And the mouths of the cannon, and grenadiers stout,
Be shown all at once to the escort without—
All now is arranged, and the net ready spread,
When the victim to make his last visit is led.
He comes with a plentiful suite of Rathores,
The chiefs crowd with rudeness within the tent doors,
While the rest of the escort remaining without,
Keep close to the tent with their eyes well about;
Nawab Mukhtar-ud-Daula has bade the chief sit,
For occasion to go forth, he taxes his wit;
And Rai Himmat Rai is too wise to be snared,
He will just step and see if the *khilat*'s[25] prepared;
Both seek the Ameer, and report that their prey
Is fast in the toils, unsuspecting foul play.
"Strike up", said the Ameer, to the fifer who stood,
With fife to his lip, "give the signal of blood!
Be the curtain now drawn!" The tent falls at the words,
The *khalasis* as bidden have let go the cords
All within are enveloped, and thus their fate meet,
The tent-fly to them is a death-winding-sheet;
And the grenadiers stand as for battle arrayed,
In the void are the cannons with matches displayed.
While the camp beats to arms, and with weapons on high,
The Rathores are surrounded, and all made to die.
Thus ever success crowns the plans of wise,
Mount! Mount! for Nagaur! be that city the prize.
The place was soon won, none were there to command,
And large was the booty that there fell to hand.

The facts were simply as follows. When the accursed Sawai Singh came with his escort of one or two thousand horse, he was brought to the Ameer's tent by the Nawab Mukhtar-ud-Daula Muhammad Shah Khan, and by Rai Himmat Rai. The Ameer had pitched his large tent for the purpose, and they took him inside, where he went and sat down with all his chiefs of note. The *sowars* and footmen he had brought for escort, stood round the tent and outer *kunats*. The tent was the net the Ameer had spread for his prey. On one side, all the ropes of it were properly fastened to the pins, but within the enclosure on the opposite side they were held in hand, ready to be dropped at a signal, and all the space within the closed *kunats* was filled with cannon, pointed, with matches lighted, and the Ameer gave order, that on hearing a fife sound, the tent should be let fall on the heads of all within, and the artillery be discharged in the faces of the escort, while

[25] A gift, typically comprising of a robe and jewels, bestowed as a mark of honor or distinction.

parties of men of known courage, should rush upon them and finish the whole. The plan succeeded completely. Upon the fated man being conducted to the tent of the audience, the Nawab Mukhtar-ud-Daula and Rai Himmat Rai went out, on the pretense of seeing if the dresses of honor and other things were all prepared. They came and reported to the Ameer that all was ready, and explained how the matter stood. The Ameer, being satisfied that he had got the victim fast in the net, gave the word to sound the fife. It sounded like the trumpet of the last day, and a confusion ensued like that of the day of Judgment.* The *khalasis* immediately let go the tent ropes and jumped nimbly on one side, and the tent went down like a shot on the heads of the fated men within. The cannons were at the same time discharged at the tent and escort, and cut the whole to pieces. The Ameer had placed detachments of select men from his battalions ready in ambuscade to rush in and finish them, and had further prepared many of his special horse in mail, having for days before made a practice of reviewing them at that hour and spot, in order to prevent suspicion. Thus the whole party were put to the sword, and the Ameer riding off to Nagaur, gained admittance at once to the city, and established his authority there, capturing an immense booty, and struck the kettle-drums and trumpets of victory.

Raja Dhonkal Singh, and the Bikaner Raja, and Sawai Singh's sons, who were all in Nagaur, fled precipitately to Bikaner and Pokhran, and the Ameer having settled a contribution upon Nagaur, stayed there some days. Leaving afterwards several battalions there from different brigades under Mohammed Ghafoor Khan, he returned himself to Jodhpur, where he was extremely well received by Raja Man Singh, to whose officers he made over the fort and city of Nagaur. The Raja professed himself to be under such obligations for this service, that he assigned for the Ameer's residence some houses within the fort of Jodhpur, and of the sum of thirty-five lakhs which it had been agreed in writing that the Ameer was to receive for getting rid of Sawai Singh, and expelling Raja Dhonkal Singh from Nagaur, about half was paid down, and devoted by the Ameer to the discharge of the arrears due to the troops, and the rest was promised by Raja Man Singh in a short time. [. . .]

[. . .] The Ameer having had an interview with Maharana Bhim Singh, the ruler of Udaipur, represented to him that a main cause of his country suffering was, that it was the prey of all strange armies passing through it, and of those who were invited by its defenseless state to come there, and pillage, and live at free quarters. It was, therefore, obviously for the Rana's interest to take one of his brigades into pay, and so restore order, and make his authority respected. The brigade would both enforce the collection of his revenues, and save him from the insults, and over-bearing conduct of every military chief, that chose to pass through Mewar. The Ameer offered to be responsible for remedying all the evils of which the Rana complained, and to furnish a brigade for

* This atrocious act of cruel villainy was perpetrated on 4th April, 1808, and astonished even Rathore perfidy. In the promiscuous slaughter, occasioned by the firing of grape through the tent as it was falling, several of the Ameer's men met their death. The *nautch* girls and their attendants, who were in the tent, were enveloped with the rest, and some Pathan *sardars* also were slain along with the Rajputs. The life of friend or foe was but of small account with the Ameer, when a political object was to be gained. *[This footnote was inserted into the English edition by the translator, Henry T. Prinsep.]*

the purpose, on the condition of receiving a share of the revenues. The Rana thinking the offer a godsend, agreed at once to give a quarter (four *annas* out of every rupee) of all his collections, and further made an exchange of turbans with the Ameer in pledge of friendship.

The Ameer having thus arranged this matter to mutual satisfaction, and having won the Rana to his confidence, told him, that his quarrel with Raja Man Singh would never be settled, so long as his daughter lived, that it behooved him, therefore, out of regard for the interests of his Raj, no less than for the honor of his family, to put her to death. "If you do not," the Ameer added, "it will be my duty, connected as I am with Raja Man Singh, to seize her by force, and carry her away in a *palki*[26] to Jodhpur, that the Raja may there complete his marriage with her." The Rana at first said, "I would willingly give my own life if the sacrifice were required, but I can never consent to my daughter marrying that chief, and as for your carrying her off by force, it would disgrace my family in perpetuity". "But", he added, after reflecting on the matter, "if you will pledge yourself to get for me Khalee Rao[27] from Raja Man Singh, I will in that case contrive to get rid of my daughter after you shall have gone, using such means as shall create as little odium as possible." The Ameer agreed to the condition, and the Rana, after his departure, caused poison to be mixed with his daughter's food, and so administered it to her. It happened, that what she took was not sufficient to effect the purpose, and the Princess guessed the object of her father, whereupon she sent him a message, that as it was a matter that concerned the good of his Raj, and the honor of his family, and it appeared that her living longer was inconsistent with these in her father's opinion, there was no occasion for him to have gone secretly to work, for that she was prepared to die by her own act immediately. Accordingly having bathed, and dressed herself in new and gay attire, she drank off the poison, and so gave up her precious life, earning the perpetual praise, and admiration of mankind.[*]

---

26 A palanquin or covered litter.

27 A reference to Ghanerao, a fief of Udaipur that Man Singh had seized.

* Both Colonel Tod and Sir John Malcolm give highly wrought accounts of the tragic end of the unfortunate princess Krishna Kumari, but neither gives the date, which seems to have been in June or July, 1810. In the Policy of Asia, a woman's life is but of small account, and more especially so amongst the Rajputs of Western India, who habitually destroy their female children. Viewed with due allowance to this state of feeling and morality, the advice given by the Ameer had much to palliate, if not excuse it. The death of this princess led to the pacification between Jaipur and Jodhpur, and removed the great source of quarrel and confusion from one end of Rajasthan to the other. The princess, according to Rajput notions, could have had no other husband, but one or other of these two Rajas, and as neither was possible, death was her only resource. Only the other day, an overture was made for a marriage between the present young Raja of Jaipur and a princess of Bikaner. The match was broken off by some court intrigue, and as a necessary consequence the princess took, or was made to take, poison. *[This footnote was inserted into the English edition by the translator, Henry T. Prinsep. The princess died on July 21, 1810.]*

An Extract from a Speech by Shyamal Das of Mewar[1]

I am commanded by all the Rajputana *sardars*,[2] *mutamids*,[3] and Charans,[4] here assembled to convey their thanks to the British Government. I will first quote from history to show the difference between the rule of former days and that of the present times, from which the good treatment which Rajputana has received at the hands of the British Government can be seen.

When the country was ruled by the Hindus the arts and sciences flourished, but as there was no single emperor at the head, the people suffered somewhat from the attacks one prince directed against the other. Afterwards dissensions arose between the believers in the Vedas and the Buddhists, which resulted in much bloodshed. The arts and sciences were neglected in consequence, and there was depletion of wealth. Then came the onsets by the Mussulmans in which Mahmud of Ghazni and others reduced the country to decline, as can be learnt from the books issued under their names. After this ruin the Pathan dynasty from Qutbuddin to Ibrahim Lodi established its sway. The state of these times can be described in a few words. For instance, in the *Futuhat-i-Firoz Shahi*,[5] Feroz Shah Tughluk writes that he killed so many Hindu *fakirs*[6] as to cleanse the world and render it pure. Religious bigotry impelled these people to the commission of such tyrannical deeds.

The emperor Babur next founded the rule of the Mughals, and during their tenure of power much blood was spilt. Sher Shah, after driving out Humayun, depopulated Rajputana and besprinkled the soil with the blood of the Rajputs. Of the Mughal emperors Akbar was certainly good to all, but as the administration of justice was weak tyranny was sometimes exercised, as for example, when at the taking of Chittor 40,000 inoffensive subjects were put to the sword, as is proved from the *Akbarnama*.[7] Akbar's son, Jahangir, writes that some Kahars[8] having come in the way when he was out shooting, he had their legs cut off. Jahangir's son, Shah Jahan, who is considered one of the best emperors, used to make men fight with cheetahs and tigers. It is written in history that this emperor directed three men to attack certain wild beasts with swords.

---

1 "Adoption by the States of Rajputana of Important Reforms," India Proceedings, Foreign Department, Internal A, July 1888, No. 19B. Shyamal Das was the *kaviraj* (court poet) of the Udaipur *darbar*. He produced *Vir Vinod*, the first comprehensive prose history of Mewar. This speech was given on March 10, 1888, two months after Shyamal Das's scholarly attainments had led to his being accorded the honorific title *Mahamahopadhyaya*.

2 A chieftain or nobleman.

3 A representative or agent.

4 A distinctive caste group that served as warriors and guides, and especially as bards, whose songs, stories, and poems preserved and channeled Rajput history. Shyamaldas belonged to this caste group.

5 *The Victories of Firoz Shah*, a brief autobiographical work describing the reign of Firoz Shah (1309–88).

6 Ascetics or holy men.

7 *The History of Akbar*, which chronicles the reign of the Mughal emperor Akbar (1556–1605).

8 The caste term for bearers of palanquins and carriers of related provisions especially water.

One of them, however, killed the tiger with his dagger, and for this disobedience of orders he was put an end to with the same weapon. Of the acts of the emperor's subordinates it is related of Arab Khan, the *Subadar*[9] of Gujarat, that, having invited some travellers and merchants from Europe to an entertainment, he sent for dancing girls to attend. The women made some excuse, whereupon Arab Khan had them beheaded, and, to crown matters, boasted that his family had always been distinguished for cruelty and bravery.

In the time of Alamgir[10] those professing another creed were subjected to great hardships. In Samvat[11] 1723 an edict went forth forbidding the teaching or learning of Sanskrit as the *kafirs*[12] derived great assistance from a knowledge of that language. In Samvat 1734 the *jizyah*[13] tax was imposed. When the emperor proceeded to the Jama Masjid the people complained, but instead of dispensing justice, he had the streets cleared by elephants, which trampled the people to death. In Samvat 1736 the emperor led an attack against Shekhawati,[14] where he destroyed many Rajputs and temples. In the same way over 100 temples were demolished in Udaipur, and the authors of this destruction were given the title of *But Shikan Khan* (redoubtable iconoclast).[15] Besides taking the lives, property and country of the rajas, the Mussulman emperors perpetrated the further indignity of demanding the sisters and daughters of the conquered chiefs.

Thereafter the power of the Mughal emperors began to decline, and then pray listen to what our Hindu brethren, the Marathas, did. They used to gather round the big rajas and distress them. One day it was Sindhia who applied pressure, and the next day Holkar would come with his army. These incursions were stayed by presents of ready money and valuables. Next came the exactions of Amir Khan, and after him others appeared armed on the scene. When after giving away all the jewelry of the *zenana* and other valuables the rajas could not purchase their deliverance, some of them were compelled to make over their sons and brothers as hostages. Even then escape was difficult. Failing money, the rajas had finally to part with a portion of their territory in order to free themselves from the exactions. The memory of the cruelty thus perpetrated has not yet faded away at Udaipur. In Jodhpur, Amir Khan's tyranny was such that thirty of his sepoys killed the Maharaja's guru, Deo Nath, and afterwards walked off without the slightest fear. The Maharaja of Jodhpur having agreed to remunerate Amir Khan if he would treacherously murder Sawai Singh, *thakur* of Pokhran, was forced to seize not only the gold and silver vessels of his subjects, but also their brass and other utensils in order to keep his pledge.

---

9 In the Mughal period the term referred to the governor or commander of a province.

10 The formal title of the Mughal emperor commonly known as Aurangzeb.

11 A reference to the Vikram Samvat calendar, which runs 56.7 years ahead of the Gregorian calendar.

12 The Islamic term for unbelievers.

13 A tax imposed by Muslim rulers on their non-Muslim subjects.

14 The northeastern part of Rajputana renowned for Hindu temples and architecture.

15 A Persian term, *but-shikhan* means breaker or destroyer of idols or images.

[. . .] Had the British Government not come soon to the rescue there was nothing to save Udaipur, Sirohi, Dungarpur, Banswara, and Pratapgarh from the impending ruin which threatened to engulf not only them, but the whole of Rajputana. When Colonel Tod arrived the income of Udaipur barely totalled Rs. 40,000 per annum; it has now by the bounty of the British Government been increased to 25 or 30 lakhs. Rajputana will never forget the heavy debt of gratitude it owes to the British Government for wresting it from the clutches of bloodthirsty tyrants and restoring it to prosperity. [. . .]

Glossary[*]

akhbars	native newspapers, typically in Persian or Hindustani
anna	one sixteenth of a rupee
ayahs	housekeeper; nanny
Babu	originally, a vernacular term of respect for a gentleman; later used to refer to an Anglicized native, especially in Bengal
Bai	a suffix for lady
Bakshi	officer charged with managing the military payroll, a responsibility that could include mustering and commanding troops
Charans	a caste group that served as warriors and guides, and especially as bards, whose songs, stories and poems preserved and channeled Rajput history
Chhatrapati	formal title of the ruler of the Maratha Empire
choultry	a sheltered space, such as a detached temple porch, used by travelers as a resting or meeting place
crore	ten million
dak	courier or mail carrier
darbar	the royal court
darbaris	courtiers
dargah	the tomb of a Muslim saint
Deccani	colloquial reference to Marathas, who were from the Deccan region
Deen	rallying cry used by Muslim soldiers (literally, in Arabic, the term means religion)
Dewan	prime minister
Dharma Shastras	law books (*shastras*) descending from antiquity that detail rules and duties (*dharma*) to be followed by Hindu society
dharmshala	rest house (literally, a religious sanctuary)

[*] This Glossary draws upon John Borthwick Gilchrist, *Hindoostanee Philology*, Edinburgh: Walker and Greig, 1810; John Shakespear, *Dictionary, Hindustani and English*, London: John Shakespear, 1817; Charles Philip Brown, *The Zillah Dictionary*, Madras: Christian Knowledge Society's Press, 1852; Charles Philip, *Dictionary of Mixed Telegu*, Madras: Christian Knowledge Society's Press, 1854; Duncan Forbes, *Dictionary, English & Hindustani*, London: W.H. Allen & Co., 1858, Charles Grant, ed., *The Gazetteer of the Central Provinces*, Bombay: Education Society's Press, 1870; Department of Revenue, Agriculture, and Commerce, *A Glossary of Vernacular Judicial and Revenue Terms*, Calcutta: Government Printing, 1874; Rev. T. Craven, *The Royal Dictionary*, Lucknow: Methodist Publishing, 1900.

dharna	a form of protest wherein the aggrieved party refuses to quit the doorstep until the wrongdoer makes amends
dhokebaaz	a colloquial term for a deceiver or cheater
divide et impera	a Latin phrase meaning divide and rule
dubashes	natives conversant in English who served as translators and intermediaries
Fadnavis	record-keeper; auditor; accountant
fakir	Muslim religious mendicant drawn from Sufi orders
gaddi	throne (literally, the cushion on which the ruler would be seated)
gardi ka waqt	time of troubles
guru	preceptor
har jaise ko taisi	a colloquial saying, meaning measure for measure
jagir	a grant of land and the rent accruing from it
jaidad	a grant of land where the rent is meant to finance military expenditure
jamadar	a military rank equivalent to captain. Literally, the person responsible for a group (deriving from *jama*, the Arabic term for an assembly)
jizyah	a tax imposed by Muslim rulers on their non-Muslim subjects
kafir	a person who disbelieves or denies the tenets of Islam
Kahars	the caste term for bearers of palanquins and carriers of related provisions especially water
karma	the Hindu doctrine that present and future states of being are a consequence of previous or past deeds
kasoomba	draught made of herbs including opium
kaudi	a small white seashell, which served as a coin of the lowest denomination. In the early nineteenth century, 5,120 *kauris* were equivalent to one *sicca* rupee
khansama	the principal steward or butler in a Muslim household
khidmatgar	a servant or attendant of a Muslim nobleman
khilat	ceremonial gift of dress
khalasis	a soldier or servicemen responsible for pitching and managing tents
Khatris	a caste group in North India, which includes Hindus and Sikhs
Koil Thampuran	title of the Royal Consort (or the Queen's husband) in Travancore
kos	a variable measure of distance based on custom, e.g., audible range. Typically one *kos* was between one and a half and two and a half miles
kunats	the cloth walls of a tent
Kumari	maiden

Kunwar	an unmarried or underage child
kuravanji	a traditional dance drama style
lakh	a hundred thousand
maaro	in Urdu, an order to hit or kill
Maharaja	king or monarch
Maharana	customary title of the Maharaja of Udaipur, indicating preeminence amongst Rajput rulers. Literally, it means greatest (*Maha*) ruler (*Rana*)
Maru	a Rajasthani term, deriving from Sanskrit, meaning the desert
mohurs	a gold coin, containing 190 grams of gold, and equivalent to fifteen rupees, issued by the Bengal Presidency of the East India Company
Mukhtar-ud-Daula	a Persian title meaning representative (*mukhtar*) of the state (*ud-Daula*)
munshi	a secretary or a scribe
musnud	the throne, referring to the cushioned bolster upon which the ruler leaned, derived from the Arabic word *sanad* (to lean on)
mutamid	representative or agent
naib	deputy
nautch	a dance performance or exhibition
Nawab	historically, the governor of a Mughal territory; later it became the title for rulers of independent Muslim principalities in British India
Nazarenes	a derivative of the Arabic word *nasara*, the term used in the Koran to describe Christians
niti shastra	precepts of ethical statecraft
palki	palanquin
parganas	a subdivision of a revenue district, sometimes compared with a barony
Parriars	a nineteenth-century term for an outcaste group, now part of the Dalit community, who were shunned and maltreated by caste groups
Peshwa	The principal minister in the Maratha Empire
Pindaris	horsemen who formed predatory bands when there were no employment to be had as irregular cavalry units
Pradhan	foremost minister
prasad	food blessed or sanctified by a deity
pucca haramzada	a colloquial phrase meaning “a true rascal”
Puranas	the sacred, mythical literature of the Hindus. Literally, in Sanskrit, the term means old or ancient
Raj	kingdom; state

Rajwada	the vernacular name for Rajasthan, meaning the abode or land of kings
Rana	ruler; chief
Rani	queen
Rawat	lord; noblemen
Residency	the office and residence of the Resident
Resident	the representative or ambassador of the Governor General of India to a darbar
ryot	tenant cultivator
salaam	a respectful greeting performed by slightly bowing the head and raising the right hand to the forehead
sanad	a document under the seal of the ruling authority granting privileges
sardar	chieftain or nobleman
Sarkar	government
Sarkil	the head minister, derives from the Persian *sar-i-khel* (commander or head of a military unit)
sati	practice of a widow being cremated alongside her deceased husband
shastras	Hindu law books, descending from antiquity, containing accumulated knowledge and rules to guide human endeavors
Shesho	preceptor; teacher; instructor; guide
sicca	a rupee coin, containing 176 grams of silver, issued by the Bengal Presidency of the East India Company
sowar	mounted soldier employed by a *silledar* (military contractor)
subadari	Mughal-era term referring to the governorship (*subadar*) of a province (*suba*)
swarabat	a plucked and fretted stringed instrument used in Carnatic music
taluk	sub-division of a *zilla* (revenue district or administrative region)
thakur	petty native chief; landed proprietor
thana	toll booths
tika	the vermillion mark applied to the head to symbolize blessing
vair	vendetta
vakil	lawyer; representative; emissary
watan	homeland
zamindar	landlord; revenue farmer
zenana	Persian term for the household quarters in which women were secluded

Index

Note: References in *italic* refer to figures.